# MUZZY
# FIELD

# MUZZY FIELD

## TALES FROM A FORGOTTEN BALLPARK

### By Douglas S. Malan

### Foreword by Fay T. Vincent, Jr.

iUniverse LLC
Bloomington

**MUZZY FIELD**
**Tales from a Forgotten Ballpark**

Copyright © 2008, 2009, 2014 by Douglas S. Malan

iUniverse books may be ordered through booksellers or by contacting:

iUniverse LLC
1663 Liberty Drive
Bloomington, IN 47403
www.iuniverse.com
1-800-Authors (1-800-288-4677)

ISBN: 978-1-9352-7884-9 (sc)
ISBN: 978-1-9352-7885-6 (e)

Library of Congress Control Number: 2009935868

Printed in the United States of America

iUniverse rev. date: 03/03/2014

President Page and Judge Malone Stop Conversation with "Babe" Ruth to Watch a Close Play.

During his first visit to Muzzy Field with the Boston Red Sox in 1919, Babe Ruth took time to visit with New Departure president DeWitt Page and Judge William J. Malone. (Courtesy: Bristol Public Library)

To Allison and Alexander
For your love, patience and inspiration

# Contents

# Acknowledgments

The author wishes to recognize the following people who were instrumental in the research and writing of this book: Jay Manewitz and the staff of the Bristol Public Library; Bob Montgomery and employees of the *Bristol Press*; Ed Swicklas and the Parks and Recreation Department of Bristol; and Ellen Zoppo and the members of the Bristol Historical Society.

Many gracious and accommodating people assisted in providing the images for the book: Lisa Brisson, photographer; Alan B. Delozier of Seton Hall University; Joe DiBari of Fordham University; Dayna Johnson of Seton Hall University; Peter McHugh of Columbia University; and Chris Siriano of the House of David Museum.

A special thank you goes to the friends and family who offered support and expressed interest in this project.

# Foreword

If, as Tip O'Neill once wisely noted, "All politics is local," so too it is with sports. This lovingly assembled history of a local sports field, ungraciously named Muzzy Field, in Bristol, Connecticut, has special meaning for me.

I was born in nearby Waterbury, and my father, who was a superb baseball and football player at Yale in New Haven, played many times at Muzzy Field for local semipro baseball teams during the Depression years when sports provided welcome relief from the grim realities of hard times. He later officiated football games on that field, and I grew up with deep affection for the many fields on which he served his beloved football as an official. So this book carries me back to the '30s and '40s, not long after Muzzy Field saw the Babe hit one into the river and when numerous local stars performed on the field before appreciative and knowing crowds.

Now we know Bristol as the headquarters of the sports colossus ESPN. In the old days it was the location of the huge New Departure Brake division of General Motors. The manufacturing businesses have left Connecticut, but the love of sport has not. Fields like Muzzy Field still play an important role in our culture and we still love our sports. For those of us with a love of both history and sport, this reminder of where we came from and where our fathers played is precious. Some things never change. The sound of ball on bat lingers in our memories forever. So too the sound of shoulder pads colliding is a permanent one. And the sound of appreciative crowds is the same as it always was. It is that permanence that makes sports unique.

The memories merge with the sites like Muzzy Field so that when we revisit the field we recall the events that carry such powerful messages. And what is the message? To me it is that the games never die. All else does, but the games go on and books like this one are joyful reminders of our past. We can live again in the "green fields of our mind," the loving term Bart Giamatti used to describe that place where Muzzy Field really exists.

*Fay T. Vincent Jr.*
*October 2007*

# Preface

The otherworldly glow hovered between the treetops and the base of the inky clouds on that August night, one of my first in Connecticut.

I was driving new roads in unfamiliar territory, enjoying a cool, low-humidity evening that was rare at that time of the year in the places I had previously lived more than a thousand miles away.

But nothing is more familiar than the ambient lights of a ballpark that beckon the observer to its gates where, inside, the game becomes a universally spoken language among strangers. So I drove toward them.

On the quiet streets of my new home, Bristol, meandering among downtown buildings, unpolished but proud, I approached a ballpark that suddenly emerged below the spires of massive evergreen trees that hugged its walls.

It is profound in its mixture of sturdy brickwork and bold green. It is a serious ballpark with its spacious power alleys stretching four hundred feet in straight-away center field. It is quirky with home plate facing northwest, allowing the setting sun to challenge players as it sinks behind the left-center field trees, most notably the massive, ancient oak that once was in play inside the fence.

Nestled in the clearing on the edge of ancient Rockwell Park, Muzzy Field is a natural preserve abutted by a modest working-class neighborhood. To me it has a feeling of quintessential New England.

The idea for the book was not hatched that night; in fact, it took three more years before my first trip to the Bristol Public Library revealed detailed information about Babe Ruth and the 1919 Boston Red Sox. While an appreciation for the ambiance of Muzzy Field was evoked immediately upon first sight, the desire to spend four years digging deeply into its history struck me only after I heard in passing about Babe Ruth's home run in 1919 and read the resulting game accounts, which led to uncovering more and more interesting stories.

The obvious soon dawned on me. Someone had to retell these stories and spread them to the people who recognize the value of such municipal ballparks rich in history and to the athletes who compete on that field without fully recognizing the magnitude of doing so.

With that, the book began modestly in October 2003.

Somewhere between then and now, I concluded that Muzzy Field is one of the lone ballparks still in use that has hosted both Ruth and Lombardi as players.

As with any project built on such research, this book would not have become a reality without assistance from many people and civic organizations. If the Bristol Public Library had not treasured the bound volumes of *New Departure News*; if the Bristol Historical Society had not found room to house bound volumes of the *Bristol Press* dating back more than fifty years; if the people involved with both groups had not been so willing to share these resources and make them readily available, sometimes on a moment's notice; if anything had been different, chances are not only would this book be woefully lacking in detailed accounts of Muzzy Field's history, it probably never would have been written.

While microfilm was an important component of the research, my ability to turn the actual pages of the newspapers and company magazines that were printed in the days after Ruth, Lombardi, and other luminaries came to town lent a rich texture to the discovery process that simplified the fact-finding mission and enlivened the subject matter. I am hopeful that energy evinces itself in the following pages.

The aforementioned publications served as the primary sources for the book. In instances when a major event took place, I consulted additional newspapers and added their most interesting reports. As the bibliography reveals, many other sources were tapped to fill in backstories and provide perspective in the description of the events.

Other newspapers in the state often reprinted versions of stories that first appeared in Bristol's print media rather than sending their own staff reporters to these events.

As a result, the importance of the Bristol reporters' work cannot be overstated. Their documentation of the events and people that shaped Muzzy Field's history stands, in many cases, as the only such recording of these magnificent stories. Without those people and their journalistic endeavors, this book would not exist. The Bristol Public Library's and the Bristol Historical Society's roles as caretakers of the city's many stories render them equally invaluable as the public's gateway to all that came before them.

It was within the walls of those institutions that I was able to bring to light stories long forgotten and in need of wider circulation.

This book does not delve much into the era of the Bristol Red Sox or anything thereafter. The stories of Bristol as a minor league city of the Eastern League in the 1970s and 1980s warrant a book unto themselves, because so much more information exists to document that entertaining era. As the late *Bristol Press* sportswriter and author, Jack Lautier, told me one evening at Muzzy Field, "It was *Bull Durham* before *Bull Durham*."

Considerably less is known about the pre-Red Sox history of Bristol's venerable ballpark. My intention with this book is to honor the history that has been largely filed away and unspoken for decades.

These are the stories of a Muzzy Field that many never knew existed, the tales of a forgotten ballpark.

*Douglas S. Malan*
*October 2007*

# Epicenter of History

The demise of the defending world champions, the Pittsburgh Pirates, was already under way when the team's train pulled into Union Station in Hartford. On that Sunday morning in June 1926, there was little indication that the ball club's brief stop in Connecticut was anything more than a relaxing off day during a two-week road trip out East.

The Pirates, traveling between Philadelphia and Boston that day, were an immensely talented team that was showing signs of inconsistent baseball, having opened their season with seven wins in April before winning sixteen of twenty-four in May. Despite their 28–21 record on June 13, manager Bill McKechnie's club struggled against the Phillies and the Braves, the two worst teams in the National League. This despite a young, potent lineup that by season's end featured six players with batting averages of .308 or higher and a staff earned run average of 3.67.

For the most part, the 1926 Pirates returned the same lineup that won the 1925 World Series in seven games over the Washington Senators. The only changes were Hal Rhyne at second base in place of Eddie Moore, and rookie Paul Waner replacing Clyde Barnhart in the outfield. The entire pitching staff remained intact. On the surface and at such an early stage of the season, the Pirates could be seen as just working out the kinks.

But there was tension in the Pittsburgh clubhouse, and their arrival in Hartford began one of the most incredible days of their unpredictable season.

McKechnie's club was in town to play an exhibition game at Muzzy Field in Bristol to benefit the Hartford Firemen's Pension Fund, arranged by promoter John Gunshanan, a former ballplayer with Bristol of the Connecticut State League. Prior to the afternoon game, the Pirates disembarked at Union Station and ate breakfast at the swank Hotel Bond in downtown Hartford where many of the city's prominent figures met them. In honor of Hartford's brief history as a nineteenth-century professional baseball town, the group held a ceremony at the Cedar Hill Cemetery graveside of Morgan G. Bulkeley, the National League's first president, before traveling west by car to New Britain for a similar ceremony in recognition of former NL president and umpire Thomas J. Lynch.

A semipro team from New Departure Manufacturing Company awaited the Pirates for the midafternoon game at Muzzy Field. As an industrial giant in ball bearing and coaster brake production and a subsidiary of General Motors that designed the first Yellow Cab in 1907, the wealthy New Departure Company offered recreational opportunities throughout the year for its employees. Its baseball program, officially launched in 1919, prospered from two key factors—plenty of wealth and a company president willing to spend money on the sport.

As a result, New Departure annually fielded one of the more successful semipro clubs in New England and enjoyed a continued run through the 1920s as the champions of Connecticut, albeit often self-proclaimed. Its roster was a collection of players who spent time in the major and minor leagues and starred for colleges throughout the Northeast. Although the company's newspaper enjoyed taking the self-righteous stance that its players were all employees at New Departure and not those playing "for mercenary motives," as the sports pages stated indignantly of the opposition, there was shuffling of players on a yearly basis, and it seems that talented ballplayers were provided with day jobs.

"Mostly the players were from other towns, and [New Departure] employed them there. They'd offer them a job. Not a big job, but they got paid," said Louis Laponte, a longtime New Departure employee and Bristol native who played shortstop for the team in the 1930s.

This was especially true once New Departure became an established power in the early 1920s, and the baseball players were held in high regard during the program's halcyon days before the Depression. Some of them resided at the company-owned Endee Inn and spent two or three afternoons a week practicing at Muzzy Field.

"Well-known players have been brought here and placed at work in the factory so that New Departure would put a team in the field which would represent the city," the *Bristol Press* wrote in April 1919.

Although Muzzy Field was technically a public facility within Rockwell Park in Bristol's West End, New Departure funded the maintenance and improvements that turned the spacious field with distant fences into one of the classiest ballparks in New England and now one of the oldest in America.

Muzzy Field in 1926 reflected the prosperity of its surroundings, humming with activity and producing a product of baseball as high in quality as that of the city's ball bearings and coaster brakes, if not as well-known nationally. Aside from

New Departure, Bristol boasted a strong industrial core where the majority of its twenty thousand residents worked. Those not employed in the factories ran the corner markets and various specialty shops in the downtown area near the field.

Many of them flocked to Muzzy Field on weekends from April to September for the entertainment of New Departure baseball, and fans came to expect the finest opposition in those traditional Sunday afternoon games. While the Pirates' appearance in June 1926 certainly created a stir of excitement from the time it was announced in May, the fact that a major league team would challenge the Endees in the middle of the major league season was not uncommon.

After all, Muzzy Field attendants had seen their hometown club host, and sometimes defeat, premiere baseball teams from the United States and Cuba that featured some of the most legendary names in the history of the game. In the eight-year span from the inception of New Departure baseball to the game against Pittsburgh, Muzzy Field served as a playground for the spectacular. Babe Ruth appeared with the Boston Red Sox in 1919 and a year later with a semipro outfit from Hartford. Martín Dihigo and other Cuban legends appeared with teams between 1921 and 1925, as did several Negro League teams. And numerous former major leaguers played against New Departure for semipro clubs from the Northeast.

The astounding parade of baseball legends during the decade culminated when the world champion Pirates arrived at Muzzy Field on that Sunday afternoon in 1926. If the visitors were unaware of the field's history, they probably were prone to overlook a team of part-time ballplayers, although several of the New Departure athletes had played for one of the four Eastern League teams in nearby Waterbury, New Haven, Bridgeport, and Hartford.

Laponte, a teenager at the time, was in the stands to see the Pirates along with nearly three thousand other fans, a somewhat disappointing figure considering the *Bristol Press* predicted upwards of ten thousand people would attend the game. Ironically, the trend toward declining attendance increased by the mid-1920s when the fans in Bristol, still considered one of Connecticut's strong baseball towns, began clamoring for more games against in-state rivals rather than teams featuring baseball's luminaries. By 1926, the acrimonious on-field relationship between New Departure and teams from Manchester or Torrington attracted as many fans as, if not more than, any appearance by a well-stocked traveling team or even a major league club.

Unbeknownst to future Hall of Famer Max Carey, he was in his final days with the defending World Series champion Pittsburgh Pirates when they visited Muzzy Field in late spring 1926 to play in what many consider to be the greatest game ever staged on the field. (Courtesy: Getty Images)

And without the help of mass media, visiting teams and ballplayers—save for Babe Ruth—rarely arrived with the hype that would shatter the quiet side streets of Bristol if the defending World Series champions were to arrive today for an exhibition game. In a factory town of proud residents with deep family roots, battling Manchester, the boys from across the river, meant more than watching an extremely talented, yet unknown, player named Dihigo.

But in retrospect, the Pirates game and many other athletic events in Muzzy Field's history shined with a brilliance reserved for amazing stories that have been lost in brittle pages of old newspapers. Though the park has undergone physical changes since it opened in 1912 and celebrated its first "official" game in 1914, the footprints of some of the all-time greatest athletes remain embedded in the field.

A motorcade from Hartford brought several of them when future Hall of Famers Waner, McKechnie, Kiki Cuyler, Pie Traynor, and Max Carey arrived on June 13, 1926. If the Pirates thought the Phillies and Braves had been a challenge that season, they certainly did not expect such resistance from these upstart New Departurites.

# Roots of Baseball in Bristol

Long before Muzzy Field became the central gathering spot for Bristol entertainment, the townspeople had become devout followers of the game. As early as 1859, Bristolites were playing baseball on the Federal Hill Green and workers were said to have called out of work at the cost of a day's pay just to play the popular game (Clouette and Roth 1984).

The Federal Hill Green initially was purchased in 1773, and Bristol, then known as New Cambridge, used the green as "a place of perade [*sic*]" and later as the playground for the Federal Hill School. But as baseball's presence took root in the rural town, the green—the only open space available for public sports—served as the hub of athletic activity (Peck 1932).

Today the green is a smaller, quiet patch of grass with some playground equipment and a rudimentary chain-link backstop. After the Civil War, players and fans gathered regularly on the lot to participate in the burgeoning national pastime as well as the locally popular game of wicket, a New England spin on the old English game, cricket. The postwar surge in popularity compelled the formation of town teams of everyone from the YMCA to Bristol's factories to neighborhood groups like the Bristol Oneidas, the Nine Brothers of Terryville, the Lobster Legs of Forestville, and the Brick Block Nines, which fielded a team of residents from the large brick apartment buildings on Main Street (Clouette and Roth 1984; Lautier 1988). A second field emerged just down the street from the steep hill on which the Federal Hill Green was perched. The Center Street Grounds served as the home of the Bristol Indians, the local entry in the professional Connecticut State League, which counted Connie Mack among its players with the 1884 Meriden squad.

Baseball quickly became a blue-collar avocation for residents who, by 1870, were experiencing the industrialization of their country town. A strong, profitable industrial base soon paralleled the quality of baseball on display, and the status of Bristol as a vibrant community further defined its role as one of the state's foremost baseball towns.

Interest in the game spiked in 1896 when New Departure, then a bell manu-facturer, fielded a team of factory workers that competed as amateurs and played a series of games against Torrington and Winsted. The 1896 Bristol Bells had their fair share of baseball talent with Ad Yale and Ed Cassian playing catcher and second base for the squad coached by Manager Piggott. Yale became a first base-man with Brooklyn in 1905, and Cassian was a former Philadelphia Phillie.

A year later, Bristol secured a position in the Class B Connecticut State League, an aggregation of five professional teams that traveled by trolley cars, owing to the proximity of the towns, with players earning $125 a month (*Hart-ford Times* 1901). Despite the natural rivalries, lackluster gate receipts from the smallest town in the league threatened to wipe out Bristol's months-old existence. After the suspension of the Bristol season on June 3 followed by the possibility of relocating to Winsted, Bristol coal and wood merchant Otto F. Strunz offered to rescue the franchise during a league meeting in Derby and bankrolled the team with other merchants, thereby keeping the team in Bristol and resuming its sea-son on June 10 (Lautier 1988; *Hartford Times* 1901). The team finished in fifth place with a 35–44 mark.

The Spanish-American War wiped out the 1898 campaign in Bristol, but its team returned to the CSL in 1899 under the direction of John Gunshanan, a left fielder from the 1897 Bristol team and businessman from Hartford whose base-ball connections would lead to important historic moments at Muzzy Field. But at the turn of the twentieth century, Bristol's professional baseball future was in doubt until a meeting at the Bristol Opera House drew a collection of well-heeled citizens who provided the funds to keep the team alive. With Gunshanan serving as manager, Bristol improved to 47–42, finishing fourth, but his constant shuf-fling of the lineup perturbed fans who wanted consistent names and faces on the field.

For all of the money put up at the beginning of the season, the Bristol fran-chise was in debt at the end of the 1899 campaign. Still, the involved business-men made certain to pay the players and anyone else who was owed money (Lautier 1988).

A new ownership group took over the 1900 season and built upon Gunsha-nan's improvements. Strunz returned to the fold with William J. Tracy (a meat market owner), John E. Kennedy (a barber), and James H. Hayes (a trolley oper-ator), by his side. The quartet hired Rhode Island native Jimmy Cooney as man-ager, and he brought with him the experience of playing 324 games for Chicago and Washington of the National League from 1890 to 1892.

Bristol's 47–46 record that year overwhelmed few, but the club returned a majority of its players in 1901 for what would prove to be the high point in the early days of Bristol baseball history.

With two future major leaguers on their roster, the Bristol Indians stormed through the league with a 65–40 mark paced by returning pitchers Homer Mock (23–10) and pitcher/dentist Dr. Frank Reisling (23–11), who would later join Walter Johnson on the Washington Senators' pitching staffs of 1909–10 after two seasons in Brooklyn in 1904–5.

The one-two punch was a force in the CSL, and if not for Reisling's encouragement, the duo might never have been team leaders for the Indians. Reisling arrived in Bristol in late May 1899 after abbreviated stints in the Ohio and West Virginia League, the Interstate League, and the Eastern League. An Ohio native who worked his way through the Ohio Medical College, "Doc" spent part of 1899 with the Hartford Eastern Leaguers before entering the CSL. He was known to be a strong hitter after fashioning a .400 average with a 15–13 mound record before the Ohio and West Virginia League dissolved in 1897, and he could play any position on the field (*Hartford Times* 1901).

Before the 1901 season, the twenty-seven-year-old right-hander coaxed Mock, another Ohioan, away from Canton where he had been pitching in an independent league. As a sturdy left-hander, Mock began playing professional baseball in 1898 when he reportedly signed with the Washington Senators of the National League. Although he never played a game in the major leagues, his performances in subsequent years caught Reisling's eye, and the doctor lured the twenty-four-year-old to the East Coast.

Two college pitchers, James Eddy and Frank McLean, joined the team during the summer and rounded out the rotation. When not on the mound, Eddy played a brilliant right field and the *Hartford Times* called him "easily the best fielder in the league as his throws in from the corner of the garden have cut off many a runner at the plate and at third."

A smooth-fielding bunch considered to be the CSL's premiere defense strengthened the pitching staff, and these two elements essentially captured the league championship for a team that did not produce strong offensive numbers and found themselves in many low-scoring games.

The team's performance was not a secret outside of Connecticut. Following the championship, the newly formed Chicago White Sox sent two telegrams asking Reisling to name his price, but the married dentist declined the offer because his practice had become so busy that he needed an assistant. He did not have time to join the major leagues. Mock, too, was courted by the major leagues, but for unknown reasons he declined to join Cincinnati's club for the close of the season.

With only two Connecticut natives on the 1901 roster, catcher Paddy O'Connor was a virtual local, hailing from Windsor Locks. He went on to play for the Pittsburgh Pirates (1908–10), where he earned a World Series championship in 1909, St. Louis Cardinals (1914), Pittsburgh Rebels (1915) of the Federal League, and the 1918 New York Yankees. But for the 1901 Bristol team, the twenty-two-year-old caught only a handful of games after arriving late in the season to fill in for injured catchers Arthur Anderson and Frank Beaumont.

Two other players on the 1901 state championship team already had spent time in the major leagues. Second baseman Red Owens played eight games with Philadelphia in 1899 and returned to the majors in 1905 with Brooklyn, hitting .214 in forty-three games. Veteran Ted Scheffler, the captain, was a thirty-eight-year-old left fielder who had played for the 1888 Detroit Wolverines of the National League and the 1890 Rochester Broncos of the American Association.

Owens teamed with an infield of seasoned professional ballplayers who all spent several seasons in minor league baseball leading up to 1901. With shortstop Hodge "Kid" Berry, Bristol was believed to have the sharpest middle infield in the league. With Edward Connors, first baseman, and Thomas Francis, third baseman, on the corners, the team boasted "by far the fastest [infield] in the league," according to the *Hartford Times*.

The collection of talent spread throughout the field, and Bristol won the pennant by four games over the Bridgeport Orators, owned by Jim O'Rourke, a Hall of Famer who won two World Series with the New York Giants and presided over the CSL.

He congratulated the team from the relatively small town of seven thousand in a letter that read, "You have won (the pennant) under admirable circumstances and conditions, free from taint and suspicion and by the strictest observance of every principle of fair play. May the example you have given us in 1901 be an incentive for emulation."

But of the CSL clubs that could emulate the team in the 1902 campaign, Bristol was excluded. Although the bills and players had somehow always been paid, the team's four-year existence was fraught with financial difficulties, and the owners jettisoned the franchise after their pennant-winning season. The club picked up operations in Springfield, Massachusetts. Derby, which finished in last place at 38–71, also folded, and the franchise moved to Holyoke, Massachusetts. Both cities promised greater gate receipts due to larger populations, and the Connecticut State League became a misnomer.

Muzzy Field's history benefited from well-connected baseball people in Bristol. Local businessman William J. Tracy, right, served as Connecticut State League president in the early 1900s. One of the league's alumni was good friend Connie Mack, left, who spent time playing for the league's Meriden entry in 1884. The two are pictured here in New York in 1911. (Courtesy: Bristol Historical Society)

As some of the players from the 1901 Bristol team entered the major leagues, Tracy took over for O'Rourke as CSL president and served from 1902 to 1906 (Lautier 1988).

Without a professional team, Bristol looked to Tracy for its baseball future. While juggling his CSL duties, Tracy formed an entry called the Flats for the Town Amateur Baseball League, a semipro circuit, and the club registered a 32–6 record in the first two seasons.

One of the team's stars was pitcher George Bresnahan, who would go on to work for more than forty years with New Departure. Considered a top-flight semipro hurler, he found early success with the spitball. Mixed with his curve, changeup, and fastball, Bresnahan turned in two pitching gems in particular during the 1903 season. Against a college all-star team consisting of players from Wesleyan University, the University of Maine, and the University of Vermont, Bresnahan allowed one hit and one walk, faced twenty-nine batters, and allowed only one to reach as far as second base. In an important contest against nearby Unionville, he pitched a sixteen-inning complete game, scattering eight hits and striking out twelve in a 2–1 victory.

Despite the financial concerns that kept the professional game out of Bristol, the success of organized teams served notice that the town had the ingredients for producing high-quality baseball. During the next decade, town leaders took steps to ensure the public an athletic facility befitting its growing size and sporting enthusiasm.

The most important maneuver was made by a town leader and businessman who had a passion for wicket and for providing Bristol residents with a top-notch park.

◆    ◆    ◆

In the same year that the Bristol Indians secured championship glory, Bristol native Adrian James Muzzy was celebrating his twenty-fifth anniversary in the dry goods business. His store was the town's most popular destination for shoppers looking for nearly anything from women's hats to carpets and other house furnishings. His Riverside Avenue store was an institution, and the lifelong businessman played a major role in town government and civic policy, serving as a founding member of Bristol's Progressive Party in 1912.

Muzzy was a strong supporter of recreational activities and like many other affluent businessmen in town, he enjoyed playing wicket, a sport whose continued domination by the Bristol team predated its first baseball championship by

nearly sixty years (Peck 1932). As a twenty-nine-year-old in 1880, Muzzy participated in a wicket match in Brooklyn, New York, against a talented local team.
The Bristol squad scored a relatively easy victory, performing with acumen
unseen by the Brooklyn players and press. During that road trip, Muzzy experienced festive crowds gathered around hotly contested ball games.

In Bristol, that celebratory atmosphere had been evident during the wicket
state championship of 1859 against New Britain when a special five-car train,
decorated with bunting and filled with bands, fans, and players, left Hartford,
stopped in New Britain, and arrived to a raucous crowd at the Bristol train station.

Such pageantry later surrounded important New Departure baseball games.

By 1901, Bristol's identity was changing. The rural characteristics of the town
were disappearing as new factories and houses sprouted downtown. Land-use
decisions were being made that would affect the future of Bristol. Even the
wealthy and powerful figures who generally profited from the decisions ques-
tioned the process when it appeared their own personal slice of privacy would be
affected by high-density development.

This was the case when Mrs. Albert Rockwell, wife of New Departure's
founder and benefactor of Rockwell Park, passionately protested an expansion of
her husband's company that stood down the hill from their stunning Brightwood
estate on West Street, a granite-walled example of seventeeth-century English
architecture secluded in wooded land along the banks of the Pequabuck River.
She protested in vain (Clouette and Roth 1984).

But industrial encroachment extended only so far, and a section of town along
Bellevue Avenue near the Federal Hill Green remained the unique and sole possession of the families who benefited most from the morphing town center.

With an influx of immigrants from Ireland, Italy, Poland, and Germany, the
face of Bristol was changing from its days as a quiet agrarian Yankee town.

Around 1910, open plots like the Center Street Grounds were threatened with
the type of housing developments that still define those areas in present-day Bristol, and a local organization formed to preserve land for public recreation. In the
same year that Fenway Park opened in Boston, the Bristol Public Welfare Association (BPWA) received its first land donation when Muzzy offered five acres
within Hickory Park north of Park Street in memory of his two sons, Leslie
Adrian Muzzy and Floyd Downs Muzzy, who died in early childhood.

A request to call the plot Muzzy Athletic Field was carried through, and the
location sat within a park, once owned by industrialist Wallace Barnes, that
hosted popular harness racing events in the nineteenth century. Soon enough,

baseball would far surpass horse racing as the town's warm weather recreation of choice.

BPWA transferred the land to the city in 1912 and field preparation began in the same year. By February 1913, town meetings were held to discuss the construction of a grandstand and outfield fence along with the placement of the playing field, which would serve only for baseball games until another Muzzy land transaction six years later.

The first game at Muzzy Field occurred on May 1, 1913, when the grammar schools of Bristol and Meriden competed in the unofficial christening, but it was more than a year later before the grounds were officially opened with an exhibition doubleheader fund-raiser.

If Muzzy Field is to be celebrated properly as a ballpark that hosted athletic figures and events of great historical significance, then the events of July 8, 1914, deserve their due documentation. If not for the fact that it was the field's first banner event, the date would simply signify a gathering of ordinary townspeople playing baseball, which, one could argue, was the purpose of the field from the outset.

A crowd of approximately one hundred watched as teams from east and west Bristol, one coached by William J. Tracy, battled it out for three innings. One highlight was Bristol mayor James Cray leaving the game after he exhausted himself chasing a triple in the spacious ballpark, whose fence had not been completed at the time.

The second game pitted two other local nines against each other, and the money raised at the gates with twenty-five-cent admission was used to help pay for grading the land, removing a few small trees, and building the fence that would have eased Mayor Cray's responsibilities in center field that day.

For a ballpark that would see more glorious days and brighter stars, the doubleheader was somewhat unimpressive. But it ushered in an era of baseball that would place Bristol on the national map after the young industrial city answered a call to help drive America's military effort in World War I.

◆    ◆    ◆

With America's involvement in World War I, Bristol factories were booming as Connecticut produced a majority of the nation's munitions for the battles of Europe in 1917. Employment numbers skyrocketed, and local factories hummed with activity. Bristol Brass, National Marine Lamp, and New Departure, which had been sold to United Motors (soon to be General Motors) in 1916, all dedicated a majority of their output toward the war effort and built new housing for families who moved to town to help meet demand for workers.

Bristol residents volunteered in great numbers for Company D of the National Guard, and by the fall of 1917 the town had sent thirteen hundred men into service.

Townspeople's attention, understandably, was on the war. Little thought or time was given to baseball, although an initial effort was made to organize a semi-pro state league that included Winsted, Hartford, New Britain, Ivoryton, and Torrington.

The 1917 Bristol squad featured second baseman/shortstop George Scott and center fielder Raymond "Nanny" Green, two players who newspapers said would help make the local entry one of the most competitive in the league.

But by July, the team and the season dissolved due to lack of players and support. Even the factory league, which abruptly ended its season in June, could not attract enough interest to remain viable. Before the end of the state league season, Scott quit baseball to join Company D in the army.

As the *New Departure News* wrote that month, "Throughout the country, it seems to be an off-year for baseball."

Muzzy Field remained quiet for most of that summer except for a highly anticipated game that took place in August between players from the old Town Amateur Baseball League teams of the early 1900s and current town players.

The game served as a fund-raiser for the Red Cross, and the old TAB team included left-handed pitcher, Judge William J. Malone, who had made a name for himself as a southpaw on the Yale Law School team, and shortstop Doc Mac-Donald, studying mental illnesses at the Middletown Insane Asylum while playing for that aggregation during the summer.

The old-timers lost, 7–5, but the game raised $122. For the rest of the summer and early autumn, pickup games dotted Muzzy Field's schedule, including the popular interdepartment battles during New Departure's Field Day celebrations. That annual barbecue and festival for employees and their families would become the largest of its kind in the country, according to the company.

Although interest in baseball at Muzzy Field remained cool in 1918, New Departure's team regularly played games every weekend, despite a proposed league that never got off the ground in the spring. They ended the season on Labor Day when the United States government cut off the major league schedule as more players were entering the war.

Under the direction of manager Maurice Kenyon, New Departure finished 14–11–1 with a light-hitting team (.232 team average) that committed fifty-two errors. If not for one of the most impressive seasons ever registered by a New Departure pitcher, the team's win total probably would have been far fewer.

Before the first game in May, word arrived from Europe that German forces had seriously wounded George Scott, Bristol native and former New Departure and TAB infielder, in the battle of Seicheprey, a small village in northeastern France. Scott's Company D was one of the first to clash with the Germans, and the unit suffered heavy casualties in the bloody fighting.

Scott survived and remained in the army, but no matter the action at Muzzy Field, the realities of war prohibited full enjoyment. Other townsmen and New Departure employees were at serious risk overseas.

The New Departure team of 1918 featured several high school and college players, including William J. Tracy's son, Francis, who played shortstop.

But the undisputed star of the squad turned out to be a young right-hander from the banks of the Champlain River in Vermont named James "Doc" Williams. Having gained pitching experience with the Barre (VT) Athletic Club and Goddard Seminary, Williams was known for pinpoint control guiding a fastball with good zip.

Although New Departure's opponents of 1918 paled in comparison to those of the 1920s, Williams put up numbers on the mound against other semipro factory teams that command attention.

His eleven-strikeout three-hitter on opening day against Bristol Brass presaged a dominant season from the youngster, and he struck out thirty-four batters in his first three games of the season while remaining composed and confident to the point that the *New Departure News* wrote, he "has a smile as disconcerting as his pitching. The louder the noise, the broader he smiles."

Williams continued to pile up gaudy statistics, and a lack of run support against tougher competition from Torrington and New Britain was the only thing that kept his misleading win-loss record hovering around .500.

In the season's most intense game, Williams stared down bitter rival Torrington on June 15 at Muzzy Field and threw a two-hitter with nine strikeouts. Despite his performance, his opponents scratched out a 1–0 victory in what the *New Departure News* called "an exhibition of baseball the equal of which has never been seen in Bristol."

Williams dropped another tough decision to New Britain in July when his six-hitter went for naught in a 2–0 loss.

By that time, professional ballplayers were trading their gloves for guns, and the Eastern League discontinued its season when the government decided that nonessential workers, such as players, would have to either work toward the war effort or fight. Along with the American League, National League, and International League in minor league baseball, New Departure vowed to play out the extent of their schedule.

Williams finished August in a blaze winning all four of his starts, notching a season-high seventeen strikeouts in a two-hitter against Jewell Belting Company at Muzzy Field, and recording sixteen strikeouts in a four-hitter on the road against the Meriden Lutherans.

In the last game of the season, New Departure lost 4–3 to Waterbury, which was reported to have been composed mainly of professional players, and Williams abruptly said good-bye to Bristol as he returned to his farm in Charlotte, Vermont.

In just one season, he posted statistics that would never be equaled by another ND hurler. Taking into consideration incomplete box scores from three games, Williams went 9–7–1 with 144 strikeouts, 18 combined walks and hit batsmen, and 83 hits surrendered in 130 innings.

Despite speculation that he might return in the spring, James "Doc" Williams never again appeared at Muzzy Field or in a New Departure uniform, and the entire team was overhauled before the 1919 season, including Manager Kenyon, who took a job in Pennsylvania.

As Bristol and the world suffered through the deadly Spanish influenza outbreak during 1918, they found reason to celebrate when the war ended in November. As Muzzy Field thawed in the spring of 1919, it would soon become something much grander than a municipal field hosting friendly ball games among locals.

# 1919: Dawn of Baseball's Golden Years

Though tempered by the ravaging effects of the flu pandemic, Bristolites joined Americans nationwide in celebrating the official end of World War I on November 11, 1918. With a majority of the boys headed home, New Departure swelled with new employees and thrust itself into the sporting landscape.

The malaise that affected the game the previous two seasons lifted under the spring sun, and the town exuded postwar pride.

"The war is over and people are ready to be amused and enthused," the *New Departure News* cried out in its March 1 edition. "Sports are coming back with a jump."

Surging interest in sports compelled the city's major industrial power to form the New Departure Athletic Association in the spring to provide year-round sporting outlets for men and women. Lester Sigourney, the sports editor for the *New Departure News*, served as president. This decision alone indicated that athletics were going to play a larger role as entertainment for the masses, and Muzzy Field would become the central gathering place. The change was evident even in the newspaper, which began dedicating considerably more space to its twice-monthly baseball reports than it had during the war.

With the blessing of sports enthusiast and New Departure president DeWitt Page, the baseball team, and all company teams, were promised full support from the NDAA. As a result, rowdy cheering sections showed their support at New Departure home and away games and would come to define some of the classic games against Manchester. Page, who was said to have arrived for games at Muzzy Field in his chauffeur-driven green Cadillac, hired Harry Drucquer, recently dispatched from the army, as the baseball manager.

Drucquer began shaping a team that carried the heavy weight of high preseason expectations. Around the state, he maintained a reputation as a fine manager who created the powerful Redwood Baseball Club in nearby Meriden while remaining well-connected with "all of the fast semiprofessional ball players in New England," the *New Departure News* reported.

The new manager wasted no time revamping the New Departure lineup. Coinciding with a spike in hiring at the company, a wealth of baseball talent flooded into Bristol prior to the 1919 season. Former major and minor league players who had since taken up semiprofessional baseball combined with talented college players to form a New Departure ball club that immediately separated itself from its predecessors.

Some of the ballplayers would become icons in the town, their names adorning present-day baseball facilities as a reminder of their influence. Two of them came to New Departure with major league experience.

Lester Alfred Lanning, nicknamed "Red" during his professional days, was a multitalented pitcher and outfielder who played for Connie Mack's woeful Philadelphia Athletics team of 1916 that finished 36–117, fifty-four and a half games behind first-place Boston. During a season in which Mack used fifty-one players, the twenty-one-year-old left-hander pitched in six games and batted thirty-three times.

He was winless on the mound with 3 losses and an 8.14 ERA in $24^{1}/_{3}$ innings, walking nearly twice as many as he struck out. The five-foot-nine, 165-pound control pitcher did not fool many hitters with his changeup in the American League, but against teams on New Departure's schedule, he was a true force.

The same went for his hitting. With the Athletics, Lanning collected six hits with two doubles and a run batted in while scoring five times. He fared much better in Bristol, and he suited up in 1919 predominantly as an outfielder.

Another former major leaguer arrived with a more colorful baseball past and quickly became a fan favorite for his playing ability and personality. James Arthur "Swat" McCabe was a left-handed hitting right fielder who stood five foot ten and weighed a shade below 190 pounds during his playing days.

He already was thirty-seven years old in 1919, but his hitting ability made him an obvious choice as a starting outfielder. One of McCabe's earliest experiences in organized baseball came with the United States Army, which he joined in 1897 after lying about his age. He then traveled through the Connecticut State League circuit, making stops in Meriden and New Britain, before breaking into the majors with the 1909 Cincinnati Reds, though it was not an easy segue.

## "SMILER" LANNING.
### Happy as a Lark Out in Center Field.

Les Lanning reached the major leagues at twenty-one as a pitcher and outfielder with the 1916 Philadelphia Athletics. He became one of New Departure's finest players when he joined the team in 1919. (Courtesy: Bristol Public Library)

After New Britain owner William Hanna sold McCabe to Cincinnati Reds owner Garry Herrmann, the outfielder audaciously, at the time, demanded a two-hundred-fifty-dollar cut of the two-thousand-dollar deal, enraging New Britain officials and the local newspapers that covered both teams. "This I positively refused to do, considering it a 'stick-up,'" Hanna wrote to Cincinnati's team counsel, August Harriman, in September 1909. "He has been badly influenced by someone, and he will probably see his error and report later ... I am very much disappointed in his actions and was in hopes our business relations would be most amiable."

McCabe's demand came after the Reds forwarded train fare for his trip west on a Friday to reach Cincinnati for a Sunday game. An angered Hanna promptly cancelled the train trip.

"It is possible he may realize how foolishly he is acting before time for the train to pull out to-night," the *New Britain Herald* reported. "(Reds manager) Clark Griffith will not stand for any monkey-doodle business of this kind from a graduate of the minors."

From the *Cincinnati Enquirer*: "When a man has a chance to jump from a class A league to the majors and spends so much time looking at a few plunks that he thinks [someone] ought to hand him for nothing that he misses a tryout, he would probably not make good; anyway, certainly not in the way of brains." Griffith was quoted as saying, "If he doesn't come this fall he will only be standing in his own light, and we will not shed any tears at this end of the line."

McCabe eventually acquiesced and landed in the Queen City. In three games, he collected six hits in eleven at-bats while committing three errors in the outfield. McCabe showed promise and returned to Cincinnati in 1910, despite his contract dispute.

Hanna's agreement with the Reds called for the National League team's officials to pay a seven-hundred-fifty-dollar down payment in September 1909 and the remaining $1,250 by May 15, 1910, so long as McCabe "proves satisfactory," Hanna stated in his letter to the Reds.

Four days before that May deadline, McCabe was in Cincinnati and wrote to Harriman on Hotel Havlin stationery. "The understanding between Mr. Hanna and myself was that I was to get $500 in case I was retained by the Cincinnati club after the 15th of May and as I think I will stay (in the major leagues) I wish you would kindly make arrangements with Mr. Hanna so that I will be taken care of."

It is unknown for certain if McCabe received any or all of the money he requested, but he certainly won no friends in the Cincinnati front office.

In his second stint with the Reds, he batted .257 with five RBI in thirteen games and played flawless defense with two assists. On opening day, April 14, against the Chicago Cubs, he got a hit off of Orvie Overall and followed up the next day by going 2-for-3 with a run scored against Mordecai "Three Finger" Brown. About a month later, he socked a double off of Christy Mathewson.

But his fun-loving ways and practical joking did not sit well with Reds management, and McCabe lost his job in Cincinnati because of what newspaper reports called "extra-curricular activities."

He returned to Buffalo of the International League where he continued to produce to the delight of the coaches, until he ignored a bunt signal during a game and swung away, cracking a double.

"He made the remark, 'What do you have one of your best hitters bunting for? I'm calling the shots here,'" said his son, Jack McCabe, born in Bristol in 1922. "He was a real fun guy. Too much at times, I think. In his older years, I think he regretted a little bit of his actions. He could've been up there [in the majors] a lot longer with his ability."

Buffalo severed ties with McCabe, who then played in Pennsylvania and Connecticut before joining New Departure as one of their most potent hitters.

Catcher Clyde Waters became a fixture behind the plate starting in 1919, and the former minor leaguer served as captain of the baseball team and played quarterback for the West End Athletic Club football team, which played their home games at Muzzy. Waters left the Winchester Repeating Arms Company in New Haven for New Departure in Bristol in March 1919, and the *Bristol Press* printed a story from the *New Haven Register* that described Waters as the most popular baseball and football player in that town as well as "one of the best catchers in the state."

The New York Yankees owned the rights to Waters, and he spent several seasons playing with the New Haven entry of the Connecticut State League while logging the 1918 season with the New Haven Colonials of the Eastern League. The Yankees never recalled him, and he built a reputation in his town of West Haven, strong enough to be selected to run for the town clerk's office.

An acclaimed football referee, Waters often worked some of the local games at Muzzy Field involving the West End Athletic Club the day after ruling a high-profile collegiate contest.

Bristol native George Scott probably was the most beloved member of
the New Departure baseball team. (Courtesy: Bristol Public Library)

Hometown hero George Scott returned to Bristol as the starting second baseman on a solid infield that included former Cleveland Naps shortstop George
Dunlop, a teammate of "Shoeless Joe" Jackson, and team leader and namesake
Nap Lajoie during the 1913 and 1914 seasons with the American League fore-
runner to the Indians. Ernest "Smoke" Halbach was at third and the tall, sure-

handed Eddie Zielke manned first base. With two former major leaguers in the outfield, Gene Gaffney filled the spot in left, and Gus Forslund was a utility player who ended up seeing action at five different positions during the season.

Pitchers on the preseason roster included Dan Harrigan and Cecil Randolph "Squiz" Pillion, a left-hander who appeared in two games with the 1915 Philadelphia A's. Neither stayed with New Departure past July, but they won three games while in uniform.

The strength of the pitching staff centered on two southpaws with considerable minor league experience. Earl Champion and Eddie Goodridge were stingy workhorses who joined New Departure in the first two months of the season and performed the bulk of the pitching duties from June to September. They frequently stymied the opposition. Goodridge, an Amherst graduate, was an athletic and economical pitcher who could strike out opponents as often as he induced them into weak ground balls. The lanky Champion fooled batters with his sidearm delivery and reportedly caught the eye of Boston Braves manager George Stallings during his 1918 minor league season in New London and Binghamton. Pittsfield was in hot pursuit when Champion joined the Endees.

The duo helped carry out the prediction that New Departure would field one of the sharpest nines in New England.

Meanwhile, Muzzy Field earned its fair share of attention as it transformed from humble beginnings into a first-class non-major league ballpark in 1919. Under the direction of grounds crew manager Percy Burnham, the pockmarked field was smoothed out with a double layer of sod under a cover of loam at second and third base while holes were filled in at first and shortstop, and the infield was leveled in general. Spots in the outfield received some fill, too, although it played a little rougher than the polished infield, according to the *New Departure News*.

William J. Tracy remained active in Bristol's baseball scene at this time as the representative of the board of park commissioners who urged downtown merchants, factory owners, and athletic clubs to provide some of the help needed to construct a grandstand with amenities modeled after Waterbury's Eastern League ballpark.

The wooden covered grandstand would accommodate twelve hundred fans, nearly five times as many as the old bleachers it was replacing. A ticket office at the entrance to the park would lead to a wooden plank walkway ascending into the aisles of the grandstand. Below the seating, there were two spacious dressing rooms; washrooms with toilets, washbowls, and showers; and windows and a concrete floor. Additional picnic grounds surrounding Muzzy Field extended west of the ballpark on a level surface near the banks of the Pequabuck River that flows behind the outfield fences.

At a cost of twelve thousand dollars, the project excited many of the town's faithful fans who united to "give Bristol a first-class athletic park," the *New Departure News* noted, and Tracy was calling on everyone to pitch in to build and paint the new Muzzy Field grandstand in time for a Flag Day celebration honoring Bristol's World War I veterans.

In early June, the town council voted to begin construction of a cinder track in the ballpark's outfield at a cost of one thousand dollars, which would allow high school athletes to compete in interscholastic meets. The track also hosted club meets with athletes from throughout the Northeast. In a town that loved its sports, Muzzy Field had the ability to host baseball, boxing, and track events, and when Adrian Muzzy sold to the parks department surrounding land for one dollar in mid-September, a football field was constructed that also served as a soccer pitch.

Undoubtedly, the 1919 season promised to be electric, and a season-opening victory over Wesleyan University in Middletown on April 19 began a two-and-a-half-month tear for New Departure. Behind pitchers Harrigan and Dutch Leonard (not the one from the Boston Red Sox), the Endees played with the kind of spark and chemistry that provided fans a reason to believe their club would place among the best in New England.

New Departure finished a light May schedule with a 4–1 mark, the only loss coming on the road in the second game of a Memorial Day home-and-home doubleheader with the New Britain Pioneers. Pillion earned the first win of the month with five innings of relief in a game with Manchester, a talented team that had handed a heavy defeat to the powerful Hartford Polis, a squad that would play a considerable role in deciding New Departure's level of achievement in 1919. It was his only decision in a New Departure uniform.

Harrigan saw action in four games and posted a complete-game, 10–1 victory over Manchester at Muzzy on May 24 during which Scott made his season debut at second base. Champion joined the team around the same time and posted a complete-game, 3–2 victory over Remington Arms of Bridgeport, scattering nine hits in his first Muzzy Field appearance. His opponents had finished the 1918 season with just one loss, to the Polis.

Lanning's first win came against the Pioneers at Muzzy, a six-inning outing with three hits allowed in a 5–1 victory. Harrigan finished with three innings of no-hit relief.

Of those five pitchers, Champion separated himself as the staff ace after his first start.

In front of a large Muzzy Field crowd on June 1, Champion squeezed out a 4–3 victory over three-time defending state Industrial League champion Bridgeport Singers, his former team, in a ten-inning affair. The left-hander pitched a complete game and scattered seven hits while Halbach won the game on a single that scored Scott.

Following a loss to the New Haven Nutmegs, Champion kick-started a lengthy winning streak for the Endees after he stared down another industrial power in the Graton & Knight Manufacturing Company of Worcester, Massachusetts. Known as the Worcester Pros, the team featured former Brooklyn Superbas/Dodgers catcher Bill Bergen, one of the most prolific defensive catchers in baseball history as well as one of its most futile hitters.

Catching ran in the Bergen family. Bill's older brother Marty broke in as a twenty-five-year-old backstop with the National League Boston Beaneaters and enjoyed four solid years in professional baseball. Unfortunately, he is known historically for more sinister reasons.

After suffering a broken hip that assuredly ended his career in 1899, Marty Bergen snapped in January 1900 and killed his wife and two children with an ax in their North Brookfield, Massachusetts, farmhouse before slitting his throat with a razor in a murder-suicide that was discovered by his father, Michael.

Leading up to his death, Bergen would leave the Beaneaters for days at a time without punishment, and he became such a divisive presence among teammates that only one Boston player attended the funeral (Francis). Although it has been written that the tragedy deeply affected Bill for his entire life, the younger Bergen put together an impressive pro baseball career following in his brother's footsteps on the field. But he was far from being a competent hitter.

In an eleven-year career that began in 1901 with Cincinnati, Bergen holds the ignominious record for lowest career batting average of any player with at least twenty-five hundred at-bats. His .170 lifetime average is more than forty points lower than the next weakest hitter, and his .194 career on-base percentage and .201 career slugging percentage both hover around the threshold for the ultimate in offensive impotence.

Bergen batted above .200 just once in his career when he hit .227 in his third and final season with the Reds. The year before he established what would be a career-high with thirty-six RBI in eighty-nine games, and in his rookie campaign he hit the first of two career home runs in 3,028 at-bats, one of the lowest percentages of home-run production for any player.

Aside from his .227 output, he managed to hit at least .190 just once in his career, and Bergen's average yearly stats were a .171 average with seventeen RBI, six extra-base hits and twelve runs scored. Oddly enough, Bergen hit twenty-one career triples and had enough speed to steal twenty-three bases.

Based on research by Joe Dittmar of the Society for American Baseball Research, Bergen also lays claim to the longest hitless streak in history. From June 29, 1909, to July 17, 1909, in the midst of one of his best seasons defensively, Bergen went forty-six straight at-bats without a hit.

To look at his career batting statistics, it is amazing that Bergen played in nearly 950 games as a regular, but that speaks to his defensive abilities.

Just as no one could approach his punchless offensive numbers, few could rival his defensive prowess. Bergen was known to possess sharply honed catching fundamentals with a knack for nabbing foul balls, and his powerful arm and pin-point accuracy allowed him to gun down runners flat-footed, a rare talent among catchers of the day. In his minor league days with Fort Wayne (IN), he single-handedly finished an inning by picking off three runners after his team had faced a bases-loaded, no-out situation.

Against the St. Louis Cardinals on August 23, 1909, historical accounts differ but claim that the six-foot, 184-pound catcher threw out either six or seven would-be base stealers out of eight attempts in a 9–1 Dodger loss. That same season, during which he hit .139 in a career-high 112 games, Bergen registered 202 assists, a figure that still ranks among the best performances ever by a catcher. He also was said to be an astute tactician behind the plate, having caught two no-hitters for the perennially losing Brooklyn ball club where he played from 1904 to 1911.

While his three seasons with Cincinnati produced some of his career-high offensive numbers, it was in Brooklyn that Bergen became a consistent defensive stalwart. In 1908, he committed only 7 errors in 614 chances for a .989 fielding percentage before following up with his stellar 1909 campaign. For his career, Bergen owns a .972 fielding percentage in 5,839 chances with 4,233 put-outs, 1,444 assists, and 108 double plays.

By June 1919, the forty-one-year-old North Brookfield, Massachusetts, native was playing for the Worcester Pros, and he became one of the first historically significant ballplayers to appear at Muzzy Field.

Champion squared off against Boston College pitcher Jimmy Fitzpatrick in front of fans who could now sit in the new Muzzy Field grandstand. In a pitcher's duel, Champion battled for ten innings and surrendered five hits before darkness and a dense mist ended the game with the score tied at three.

Not surprisingly, Bergen finished 0-for-4. Box scores and game stories do not indicate that any runners attempted to steal.

New Departure had proven their ability to compete with and defeat some of the best semipro ball clubs in the area, and newspapers did not miss the opportunity to remind readers to come to Muzzy in support of one of the most talented teams around. When Flag Day arrived and servicemen were feted at the recently completed field, the club's doubleheader sweep of the Meriden Schenks began an eleven-game winning streak that lasted nearly a month.

A return trip from the Worcester Pros on June 15 saw pitcher Lore "King" Bader take the hill against New Departure. Between 1912 and 1918, Bader pitched in twenty-two games for the New York Giants and Boston Red Sox, compiling a 5–3 record and 2.51 ERA in $75^1/_3$ innings. Mainly a relief pitcher in the pros, Bader started four games with the 1918 Red Sox, but he missed the World Series championship after playing his last major league game on July 18.

In semipro circles, Bader was a hot commodity, and Swat McCabe greeted the thirty-one-year-old right-hander by blasting a triple to the left-field fence described by the *New Departure News* as "one of the longest drives yet witnessed" at the Bristol ballpark.

In 1919, that was no mean feat.

Based on documents unearthed by the Bristol Parks and Recreation Department, Muzzy Field's enormous dimensions measured 388 feet down the left-field line, 428 feet near the in-play oak tree in left center, 441 feet to straightaway center, 371 feet to right center with a merciful short porch 322 feet down the right-field line. Home runs beyond the wall were an extremely rare occurrence.

New Departure hit Bader's offerings around most of the ballpark's open spaces that day in a 9–3 victory. The former pro gave up ten hits, five doubles, and McCabe's triple while a pitcher named Smith earned the win for the home team. Like many other pitchers, Smith held Bergen hitless in three at-bats. Again, there are no reports that the catcher threw out any runners during the game.

While Champion remained the ace, Eddie Goodridge emerged as the solid number two starter during the winning streak and established himself as one of the team's most knowledgeable baseball men.

A smart ballplayer with a leader's personality, Goodridge later became a player/manager for the New Departure club, but he showcased his managerial skills in 1919 by leading the women's baseball team in the newly formed New Departure Girls' Athletic Association.

Interest in sports was not restricted to the men, and female factory workers soon enjoyed many of the same opportunities to play baseball and basketball and compete in track and field through the generous funding from the large company. Company teams also sprouted outside of Plant A in Bristol. New Departure's Plant C, located in the Elmwood section of West Hartford, fielded Bristol rivals in men's sports and competed against industrial teams from the Hartford area in all of the popular sports such as baseball, basketball, and bowling. Women's baseball was no exception, and the *New Departure News* published Plant C's results with equal enthusiasm.

Plant A's first women's practice was held on July 5, 1919, under the direction of Manager Goodridge, and the team played their first game on August 9 at Lake Compounce amusement park against the women's team from Colt Manufacturing Company of Hartford, a game New Departure lost 10–6. Photos in the *New Departure News* show that the women played, or at least practiced, at Muzzy Field on weekdays.

Goodridge's eagerness to involve himself in several sports had been his penchant since he earned letters in four sports on the high school and prep school levels. He came to Bristol after spending part of the 1918 season with the Hartford Senators where he led the team with a .297 average and seventy-eight hits, both among the top eleven in the league. As an Amherst freshman in 1912, he joined the baseball team and played all four years as a pitcher and first baseman, captaining the squad in his senior season. He joined the football team as a sophomore and remained part of the team for three years while playing hockey during his junior and senior seasons.

Personal friends lured him to the Bristol area after his graduation in 1916, and Goodridge played baseball in the Bristol-Farmington League and also spent time with the Hartford Poli club.

In 1917, Choate School in Wallingford hired Goodridge as a schoolmaster to teach mathematics and Latin and serve as the athletic director. He joined the Senators a year later and was said to have attracted the interest of the New York Giants and Pittsburgh Pirates. He "would have gone into the major leagues" if not for his decision to enlist in the army as a private, according to the *New Departure News*. By the end of the war, Goodridge was a first lieutenant, and he briefly rejoined the Senators before coming to the New Departure Company. Long after his semiprofessional baseball career ended, Goodridge remained at New Departure as one of the company's highest-ranking executives.

But as a young left-hander in his midtwenties in June 1919, Goodridge was introducing himself to his teammates with a complete-game victory over the Bridgeport Singers at Muzzy Field. Although pedestrian in surrendering five runs on eight hits, he won a 9–5 decision while striking out six. It was the first of several victories the southpaw posted that season.

The previous day in a road game at Comstock-Cheney of Ivoryton, a hulking right-hander named Joseph "Cuddy" Murphy earned the win in his only appearance for New Departure. Murphy was a dominating lineman at Dartmouth and an overpowering right-handed pitcher who spent time with the Boston Red Sox in spring training. He played two years of professional football with the Canton Bulldogs and Cleveland Indians in 1920–21, both featuring player-coach Jim Thorpe, a future Hall of Famer and Olympic great.

Murphy's one appearance in a New Departure baseball uniform was a key 5–2 victory in ten innings over the stiffest challenger to the team's quest for the semi-pro state championship.

By the end of June, New Departure's hitting augmented their strong pitching as five regulars in the lineup were batting .320 or better, paced by Lanning's .405 (15-for-37) mark. The second-leading hitter, Smoke Halbach, strengthened his .377 average (22-for-58) by reaching base in the tenth inning of a Saturday afternoon home game against the New Haven Nutmegs. He scored from second on a grounder to first base as New Departure won, 4–3, behind Goodridge.

The left-hander pitched ten innings and surrendered ten hits with seven strikeouts and three walks. It was the first win in a weekend that featured the season's opening game with the Fisk Red Tops, a powerful team from the Chicopee, Massachusetts-based, tire company. Former minor leaguers, players still owned by major league teams, and players from powerhouse college programs such as Holy Cross filled the Fisk lineup, and their games against New Departure always were touted as some of the season's best.

On June 29, the teams did not disappoint in a thrilling contest at Muzzy Field. Rube Richards of Brown University opposed Champion, who had not pitched in nearly three weeks.

New Departure struck first in the opening frame when George Scott led off with a single, and Lanning bunted him over to second. Swat McCabe, sporting a .320 average, then smacked an RBI single over second base for a 1–0 lead. The teams played flawlessly for the next eight and a half innings as the pitchers engaged in complete-game duels.

Champion got the better of the decision with a four-hitter and four strikeouts, while Richards surrendered just two hits after the first inning and struck out six.

With one victory over both of the top nines from Massachusetts and an edge among home state teams, New Departure was in control of a fine season by the time they swept a doubleheader at Muzzy Field against an outclassed club from nearby Southington on the Fourth of July.

The next day, Goodridge highlighted the long holiday weekend with a two-hit shutout of Comstock-Cheney on a blistering hot afternoon in Bristol. The young lefty struck out seven batters with one walk, while hitting one batter, as he retired the final seventeen hitters he faced. Halbach and Eddie Zielke knocked in one run each.

Lanning capped off the long holiday weekend with a rain-shortened six-inning affair against the Waterbury Elks in which he earned the 2–1 win with seven strikeouts.

New Departure stood tall with a 17–2–1 mark and an eleven-game winning streak before they dropped two decisions the following weekend. The losses began a mediocre stretch that extended over the final two months of the season.

In the much-anticipated return meeting with Fisk at Riverside Park on July 26, another pitcher's duel ensued and the clubs played a hotly contested game. It was a rematch between Champion and Richards, but Fisk added talent to their lineup with center fielder Snooks Dowd, a hotshot infielder with New Haven who was owned by Connie Mack.

Dowd had been temporarily suspended with Joe Dugan after failing to show up for an exhibition game in Rochester that month, and Fisk quickly plugged the Springfield native into their leadoff position.

A year earlier in February, Dowd made news when he turned down an offer from New York Yankees manager Miller Huggins in order to earn his degree from Springfield High School. An accomplished athlete, Dowd later became a standout basketball forward for the Boston Whirlwinds of the American Pro Basketball League in 1925.

On a windy afternoon at Riverside Park, Champion and Richards put up numbers nearly identical to their first meeting. Only an error by Scott in the fifth allowed two Fisk runs to score as the Red Tops took the game. Richards pitched a four-hit shutout and struck out three while Champion scattered four hits and struck out five.

Late in the game, Scott was called out on a double when he failed to touch first, thereby ending a New Departure rally in another well-played game. Dowd finished 1-for-4 on a smash that was knocked down by the bare hand of shortstop George Dunlop.

New Departure recovered at home the next day, ending the month of July with a 12–0 win over American Chain of Bridgeport in which right fielder Eddie Goodridge went 4-for-5 with a double and a stolen base while Otto Townsend, a minor league right-hander who joined the team on July 19, got the win and scattered eight hits. For Goodridge, there was a measure of revenge considering American Chain roughed him up in a 9–6 loss on July 13.

The August schedule posed some serious challenges for a club that had faltered after a long winning streak. With a two-game lead in the season series against Comstock-Cheney, New Departure traveled to Ivoryton on August 2 for a pivotal rematch. New Departure pitchers limited Comstock-Cheney to two runs in the earlier meetings, and Goodridge was called on to stop a hot team that recently defeated the Hartford Polis, 14–7, and Fisk, 2–1, in fifteen innings.

Similar to his last start against Bridgeport, however, Goodridge came out shaky, and Comstock-Cheney hammered him for five runs on seven hits in two innings. Townsend relieved the home team and held them at bay while New Departure chipped away at the lead, scoring three runs with a two-out rally to tie the game in the sixth. But in the ninth inning, Scott dropped a pop-up, and that base runner eventually came around to score on a single, sending Townsend and the team home as tough-luck losers.

The next day at Muzzy Field they rebounded against Greenfield (MA) Tap & Die. Champion and Lanning combined on a two-hitter with six strikeouts while Lanning belted a double and a triple. Champion started the game and pitched $5^1/3$ innings before Goodridge, playing right field, and Zielke, playing first, collided trying to catch a pop-up. Zielke left the game, and Champion moved to right.

Of the two singles surrendered by the southpaw duo, one came from Greenfield shortstop Wally Kopf of Dartmouth, born in Bristol and the brother of Larry Kopf, shortstop for the eventual 1919 World Series champion Cincinnati Reds. Wally later left Dartmouth and collected a single in three at-bats as a third baseman with the 1921 New York Giants. At Muzzy Field, he also finished 1-for-3.

Riding a four-game winning streak following an easy win over the New Britain Pioneers, New Departure entered the first game of a three-game series against the vaunted Polis of Hartford during the second weekend of August. The Polis were one of the teams in the area by which clubs gauged their legitimacy as championship contenders, and their appearance at Muzzy drew three thousand fans for each game.

Poli manager Curtiss A. Gillette was known to be a well-connected baseball man, and his teams usually were filled with premium talent borrowed from the Eastern League. New Departure's Goodridge briefly played with them, and they arrived in Bristol with former Bearing Maker pitcher Squiz Pillion playing right field.

If New Departure wanted to prove their worth as a formidable nine, they needed a strong showing against the Polis.

Pillion drove in a run during the game to give the Hartford team a 3–2 lead in the bottom of the ninth when McCabe reached base for New Departure. He advanced to third on a base hit and overran the bag as the ball came in behind him. McCabe scrambled back, and the *New Departure News* reported that the fans and players agreed with umpire Butch Barry, who called him safe. With hot-hitting Clyde Waters (9-for-14 in his previous four games) due at the plate, New Departure seemed to be in prime position to tie the game.

But just as Barry called McCabe safe, the other umpire, Hugh "Red" Rorty, called him out, and there was an uproar among New Departure fans and players. Manager Harry Drucquer of New Departure consulted with Gillette, and in what would now be considered a stunning show of sportsmanship, Gillette "agreed that the regretted decision … by Red Rorty should constitute a good reason for setting the game aside," the *New Departure News* reported. The results were thrown out, and the teams agreed to begin the three-game series two weeks later.

McCabe and Rorty had a history. When both were in the Connecticut State League, McCabe was fined one hundred dollars and suspended for laying hands on the umpire after a disputed call. McCabe "almost choked Red Rorty into insensibility for calling what he considered a bad decision," according to the *New Britain Herald*. Whether that incident had anything to do with the ruling during the Poli game remains unknown.

After the postponed game, New Departure faced a stiff rematch with Greenfield (MA) and another pivotal meeting with Comstock-Cheney, fast becoming their arch nemesis during the 1919 season.

Goodridge got the ball for the road game in Massachusetts on Saturday, August 16, and he responded with a dominating complete-game performance in which he struck out eleven and scattered four hits in a 6–0 victory. Kopf secured one of those hits with a single, but he was thrown out at home as part of a double steal.

The momentum of a season sweep of Greenfield, however, did not follow the team to Bristol where Comstock-Cheney notched a key 4–2 victory against Townsend and Champion, equalizing the season series at two games apiece.

Seeking to regain their footing going into the first game against the Polis, New Departure brushed aside the New Haven Nutmegs at Muzzy Field on Saturday behind Goodridge's complete-game six-hitter. The rematch against the Polis again had Muzzy Field bursting at the seams, and New Departure came out with a surprisingly quick and lethal flurry of runs.

They pounced with three in the first inning and finished with ten tallies on fourteen hits in a lopsided shutout victory. On the mound, Champion silenced the Polis with a six-hitter and five strikeouts, and Eddie Zielke finished with two triples and two RBI. Pillion played center field for the Polis and finished 0-for-3.

With a reported crowd of several thousand Bristol, Hartford, and Meriden residents, the Bearing Makers' victory caused the *New Departure News* to chirp that it was "one of the brightest days in … history" for the hometown team.

Few teams bested the Polis, much less by ten runs, but New Departure turned the trick twice when Champion returned to the mound on August 31 for the second game of the series. New Departure enjoyed a similar combination of flawless pitching and explosive offense as they scored twelve runs on thirteen hits in damp conditions while the left-hander locked down the Polis with a four-hitter in a 12–2 win.

The Bristol factory team solidified themselves as the premiere club of Hartford County, and they had two games in September that would help determine if they were arguably the top aggregation in the entire state and maybe all of New England.

Energy was high in September as preparations for New Departure's fourth annual Field Day—a remarkable all-day festival of food, entertainment, and athletic competition enjoyed by employees—were finalized, and fans of the baseball team celebrated the routing of the Polis.

New Departure's business interests continued to enjoy a postwar spike. Early in the month, the company purchased eight acres of land in Meriden for $2.5 million on the site of the Meriden Woolen Company and set about expanding its operations to a third location in central Connecticut. Already with factories in Bristol, Elmwood, and other parts of the United States and Europe, the 70,000-square-foot Meriden plant would support more than one thousand workers in the renovated four-story brick mill building. Ultimately, the Meriden Endees became one of Bristol's chief baseball rivals in ensuing years.

Not even a three-game slide leading up to the important New England championship game during Labor Day weekend could dampen the spirits of those affiliated with New Departure. Although meaningless in the bigger picture of the season, the Bearing Makers' home-and-home series with the Meriden Schenks is worthy of note just for its incredible pitching performances.

The morning game, a 3–0 Schenk victory at Muzzy Field, pitted Otto Townsend against Sammy Hyman of Georgetown. The college star got the better of the battle with eleven strikeouts in nine innings while Townsend surrendered only five hits.

An afternoon trip to Hanover Park in Meriden resulted in a two-all tie after fourteen innings in which Goodridge and Jack Barron battled to darkness. Goodridge allowed only four hits and struck out seven in fourteen innings, while Barron gave up fifteen hits in a complete-game effort and caused New Departure to strand fifteen runners on base.

Though he probably was exhausted after such a marathon performance, Goodridge was back on the mound two days later following a loss to the Bridgeport Singers in which McCabe pitched.

The New England championship was the third game of the summer between Fisk and New Departure. The previous two games had been classic pitchers' duels directed by Earl Champion and Rube Richards in which both teams posted a shutout and three runs total were scored.

But rather than give Champion a third shot at the Massachusetts rivals, manager Harry Drucquer sent five-game winner Goodridge to the hill at Muzzy Field while Fisk stuck with Richards as the starter. Although New Departure notched some impressive and important victories from July on, the team was not playing with the same winning consistency as they had in the first twenty games of the season. The Bearing Makers' record stood at 23–9–2 entering the game but just 6–7–1 since July 6, and the inconsistency plagued them in the Fisk contest.

Both pitching staffs were roughed up in the first three innings. Goodridge's performance unraveled in the third when three New Departure errors: two fielder's choice plays, a walk, and a single led to five quick runs for Fisk. But in the bottom of the inning, New Departure pulled within 5–4 and chased Richards with four singles and a double.

Goodridge and the defense settled down while the left-hander ended up surrendering eleven hits in nine innings. Fisk reliever Art Johnson quieted the bats after the third frame, and New Departure mustered only five hits the rest of the way, dropping a 6–4 decision and their chance to argue that they were New England's finest.

The Bearing Makers still had their opportunity to become state champions a week later at Muzzy Field in the fifth game of the Comstock-Cheney series. Entering the contest, New Departure's lineup boasted two .300 hitters in Les Lanning (.349 with forty-six hits) and Swat McCabe (.300 with forty-one hits). Smoke Halbach hovered near the line at .299, and Waters (.280) and Zielke (.276) both were hitting at respectable clips.

For the September 14 state championship game, Drucquer imported talented pitcher Freddie Reiger of Pittsfield's Eastern League entry. Reiger won twenty games with the franchise's 1916 Eastern League championship team when it was based in New London.

Against Comstock-Cheney, Reiger did not disappoint his new teammates as he fired a five-hitter and struck out nine batters, assisted by third baseman Halbach who turned in what the *New Departure News* called "the most spectacular play of the season" on a diving play. At the plate, Reiger also doubled and scored a run as New Departure won the state pennant in easy fashion, 5–0.

For a team trumpeted in the preseason as one of the most talented around, the Bearing Makers were able to prove as much on the state level. But one of the most important games of Muzzy Field's history still awaited them.

New Departure's annual Barbecue Field Day celebrations in September epitomized the company's attempt to create a personal connection between employee and factory while engendering a sense of family ties. The company went to great lengths to provide food, games, and entertainment in a festival-like setting that ranked as one of the largest corporate gatherings in America.

The *New Departure News* regularly reported on the developments during the planning stages that began around July, and reminded employees that the fifty-cent admission fee was a pittance considering the amount of money spent to throw the party. And it was quite a party.

News agencies descended on Bristol every year to document the gathering and later show the footage in theaters throughout North America. Magazines such as *Collier's Weekly* provided additional national coverage. The 1917 soiree attracted Pathé Weekly News Service of Great Britain, Hearst-Selig, and a newly formed film studio called Universal. Dignitaries from the automobile industry, including General Motors founder and president William C. Durant and Walter Chrysler, were frequent guests of New Departure Company and partook of the food that came to be known certainly as part of the largest barbecue in the Northeast and possibly the entire East Coast.

Bristol had a long history of such barbecues. Wealthy farmer Gad Norton, who owned Lake Compounce in its early days, began renting out the recreational area for picnics and boating around 1846. He hired cooks well-versed in Southern cuisine and started to offer barbecues and shore dinners to local organizations that rented out Lake Compounce for their outings (Clouette and Roth 1984).

A waitstaff of two hundred and fifty ensured that the barbecued sheep and other food were served hot and quickly, a reflection of New Departure's speed and efficiency as a factory, according to its newspaper, and a tightly choreographed march of employees from Muzzy Field to the Page Barbecue Grounds began after the morning baseball game and field events.

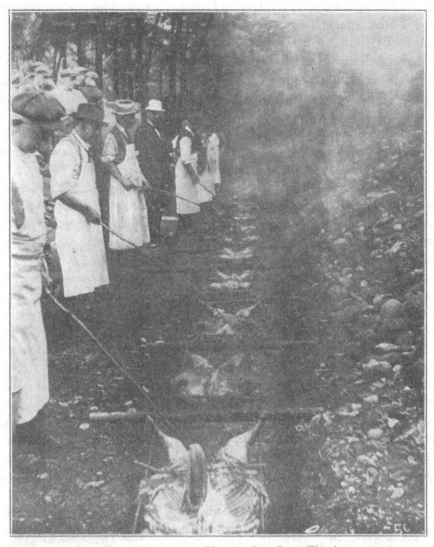

Cooking the Sheep on Skewers Over Long Firepit.

Pit masters tend to the spring lambs that were shipped from Chicago for the New Departure Barbecue Field Day in 1919. The slow roasting began before dawn, and the massive luncheon drew thousands of New Departure workers to the Page Grounds, a day before the company's baseball team battled Babe Ruth and the Boston Red Sox at Muzzy Field. (Courtesy: Bristol Public Library)

At the Page Grounds, one serving table accommodated every three tables of guests, and the company took pride in its ability to devise a system that left no one waiting hungrily.

The New Departure Orchestra and other guest bands, such as the one from Colt's Manufacturing in Hartford, provided the music, and special songs were written and sung during the event. In 1917, the tune "When the Sheep Goes Down in Bristol," with its lyrics "and our spirits start to rise/oh, what's a sheep bake but another paradise," fed off the energy and excitement that accompanied the day's events.

Traditionally, the sheep roasted over charcoal for eight hours in trenches, and head chef Thomas Ryan and his staff constantly basted the meat with a butter-based mop sauce. The rest of the menu varied yearly but always included plenty of soft drinks, side dishes, desserts, and cigars. It was an immense tailgate party for thousands of people, and of course, the company did not skimp on the baseball games that always were played during the weekend, especially in 1919.

War and an early morning rain muted the celebration of 1918, which raised $1,250 for the war effort, but a year later, the Barbecue Field Day was being hailed as the finest corporate party in the country. New Departure strived for perfection and top-notch service in everything it placed on public display, and president DeWitt Page saw to it that the weekend of September 20–21 included the choicest of everything.

On Thursday, the *Bristol Press* reported that the entire city was buzzing about the signed agreement that would bring the defending world champion Boston Red Sox to Muzzy Field for a game on Sunday afternoon. The newspaper noted that the athletic event certainly was the biggest ever to occur in Bristol, and fans could expect to see a team that while struggling that season was being considered the favorite to win the American League pennant in 1920.

"Manager Barrow of the Red Sox has notified the local management that he will present his best possible line up which is to include the famous home-run King, Babe Ruth," crowed the *Bristol Press* in its September 16 edition. "As far as is known, this is the first time that a team from the Big Show has ever made its appearance in Bristol."

It did not matter that Boston was on its way to a sixth-place finish in 1919, and the prognostications for the next season were unnecessary for creating excitement. New Departure management's willingness and ability to strike a deal to bring the Red Sox to town was enough.

Boston's schedule had them playing a doubleheader against Chicago at Fenway Park on September 20 before traveling to New York for a doubleheader against the Yankees on September 24. In between, they would compete against New Departure at Muzzy Field, and Red Sox manager Ed Barrow sent a letter to New Departure management assuring the fans that they would see Boston's finest players, including twenty-four-year-old power-hitting pitcher Babe Ruth, who debuted in the major leagues exactly one week before the official opening game at Muzzy Field.

In the deadball era, the Babe's magnificent power instantly separated him from other players, and his home run totals astonished observers. On September 20, designated "Babe Ruth Day" at Fenway Park, Ruth smashed an opposite field shot over the Green Monster, and the Knights of Columbus presented him treasury savings certificates worth six hundred dollars. The *Bristol Press* ran large photos of him leading up to the game but mentioned only his exploits as a power hitter. Because such astounding blasts were rare, everyone wanted to see Ruth unload on pitchers, and by the end of the season he was "the greatest individual calling card" in professional baseball (Smelser 1975).

Interestingly, the Bristol newspaper trumpeted the arrival of first baseman Stuffy McInnis and shortstop Everett Scott more than the Babe. McInnis was completing a superb season in which he posted a .995 fielding percentage with 1,318 chances while hitting .305 with 58 RBI. Ruth, meanwhile, accumulated his own stellar defensive numbers with 222 put-outs, 14 assists, 6 double plays, and a .996 fielding percentage in 111 games in the outfield. The article briefly mentions Ruth and his .326 batting average in the last paragraph, but fans knew the caliber of individual talent that was coming to Muzzy Field.

Not everyone warmed up to Ruth so quickly, however. Some considered baseball a gentlemanly sport relying on the strategy of the hit-and-run, the finesse of bunting, and the theory of sacrificing oneself for the team to score a run. Ruth's approach flouted that thinking with one swing of his mighty bat, and it was not uncommon for purist fans to consider his style coarse and roguish.

"The term 'inside' baseball was almost sacred, and John McGraw was its high priest," Robert W. Creamer wrote in his biography of Ruth. "It meant playing for a run, a single run. You bunted safely, stole second, went to third on a sacrifice and scored on a fly ball to win 1–0. An exaggeration, of course, but that was the ideal."

Considering New Departure staked their success on this offensive philosophy and strong pitching, it is possible that some of their followers, who might have worked at the newspaper, found more admirable the performance of other Red Sox players. Boston's manager believed Ruth would change his approach to the game after 1919.

In a season in which Ruth outpaced entire teams offensively, bashed a then-record 29 home runs, and batted .322 with 75 extra-base hits and 114 RBI, Barrow told a *Hartford Times* reporter leading up to the game in Bristol that Ruth "will become a .400 hitter … just meet the ball and will bat them to left field as well as Ty Cobb" by shortening his swing and becoming more of a contact hitter.

The Red Sox manager went on to say, "[Ruth] will not be trying to knock the ball out of the lot after this season. He will be content with his [home run] record because it will be far and away out of the reach of any other batter the game is likely to develop. [Outfielder] Harry Hooper agrees with me that if Babe shortens up and is content to just meet the ball, he will develop into one of the greatest hitters—already he is the greatest of all sluggers—the game ever has had."

Barrow added that he got after Ruth during the season to try to hit to the opposite field to drive in runs rather than relying on the long ball, but "then he started to get the home runs, and every time he went to bat he naturally wanted to knock the ball out of the lot."

Despite the manager's desire to turn his young budding superstar into a spray hitter, Bristol fans eagerly awaited the Babe to see whether he could conquer the mammoth dimensions of Muzzy Field, something no other batter had done.

But before the Red Sox rolled into town for an historic exhibition, thousands of New Departure family members and guests would indulge in the company's prodigious picnic among the birch trees surrounding Page Grounds. The factories shut down for the entire day and workers received a half-day's pay. For weeks leading up to the event, the *New Departure News* strongly encouraged all workers to pay the fifty-cent admission fee, which went toward the company's relief aid program for ill employees, and turn out in huge numbers with their families.

The company ordered 176 spring lambs shipped by refrigerated railcar from Chicago to be barbecued in a quarter mile of portable steel smoking trenches for 4,300 people. Chief Chef Ryan used butter by the hundreds of pounds for the mop sauce, and twenty-four thousand ears of fried corn accompanied the meat that smoked for eight hours from predawn Saturday to 12:30 PM. Sweet potatoes, Irish potatoes, pickles, vats of soft drinks, pies, cheese, and cigars completed the menu, which was served while factory orchestras provided music prior to the boxing and wrestling matches. It is unknown if the cigars served were from Babe Ruth's factory, which produced five-cent stogies made of Connecticut tobacco.

The 1919 New Departure Field Day barbecue at Page Grounds attracted thousands of workers and their families and was considered the finest corporate picnic in the country. (Courtesy: Bristol Public Library)

While preparations were made for the afternoon festivities at the barbecue grounds, people flocked to Muzzy Field for competitions such as the greased pig contest, foot races, and other track and field events. Employees vied for prizes that included gold watches, cuff links, cigar cutters, mirrors, toilet seats, and of course, a pig.

A decorated train from Hartford arrived early in the morning carrying employees from Plant C in Elmwood along with the band from the Colt Armory in the capital city. New Departure's Plant A orchestra and employees marched the short distance from the factory to the train station to greet the group while the band played "Hail, Hail the Gang's All Here."

The group then paraded to Muzzy Field where the annual baseball game between the Elmwood and Bristol plants took place. Against a talented Plant C team that lent players to the Polis that summer and won the Hartford Industrial League championship, Eddie Goodridge fired a one-hitter with five strikeouts, and Plant A broke a two-year losing streak with a 4–0 victory.

But considering the scope of activities during this day-long carnival that stretched across town, the inter-plant baseball game was just a small detail. New Departure was determined to host a monumental party on all fronts, and there was no shortage of superlatives used to describe it.

"Not even the Barnum and Bailey three-ring show, nor the antics of the Ding-A-Ling Circus performers will have anything on the numbers of the 1919 barbecue program," the *New Departure News* boastfully predicted in its September 20 issue.

National weeklies *Collier's* and *Leslie's* were on the guest list along with two film companies that again would document the events and show them in movie theaters throughout the country.

The biggest barbecue in company history also was called the "greatest factory festal occasion ever held in the East" and the "biggest industrial holiday program in the country," and the food was considered "one of the greatest spreads ever served at one time in the United States."

High praise, indeed, even from the always-positive slant of the *New Departure News*. But the words illustrate the general excitement that accompanied this special weekend in a new and exciting postwar life enjoyed by many Bristolites.

Following the athletic events and in distinctive New Departure fashion, employees lined up according to their specific departments, and a well-orchestrated parade proceeded to the barbecue grounds in a timely fashion that would have them arrive just as the steaming hot plates of food were ready to serve.

By all accounts, everything went off without a hitch, and many of those festive employees continued the party through the next day by either playing against the Red Sox or watching from the stands at Muzzy Field.

For Red Sox players, the trip to Bristol was a quick one. It also was an opportunity to play on a Sunday, which was prohibited in Boston at that time. Several made the trip from Boston by car and left after the game. Babe Ruth traveled round-trip in his Jordan.

The Sunday afternoon game offered fans a peek at a major league team, the first to visit the Bristol ballpark, and they arrived in droves. Newspapers reported between five thousand and six thousand fans filled the grandstand and spilled out along the foul lines to catch a glimpse of Ruth and his teammates.

Besides Ruth at first base, Harry Hooper played right field and acted as the team's manager while second baseman Red Shannon filled the shortstop position against New Departure. "Sad Sam" Jones, a twelve-game winner as a starting pitcher for the 1919 Red Sox, played left field. The rest of Boston's lineup comprised players who mainly came off the bench in 1919, including Mike McNally, second base; Joe Wilhoit, center field, who enjoyed a sixty-nine-game hitting streak with Wichita of the Western League that season; Roxy Walters, third base; Norm McNeil, catcher; and Bob McGraw on the mound.

Several of the Red Sox players were soon to be traded to the Yankees in ensuing years, most notably the Babe. His infamous transaction put him in pinstripes by January 1920, making his appearance at Muzzy Field in September 1919 one of his last in a Red Sox uniform.

The six-foot-two, left-handed Wilhoit had experienced an historic summer out West with a hitting streak that still stands as the longest in professional baseball, though largely unrecognized because of the Western League's independent status. A journeyman outfielder, Wilhoit played in the 1917 World Series with the New York Giants, the third team—along with the Braves and Pirates—that employed him during that season. He played in sixty-four games with the 1918 Giants and batted .274, but he lacked consistency and the thirty-three-year-old spent the bulk of 1919 back in his native Kansas.

He started slowly that summer, author Bob Rives wrote, hitting only .198 in the first twenty-five games. Then, for nearly ten weeks, Wilhoit could not stop hitting. He racked up a .515 average (153-for-297) during the streak, finishing the season with a .422 average that paced all marks in pro baseball. In the post-streak furor, the Red Sox outbid other teams for Wilhoit's services after the minor league season ended in September, and he responded with six hits in eighteen at-bats during his six games in Boston.

Barrow's club had struggled for consistency during the season, but Wilhoit arrived at a time when the Red Sox were reeling off their longest winning streak (nine games) and posting a season-best .591 winning percentage during the month.

Wilhoit finished the season with Boston, never to return to the major leagues, and he batted .257 in 283 career games. But coming into the game at Muzzy Field, the unpublicized Wilhoit, whose exploits went unreported by local press, was the hottest hitter on a team with two future Hall of Famers, one a growing legend.

New Departure countered Boston with Eddie Zielke at first base, George Scott at second base, George Dunlop at shortstop, and Gus Forslund at third base. The outfield consisted of Les Lanning in left, Gene Gaffney in center, and Swat McCabe in right. Pitcher Freddie Reiger made his second start for New Departure with catcher Clyde Waters calling the game.

Several thousand fans packed Muzzy Field early to watch Ruth take batting practice in the spacious ballpark that had never allowed a home run over its walls.

To the delight of the spectators, Ruth quickly cemented his place in the park's history with lusty smashes off of batting practice pitcher Heinie Wagner, an infielder for the 1912 World Series champion Red Sox club.

Once the game started, New Departure's defense played sloppily. The first scoring came in the third inning when McNeil reached base on a throwing error by Forslund that moved him to second. After McGraw walked, Jones bunted a ball that hugged the line, threatening to roll foul.

Waters picked up the ball and gunned out Jones at first. Trying to make a smooth double play, Zielke wheeled and threw to second, but no one covered and the first baseman's throw sailed into left field, scoring a run. McGraw was moving toward third when Lanning came up throwing, but he sailed it wide and a second run scored on the play's second error and the inning's third.

Defense placed Reiger in a quick hole, and after McNally grounded out to third, Hooper smacked a single to left-center. Into the batter's box stepped Ruth. He had already proved he could conquer the distant walls of Muzzy Field in batting practice, and with Reiger on the ropes, he delivered the knockout punch when he blasted a pitch over the right-field wall toward the banks of the Pequabuck River, giving the Red Sox a 4–0 lead and sending even New Departure fans into a frenzy as they witnessed one of the longest home runs they had ever seen hit. The ball was never found, possibly landing in the river more than five hundred feet away and floating downstream.

McGraw helped himself in the next inning with an RBI double.

New Departure scored their first runs in the eighth inning when the Red Sox gave away a couple of tallies. Ruth booted Lanning's grounder, and McNally did the same to Dunlop's roller before Forslund singled to right to score the lead runner. Gaffney's sacrifice fly made it 5–2, but New Departure gave back an unearned run in the ninth for a 6–2 deficit.

The home team threatened to stage a fierce rally in the ninth, loading the bases with one out before Dunlop grounded into a game-ending double play.

In all, the teams combined for eight errors in a game that lasted one hour and twenty minutes. New Departure managed ten singles off of McGraw, but Gaffney was twice gunned down at the plate by Jones and Wilhoit as he tried to score from second on singles. The right-handed McGraw, who did not win a game in ten appearances during the regular season, secured the victory and struck out two with three walks while stranding nine New Departure runners.

McCabe, Forslund, and Reiger picked up two singles apiece, while Hooper and Ruth also had two hits apiece.

INSIDE DOPE.
"Sig" and "Babe" Ruth Exchange Views.

Babe Ruth and New Departure Athletic Association president Lester
Sigourney during Ruth's first appearance at Muzzy Field in 1919. Ruth
became the first hitter to clear the walls of the spacious Bristol ballpark
when he hit a blast off New Departure pitcher Freddie Reiger. (Courtesy:
Bristol Public Library)

Reiger gave up nine hits and one walk and struck out two in the loss. Ruth added a single and a stolen base to his historic round-tripper.

"It was a tremendous slam and the Bristol folks for many years to come will rave about that drive made by the Sultan of Swat," the *Bristol Press* reported in 1922.

Following the game, the *New Departure News* quoted Ruth's and Hooper's praise of Bristol—its fans, players, and ballpark—during their brief stay. Ruth specifically mentioned Zielke's defensive work at first and suggested expanding the infield dirt area toward the outfield grass, "otherwise you have a pretty good diamond."

Babe Ruth and Eddie Goodridge at Muzzy Field in 1919. (Courtesy: Bristol Press)

Ruth added, "It has surely been a pretty nice greeting you Bristol people have given our team today. It was as nice a crowd as we have played before in any place outside of the big cities. It is also good to play a team like yours and feel that there are not more 'ringers' than regular players. Your team was playing for the sport of the game, I understand, with no outside man except one (Reiger) who played with you before. That's real sportsmanship. Personally I appreciate the glad hand extended, and I feel that every member of the team of which I am a member realizes the good feeling toward the visitors that Bristol fans as a whole displayed."

Ruth went on to tell the reporter that he was driving back to Boston with Wagner before traveling to New York, and he left encouraged by what he saw in Bristol.

"I have certainly been pleased to meet the Bristol fans and congratulate the city on its team and also in having the company that has made possible this fast ball for Bristol," he said. "Both the company and the city have reason to feel proud of the baseball interest here."

Hooper heaped similar praise in his comments and repeated his appreciation of the reception given his team.

"You have a nice crowd and believe me we shall be pleased to send our baggage to Bristol on some future day. You have given us a royal welcome," Hooper said. "The crowd has been with the home team, yet gave the visitors the glad hand. It has certainly been a most enjoyable short stay.

"If you have the backing during the season that this crowd indicates, you should certainly be pleased. I congratulate the New Departure Manufacturing Company on the commendable stand it has taken in providing such good ball for Bristol fans."

He finished by saying, "Go to it boys, and next year you will have a team that will not only clean up the State Championship, but it will give us bigger league players a stiff battle. You certainly have a good baseball city and a good team to build on for the future."

Reiger took the mound in the final two games of the season, pitching admirably in tough luck losses during the first weekend of October. Against the Meriden Schenks, he lasted eleven innings and struck out eight while surrendering two runs on seven hits in a 3–2 loss against Brooklyn Dodger pitcher Rube Marquard at Hanover Park in Meriden.

That night at Lake Compounce, the company hosted a barbecue for its New Jersey brethren, Hyatt Roller Bearing of Newark, also a division of General Motors. Hyatt had earned the New Jersey Industrial League championship and battled Reiger for nine innings on Sunday afternoon at Muzzy Field.

In a 2–0 loss, Reiger scattered five hits and struck out five, but his 1–3 record for New Departure belied his strong individual outings.

The Endees finished the season with a 27–13–2 record, impressive overall despite playing under .500 ball after July 4. Still, the club commanded respect from all opponents and proudly represented the company throughout the season. For that, NDAA president Lester Sigourney hosted a team banquet and weekend stay in New York City in October and told the club that its season-long performance would be long remembered in the history of the company.

Individually, the Endees players posted some noteworthy statistics. Les Lanning led the team with a .336 average, fifty hits, and only eleven games in which he did not collect at least one base knock. Swat McCabe hit .301 and shined in right field with fifty-six put-outs, eight assists, and only one error. Eddie Zielke, who earned praise from the great Babe Ruth, played a nearly flawless first base with a .989 fielding percentage in 432 chances while hitting .255.

Smoke Halbach (.288) and team captain Clyde Waters (.270) contributed solid offensive numbers while serving as mainstays in the lineup. Gene Gaffney (.241) provided reliable defensive play in the outfield as did spot starter Eddie Goodridge (.243), who earned more plaudits for his 6–2–1 record on the mound. George Scott struggled at the plate with a .194 average but managed to utilize his speed after drawing twenty-eight walks in thirty-seven games.

George Dunlop hit .240 with a .913 fielding percentage in nearly two hundred chances, and utility man Gus Forslund (.179) played five of nine positions throughout the season with an aggregate .910 fielding percentage.

Earl Champion, the staff ace, finished 7–1–1 and along with Goodridge and Lanning (4–0) formed an impressive pitching trio for the home team.

Though it ended on a down note with three consecutive losses, New Departure shot to the forefront of semipro teams in Connecticut by winning the state championship with a stable of talented players. The company's dedication to the sport—in money and spirit—meant that all those involved would strive toward providing the best on-field product in both dugouts. The 1919 season ushered in an era when Muzzy Field hosted players who became preeminent figures in baseball history, its home team among the most competitive in the Northeast.

# 1920: The Return of Ruth

The next year, New Departure unveiled their most ambitious schedule with fifty-one games against the Eastern League Hartford Senators, powerful semipro outfits from Massachusetts, the top-notch clubs affiliated with General Motors, and the most talented teams around Connecticut.

For the biggest games, fans could purchase tickets in advance at Judson's Newsroom or Walsh & Hollfelder's Smoke Shop on Main Street in Bristol.

There were few changes on the roster. Earl Champion, Eddie Goodridge, and Les Lanning again made the bulk of the mound starts, and the familiar faces behind them rarely changed throughout the season.

One notable exception was the departure of former Cleveland Indians shortstop George Dunlop, who joined an outfit in New Britain, Connecticut, and also played for a team in Meriden. Another former major leaguer filled his spot admirably. William "Doc" Murray played eight games with Clark Griffith's 1917 Washington Senators, and the Brown University grad provided great range and slick fielding for the New Departure defense.

Another newcomer, Tommy Bowden, added to the mix. A third baseman and shortstop, Bowden hit at a torrid pace in the first months of the season and finished as the team's batting leader. When Murray left the team in August, he played shortstop for the rest of the year.

Changes also had been made to Muzzy Field. During his visit the previous autumn, Babe Ruth commended the field but said the dirt areas around the bases could extend deeper into the outfield for the benefit of the infielders. Considering Ruth's clout, his opinion was taken seriously.

New Departure opened the season with a highly anticipated game against the Hartford Senators, managed by one of Ruth's former Red Sox roommates, Dan Howley. Speedy outfielder and former Boston Brave, Fred Bailey, who hit .185 in sixty major league games from 1916 to 1918, was the biggest name for the visitors.

A late-April crowd of fifteen hundred attended the game and saw the home team blow a 3–0 lead and a no-hitter in the ninth inning, losing 7–3.

Former Senator Andy Meyerjack pitched the first three innings, followed by Champion's three frames. Reliever Art Johnson allowed four hits and two walks in the ninth, and the New Departure defense committed two errors behind him. The deflating performance began a season in which the Bristolites failed frequently to put away big games. Many of the games involved Johnson, who played a part in numerous important contests with and against New Departure during the 1920s.

Despite the loss, the *Bristol Press* glowed after hearing compliments about Muzzy Field.

"When an old veteran like Dan Howley tells us that he is sorry Hartford does not have as good a field, clean grandstand, etc. as has Bristol, it tickles the pride of local lovers of the national sport," a story stated in the April 30 edition.

New Departure finished the year 30–18–3, a competitive mark that placed them in the thick of the state championship race. Against Massachusetts teams, however, the Endees were 4–8 and out of the running for the New England title after an August loss to Art Johnson and the Fisk Red Tops. Their lone series win came in a three-game set with the Worcester Pros, and they split two games with the Cornets of Lynn, Massachusetts, a team that entered September with a gaudy 30–2 record and an imposing pitching staff.

Among the premiere Connecticut teams, New Departure never got the upper hand. They split a two-game series with the Bridgeport Singers and drew even in a grueling eight-game set with their bitter rivals from Torrington.

Though no mythical championship was earned, the season was not void of interesting highlights, most notably Babe Ruth's second and final appearance at Muzzy Field.

Individually, Eddie Goodridge established himself as the staff ace by winning his first ten starts and eleven of his first twelve as New Departure raced out to a 17–5 mark by July. Goodridge was hitting a team-high .370, but his and the team's fortunes rapidly spiraled downward following a loss to the Chevrolet team from Tarrytown, New York, on July 18. Sometime after that loss, Goodridge contracted ptomaine poisoning, and he missed several games over the ensuing weeks. He returned weakened and finished with a 15–7–2 mound record as his batting average plummeted more than sixty points.

New Departure dropped two pivotal games to Fisk in August after Goodridge shut down the Red Tops, 6–2, on a seven-hitter in front of eighteen hundred hometown fans in late June. He struck out four in a battle with Fisk pitcher Rube

Richards, who surrendered four runs in the seventh inning to break a tie. Former New York Giant Wally Kopf managed a single off of Goodridge.

Aside from the opening day loss to the Senators, New Departure was sharp early in the season, even in the losses. Nearly thirteen hundred fans saw a rare loss in May when Art Johnson claimed a 1–0 victory over New Departure as a pitcher for the Hendee Indians of Springfield, Massachusetts, an outfit that folded from bankruptcy a month later.

Almost as many fans gathered at Muzzy Field on a beautiful spring day to see the Bridgeport Singers, Meyerjack's and Champion's former team, win 3–2 behind thirty-four-year-old lefty Pete Wilson, who was 8–9 with a 3.25 ERA in 20 games for the New York Yankees of 1908–9. Wilson tossed a four-hitter with four strikeouts while Champion left after five innings with a wrenched shoulder. Goodridge kept New Departure within striking distance by fanning seven batters in four innings of relief, but a triple that bounced over McCabe's shoulder in right field preceded a throwing error by infielder Smoke Halbach that sent home the winning run in the eighth inning.

June began with a 7–1 win at Manchester, featuring major league veteran Herman Bronkie as a player-coach in a longtime rivalry that would become intense and sometimes nasty later in the decade. Even the docile *Bristol Press* got involved in the sniping by printing that Bronkie "appears to be the only real ball-player our rivals could boast of."

A week before New Departure's lone win against Fisk, Goodridge limited the Worcester Pros to five hits while striking out eight in a 3–1 win at Muzzy. He allowed one base runner after the fifth inning and received stellar defensive play from Doc Murray. Worcester's defensive whiz Bill Bergen—the former Dodgers and Reds catcher and notoriously poor hitter—managed a single while Clyde Waters and Lanning hit doubles for New Departure. Eddie Zielke hit a triple to the cinder track that had been laid out near the wall the previous July.

Muzzy Field was the town's epicenter of outdoor activity. A track meet on July 4 attracted fifteen hundred people by *Bristol Press* estimates, and the field hosted baseball games involving town teams in the Twilight League and local factory leagues as well as junior high school games. The city's population exceeded twenty thousand in 1920, an increase of more than 50 percent in ten years, and the growing city latched on to the entertainment offered in the West End ballpark (Clouette and Roth 1984).

On July 2, the local newspaper announced that negotiations were in the works to bring a major league team to town at the same time that the New Departure

Company was planning its huge annual barbecue. The expectations, however, were never fully realized.

On the field, the Endees dropped off and finished 13–13 after mid-July. The swoon affected everyone. Swat McCabe, who was hitting .359 late in the month, ended the season at .256 as he battled a back injury. Eddie Zielke's .337 average dipped to .284, though he collected a team-high fifty-five hits, fifteen stolen bases, eight triples, and eight doubles. Tommy Bowden carried a .370 average in July and finished at .317 with ten doubles and ten steals.

The last half of the season, however, did not pass quietly.

The big leagues banned the spitball in 1920 for providing an unfair advantage to pitchers, but in the semipro circuits the spitball was an acceptable and celebrated part of the repertoire. Pete Wood, whose brother "Smoky Joe" Wood was in the twilight of a distinguished pro baseball career in 1920, embraced the pitch and used it to knock out New Departure during one of the highly anticipated meetings with the Fisk Red Tops. The ubiquitous Art Johnson, who played in six New Departure games for five different teams, also had great command of the pitch.

After ptomaine poisoning shelved Goodridge, New Departure imported a semipro player from Boston named John "Nixie" Carney, a right-hander whose spitball, fastball, and curve came together in one historic game at Muzzy Field.

The Bridgeport Singers returned to Bristol on August 1 with former Yankee Pete Wilson on the hill looking for his second win over New Departure. The two pitchers locked up in the best game of the 1920 season.

Hits were at a premium as Wilson pitched with the same command he displayed in May, but Carney was doing him one better. While New Departure squeezed out a couple of runs on triples by Zielke and Murray and a double by catcher Clyde Waters, the Singers' best chance to get on base was from walking.

Carney threw the first no-hitter in Muzzy Field history and walked four batters in a 2–0 New Departure victory. Though he finished with a pedestrian 5–5 record in 1920, Carney's last start was another gem, a four-hitter with seven strikeouts in a 2–0 home win over Torrington in the last game of that series. He spent two months on the New Departure baseball team and never played for them again.

John "Nixie" Carney threw the first no-hitter in Muzzy Field history in 1920 when New Departure scored a 2–0 win over the Bridgeport Singers and pitcher Pete Wilson, a former member of the New York Yankees. (Courtesy: Bristol Public Library)

The win over Torrington on September 26 denied that team the outright state championship and capped a give-and-take series that produced no definitive leader. Both teams won four games, and both teams won two of them on the road. In 1920, Torrington was in the upper class of Connecticut semipro baseball with a stable of former Eastern League players, all of them from the Hartford Senators.

Men such as Billy Dwyer, Andy Meyerjack, Tom McLeod, Ray Holden, and Nick Rubino attracted fans to Fuessenich Park, an historic ballpark in its own right, and produced a consistent winner for manager Jack Miran. In the sixth game, Torrington used thirty-seven-year-old right-hander Andy Coakley to subdue New Departure in a 3–2 win at home. At the time, Coakley was head coach at Columbia University and described in the newspaper as a New York Yankees scout. From 1902 to 1911, he won sixty games for four different big league teams, including the Yankees, and lost a 9–0 game to Christy Mathewson in the 1905 World Series, his only appearance in the Fall Classic, when his Philadelphia A's defense committed five errors. A couple of years after his game against New Departure, Coakley was coaching a sophomore power-hitter at Columbia named Lou Gehrig.

Holden hit two home runs in the series, including an inside-the-park shot at Muzzy Field that was the first round-tripper since Babe Ruth's clout in 1919.

By that time, New Departure had no chance of earning the New England championship; Art Johnson assured that with a two-hitter for Fisk in late August when the Red Tops scored five runs in the eighth inning off of Eddie Goodridge. The next day, Rube Richards limited ND to two hits and never allowed a runner past second as Greenfield Tap & Die won the season series at home.

The downslide extended beyond the playing field. On August 31, New Departure announced reluctantly that the annual barbecue event was cancelled for 1920. A "slight depression in business" caused the company to "temporarily [lay off]" some workers, and despite the thousands who attended the celebration in 1919, factory officials were not certain that it was worth the effort. In all, it was "no time for fun and feast," as the company's press release read in the *Bristol Press*.

The baseball team turned things around with a series-clinching win at Muzzy Field against the Worcester Pros before posting two shutouts after the Labor Day games with Torrington. After whitewashing the Meriden Schenks, 5–0, the second shutout, a 3–0 decision, came against the Cornets of Lynn, Massachusetts, in the Bay Staters' first appearance in Connecticut.

With a 30–2 record, Lynn was loaded with talent and already owned a victory over New Departure from early September. Walter Hunt pitched that game, a 3–2 decision, and entered the second one with a fifty-four-inning scoreless streak. The Atlanta native was studying for the ministry at the Newton Theological Seminary, but the 14–0 right-hander refused to play on Sundays, meaning he would be unavailable for the second contest.

"Nixie" Carney threw a five-hitter, and Goodridge added an RBI single in the victory. Gene Martin, an outfielder who joined the team for the first Lynn game, went 3-for-4 with a double and a run scored.

Martin was not the only new addition late in the season. Doc Murray and Clyde Waters both departed the team in August to play in the Eastern League, and Billy Harkin from Boston and Charlie Woodtke of the old Meriden Redwood club filled their positions. In September, catcher Art O'Connell of Bridgeport's American Chain team joined the Endees with Martin, also of Bridgeport.

With a slightly altered lineup, New Departure hosted a General Motors tournament on September 19 against the Hyatt Roller Bearing Company of Newark, New Jersey, and the Chevrolet team from Tarrytown, New York. The three teams were considered the best in the country among GM clubs.

The doubleheader started at 2:00 PM with Hyatt battling New Departure, the winner facing Tarrytown at 4:00 PM. Walsh & Hollfelder's Smoke Shop announced the games with enormous advertisements in the *Bristol Press*, proclaiming that forty-five GM teams had been whittled to the best three. Tickets cost fifty and twenty-five cents, and the games drew between twenty-two hundred and three thousand fans depending on which local newspaper one relies.

Hyatt's lineup included Bert Daniels, a thirty-seven-year-old outfielder who played five seasons with the New York Yankees and Cincinnati Reds. In 523 games, Daniels hit .255 with 486 hits, 295 runs scored, and 130 RBI. He collected 76 doubles and 40 triples and stole 159 bases between 1910 and 1914.

A pitcher named Carlson, a former member of the Jersey City entry in the International League, opposed Eddie Goodridge on the mound.

Scoreless through the first five innings, George Scott came in as a pinch runner and scored both runs. The game-winner followed his single and stolen base. Gus Forslund smashed a line drive to third that ricocheted between the third baseman and shortstop. As the infielders fumbled the ball, Scott tore around third base and scored from second.

Goodridge limited Hyatt to a run on three hits and struck out six while holding Daniels hitless in four at-bats.

Another anticipated rematch with Tarrytown loomed. New Departure had yet to figure out Gus Helfrich, the spitball pitcher who surrendered five runs on fourteen hits with thirteen strikeouts and four walks in two complete games. The *New Departure News* considered Helfrich the best semipro pitcher to appear at Muzzy Field in 1920.

Helfrich had been the property of the Chicago White Sox and pitched for Hartford of the Eastern League, Portland of the Pacific Coast League, and Nashville of the Southern Association during the 1910s.

Fans at Muzzy Field certainly got their money's worth from a tight Hyatt duel and a second game that entered the ninth inning deadlocked at 1–1.

Helfrich and Nixie Carney surrendered little to the opposition, but Tarrytown broke through with four runs in the ninth to win. Helfrich struck out five and gave up four hits as Tarrytown reigned supreme among GM teams. By beating New Departure for a third time, he joined Art Johnson as the only two pitchers to achieve that feat.

The following week, New Departure split the last two games with Torrington, leaving a sour taste at the end of a long season. But all of that changed when New Departure management announced an agreement forged with Curtiss Gillette of the Hartford Polis. The teams would play two games during the October 2 weekend, and the Polis would come to Muzzy Field with New York Yankees superman Babe Ruth in their lineup.

◆     ◆     ◆

By 1920, Ruth had changed the game of baseball. He obliterated the home run mark he set the previous year by blasting 54 and driving in 137 runs with a .376 batting average, numbers that again outpaced entire teams.

Everything Ruth did was grand, and his celebrity status made him the ultimate attraction not only in cities around professional baseball but also for semipro baseball managers looking to stuff their grandstands and pockets with paying customers trying to catch a glimpse of him. Teams from New England, New York, Pennsylvania, and the Midwest sent telegrams to Ruth's personal business manager, John Igoe, hoping to secure the home run king for an appearance.

He was scheduled to play seventeen games after the regular season for a reported sum of fifteen hundred dollars per game before embarking on a tengame tour of Cuba in mid-October that would pay him twenty-five thousand dollars.

Igoe showed this stack of telegrams to New Departure and Poli management when they made a pitch for Ruth to play a game in Connecticut. For more than two weeks, negotiations stalled until Gillette traveled to New York to meet Ruth at his Manhattan apartment. At first, Ruth refused to undermine Igoe by talking to Gillette, but when the Poli manager mentioned the New Departure team and Muzzy Field, Ruth recalled the wonderful reception given him by Bristol fans and players during his visit with the Red Sox in 1919, according to newspaper reports.

He placed a phone call to Igoe and agreed to play in one game at Muzzy Field, his only Connecticut appearance of the season. The *Hartford Courant* reported that Gillette beat out "at least thirty other ambitious baseball men in the scramble to engage the player for that date."

One of them was George Weiss, a keen businessman and owner of New Haven's Eastern League team. During his days at Yale University, Weiss operated a semipro team that frequently outdrew the Eastern League club at the gates. Weiss more than doubled Ty Cobb's appearance fee to lure him to New Haven, and the budding executive knew how to please the fans, according to author Mark Gallagher.

After his stint with the Eastern League club, Weiss joined the New York Yankees and became a Hall of Fame general manager as the Yankees won nineteen pennants and fifteen world championships in his twenty-nine years.

The *Bristol Press* announced in its Tuesday, September 28, edition that Ruth and the Polis would meet New Departure Saturday afternoon, changed from Sunday due to Ruth's schedule. Representatives of the two teams met at the Hotel Bond in Hartford and sent "a very sizable check" to Igoe, and Ruth closed out his first season with the New York Yankees on September 30 by socking his fifty-fourth home run in the ninth inning against the Philadelphia Athletics.

After resting in New York, Ruth traveled to Springfield, Massachusetts, the next day with Igoe for a game between the Polis and the Springfield Ponies of the Eastern League. This game was a last-minute deal struck by Gillette and Ruth, and not even a severe rain and wind storm that swept through Connecticut early in the morning changed the schedule. There was, however, an incident in Meriden, Connecticut, that could have changed the course of baseball history.

On his way from New York to Springfield in his new twelve-thousand-dollar Packard, Ruth collided with a truck employed by City Trucking Company of Worcester, Massachusetts, and he "narrowly escaped serious injury," according to the *Bristol Press*. It was never reported that the stormy conditions contributed to the accident.

"He landed in a field with his car wrecked even to the steering post being ripped out," the story reported. "Ruth was given a lift by a passing autoist and went on his way to Springfield, leaving his car to be hauled to a local garage."

Meriden's *Daily Journal* headlines on the first day of October blared, "Champion Baseball Swatter Near Death," after Ruth passed through town and under a culvert where he "found himself headed for a Mack truck."

The Packard's front end was demolished, its radiator punctured, windshield shattered, and headlights broken.

The story reported that everyone escaped with minor scratches from the windshield, but it was not the first time Ruth had a close call in 1920. In early July, Ruth, known to be a wild driver, ran his car off the road in Wawa, Pennsylvania, when he took a curve too fast at two o'clock in the morning. The car overturned with his wife Helen and Yankee members Frank Gleich, Fred Hofmann, and Charley O'Leary inside. No one suffered any serious injuries (Creamer 1974).

Ruth made his way to Springfield in time for the Friday afternoon game, and fans met him with jubilation.

"Followed through the streets by hundreds of kids and a few who had been kids a long time ago, Ruth was the pride and hope of everything that is good and clean in baseball," a *Hartford Courant* story read.

Ruth excited the Springfield crowd by playing four positions (left field, pitcher, catcher, and first base) and collected a double and single in five at-bats. After the game, he left for Hartford and checked into the Hotel Bond with Igoe, and another large crowd of people awaited the celebrity's arrival.

"The lobby of the Bond was full of persons of all ages and both sexes who gazed upon the redoubtable Babe with much more awe than a *Courant* reporter saw another crowd in the same lobby last year gaze upon John D. Rockefeller," a *Hartford Courant* story reported, adding that Ruth signed the hotel register "in a fine Spencerian hand about which there was almost a suggestion of the feminine."

The story went on to say that Bond management benefited from a speaking engagement by U.S. Senator Henry Cabot Lodge a few blocks away because only a man of Lodge's esteem "could have diverted from the Bond a mob so huge that it might have smashed things in its enthusiasm to enter."

Ruth lounged in a hotel lobby chair, smoking a cigar. He was dressed in a "dark suit of conventional cut, blue and white striped shirt, soft collar, dark, unobtrusive tie and black hat" and spoke little of the Black Sox hearings being conducted in Chicago. Instead, he talked about the car accident in Meriden that left him limping slightly.

"I got a crack in the face in that smash, too," Ruth told the reporter. "But that car, that car! It was a beauty, and I'd had it just four days."

The next day, October 2, Ruth and the Poli club arrived in Bristol for a 3:15 start in the first of the two-game series. New Departure imported Gus Helfrich, the star spitball pitcher from the Tarrytown, New York, team, to oppose George "Kewpie" Pennington, an accomplished right-handed hurler for the Hartford Senators who pitched in one game for the St. Louis Browns in 1917.

The Polis lineup also featured Lore "King" Bader, a former New York Giants and Boston Red Sox pitcher, batting leadoff and playing right field, and New Departure started many of their regular players. But the buzz, understandably, surrounded Ruth.

Reserved seats sold out in twenty minutes at Walsh & Hollfelder's, and the *Bristol Press* printed mandates about where to park on the day of the game in anticipation of the thousands of fans who would arrive from around the state.

"Muzzy Field is an ideal field for the staging of such an attraction, being one of the largest and best ballparks in the state," an anonymous reporter wrote in the *Hartford Courant*. "There will be special train and trolley service so as to handle the large throng that will turn out to see the home run king."

New Departure management wanted to make clear that the event was scheduled solely for the fans.

"This is not a money making affair for the New Departure Athletic Association," NDAA president Lester Sigourney told the *Bristol Press*. "We simply put on as big an attraction as we could find in order to emphasize our appreciation of the support that has been given our team this year by Bristol fans."

NOT SO FAST, "BABE."

The Yankee Fence-Buster Tries to Go From First to Third on Bunt But Is Doubled Up, Zielke to Bowden.

Babe Ruth at Muzzy Field, 1920. (Courtesy: Bristol Historical Society)

The crowd of thirty-two hundred mostly wanted to see the Babe belt a few home runs out of spacious Muzzy Field, and he blasted four in batting practice off of Bader, one that cleared the wall by at least twenty yards, according to the *Bristol Press*.

During the game, however, Helfrich kept the reins on the Polis lineup much as he had done to New Departure on three occasions that season. Ruth smacked two doubles and two singles in his four at-bats, but Helfrich allowed only two other hits and struck out nine as New Departure won, 7–0.

The infield registered every putout, and Helfrich's most impressive inning was the fifth when Ruth led off with a double only to be stranded by the next three batters who never lifted a spitball out of the infield.

Eddie Zielke, the first baseman who caught Ruth's eye the previous year, hit two triples and a double while driving in four runs and scoring two as New Departure's offensive catalyst.

Ruth played every position but pitcher and committed one error while at third base. Eddie Goodridge, who scored three runs, hit a grounder that Ruth booted, and "the big fellow started to wipe his hands on his uniform and claimed that the ball was all wet," the *Bristol Press* reported.

"BABE" LIFTS ONE A MILE HIGH
Foul Ball Goes Way Up Among Clouds and Causes Spectators to Wonder if It is Ever Coming Down.

Babe Ruth delighted fans in Bristol when he chose to return to Muzzy Field in 1920. Ruth played eight positions for a semipro team from East Hartford and collected four hits in the game, which his team lost. He blasted four home runs out of the spacious ballpark during batting practice. (Courtesy: Bristol Public Library)

## GIFT TO "BABE" RUTH
President Sigourney of Athletic Association Surprises Big Champion with a Fine Speech and Bristol Steel Rod.

As appreciation for returning to Muzzy Field in 1920, New Departure Athletic Association president Lester Sigourney presented Babe Ruth a steel fishing rod manufactured in Bristol. (Courtesy: Bristol Public Library)

In all, the fans got their money's worth seeing the Babe perform and New Departure win handily. Ruth began his barnstorming tour the next day in possession of a Bristol Steel Fishing Rod presented him before the game.

New Departure finished the series against the Polis with a road game on October 3. The ten-inning affair ended tied at five, and neither team could claim the Hartford County crown. Goodridge opposed Bader on the mound, and the Polis lineup included twenty-four-year-old New York Yankee "Muddy" Ruel as catcher. About two months prior, Ruel was behind the plate when Carl Mays struck and killed Cleveland's Ray Chapman with a pitch at the Polo Grounds.

Goodridge completed the New Departure season the next weekend with an 8–2 victory in Newark against Hyatt Roller Bearing, winning the season series.

# 1921: Barriers Broken

Eddie Goodridge was becoming the most consistent and versatile player for New Departure, adding team manager to his duties for the 1921 and 1922 seasons. In the wake of his team's thirty-win season, Goodridge dealt with several personnel changes and a demanding schedule against out-of-state teams.

Swat McCabe's back injury in 1920 sidelined the thirty-nine-year-old right fielder for all but one game in 1921, and he would eventually sit out the entire 1922 season. Tommy Bowden, the team's leading hitter and fill-in captain from the previous year, left New Departure to play third base for the Bridgeport Singers, and the team's number two starter, Earl Champion, joined rival Torrington after spending part of the 1920 season on the injured list.

Like a modern major league team in the off-season, New Departure signed several players to bolster their lineup. Pitcher Hal Justin brought considerable minor league experience to Bristol, and Eddie Goeb, who performed admirably on the mound for the New Britain Pioneers in 1919 and also played outfield, formed the rotation with Tony Welch, signed in May. Goodridge, Gus Helfrich, and Pete Wood made ballyhooed starts for New Departure, but Helfrich and Wood performed considerably worse for the team than they had against them in previous years.

Doc Murray never returned to the club, and shortstop Joe Holcomb signed in April after spending the previous season in the minors in Montreal. Second baseman Bill Tamm of Providence signed in May and briefly replaced Gus Forslund, who had a short stint on the injury list with a split finger. Speedy left-handed hitter Jim Green (or Greene as the newspapers sometimes spelled it) joined the team from New Britain to replace McCabe.

Other New Departure veterans included Clyde Waters, Smoke Halbach, Eddie Zielke, hometown boy George Scott, and Les Lanning, who started the year on the injured list and played very little during the season.

The Bristol club filled their schedule with sixteen games against teams from the powerful Massachusetts Industrial League and continued to enhance their rivalry with Torrington while the relationship with Manchester became evermore bitter.

In 1921, Muzzy Field experienced another historic first when all-black teams took the field against New Departure; one of them, the Cuban Stars, featured men who are considered now to be some of the finest players in the history of the game.

The home team earned no championships and fared rather poorly against the best in-state aggregations, but they held their own with eight of Massachusetts' industrial teams, considered by some reporters to play a brand of baseball superior to Connecticut's. Against those teams, New Departure fashioned a 10–6 record.

Overall, New Departure finished 24–17, their lowest winning percentage in the glory days of 1919–1926, but the local press wished to remind fans that the economic situation of the day hampered many other teams in the area.

"The New Departure ball club is fortunate in having one of the very few industrial semipro teams in the East which is supporting a first-class team this season," a story read in May.

In their third game of the year, "an innovation in local baseball" was displayed at Muzzy Field when the Elm City Giants of New Haven, "the colored champs of New England," as the *Bristol Press* called them, arrived with a lineup of former college stars, some who had minor league experience.

In his first start of the season, Hal Justin limited the Giants to eight hits and struck out three in a 6–2 New Departure victory. Elm City's starter named Logan walked five and surrendered eight hits in a complete-game effort. Zielke smashed a double and triple for the home team and scored a run while Waters and Forslund both collected two hits and scored once.

Published details about Elm City were sparse. Their lineup included Twyman in left field with a triple in four at-bats; Moore behind the plate, hitless in four at-bats; Ching at second base with a triple and a run; Gibbs at first base with two hits; West at shortstop with two hits, including a triple; Redmond in center field, hitless in two official at-bats; Lawrence at third base; Scipio in right field, hitless in two official at-bats; Logan as the starting pitcher with a hit; and Wilson, the relief pitcher, with a hit and a run.

Though the game's play-by-play was not particularly notable, the presence of the Giants opened Muzzy Field to future games against all-black teams that helped define the ballpark's legacy.

Three more were played in 1921, starting with Elm City's return visit to Bristol on August 14. Again, the game was not memorable, except in for its poor play. In a sloppy 10–6 New Departure win, the teams combined for fifteen errors, attributed to what the *Bristol Press* described as "temperamental fielding" that sometimes resulted in "all kinds of circus stunts as well as unusual features," such as "two double plays and a couple of tumble tom plays."

The newspaper implied that New Departure's fielding woes were a result of Elm City's in that the Giants were more interested in appearing flashy than functional defensively, and New Departure started to play similarly. Whether this was truly the case remains unknown, but it highlights an attitude common around the country at the time. Whenever an all-black team arrived in Bristol, the *Press* heralded their talent, but not without writing parts of the stories using minstrel dialect, referring to players with racist terms or describing their performance with words such as "circus" and "antics."

Tony Welch opposed Langford in the second meeting; neither was sharp in his complete-game performance, except at the plate. Langford scored two runs with a hit, and Welch belted a double as part of three hits and three runs scored. Smoke Halbach added a triple in his three-hit day, and George Scott scored three runs for the victors.

Elm City's lineup included Twyman in left field with two hits and two runs; Gibbs at first base, hitless in five at-bats; Lawrence at third base, hitless in three at-bats; West at shortstop, hitless in three at-bats; Redmond in center field, hitless in two at-bats; Conquest in right field with three hits and a run; Moore behind the plate with a hit and a run; and Langford pitching with a hit and two runs.

Eight days later, the *Bristol Press* announced "a rare baseball treat" after Eddie Goodridge convinced owner Nat C. Strong to bring his Cuban Stars to Bristol on their way up to Providence for a weekend game. At first, Strong hesitated because he felt Bristol was too small a city to pay dividends, but Goodridge convinced him otherwise.

The *Bristol Press* informed readers of the game's high profile. "Bristol is very fortunate in being able to attract a team of so high a calibre [*sic*]. Bristol again comes up in line with the big cities when we have the rare privilege" of seeing the Cuban Stars, an independent organization based in the East in 1921. Another Cuban Stars team, designated by historians as the Cuban Stars (West), played as a member of the Negro National League at the time.

The Stars who arrived in Connecticut included some of the same players against whom Babe Ruth competed after he left Bristol for his barnstorming tour of 1920. Several of them are immortals in the pantheon of Cuban legends, and their exploits are well documented by several historians.

Starting infielders included Tatica Campos at first, Julián Terán at second, Julián Fabelo at third, and Pelayo Chacón at shortstop. Chacón, like the other players, spent the winter months playing for Cuban powerhouses such as Santa Clara and Fé, and he had won the previous year's batting title with the Fé ball club.

A diminutive five-foot-eight 140-pounder, Chacón was considered a superb defensive player with smarts, speed, and range. At the plate, his bat control made him a fine executor of the hit-and-run. Major league scouts sought his services, but like many equally talented players of the day, his skin color prohibited anyone from signing him. Chacón played from 1909 to 1931, batting .350 (1911–12) and .364 (1920) in exhibitions against John McGraw's New York Giants and finishing his career as one of Cuba's top base stealers. He later parlayed his baseball acumen into a successful career as a manager in Cuba.

Under Chacón's tutelage, Martín Dihigo became one of the greatest players of all time, and Chacón moved to Venezuela in the 1930s and helped develop that country's professional baseball league. His son, Elio, broke into the American major leagues in 1960 and played two seasons with the Cincinnati Reds before suffering through the 1962 season with the New York Mets. Against New Departure, Chacón probably served as captain and manager, roles he filled often in his history with the Cuban Stars.

Campos played sixteen years at every position but shortstop in his career. Fabelo had been the regular shortstop prior to Chacón's arrival and lasted eight years stateside in the Negro Leagues. He and Terán were near the end of their careers in the United States by the time they arrived at Muzzy Field.

As talented as the infield was for the Cuban Stars, the outfield was more formidable. The island's answer to Babe Ruth was Alejandro Oms, who played center field against New Departure. Nicknamed "El Caballero," or "The Gentleman," for his graceful and quiet style, Oms was a left-handed line-drive hitter with extreme power who had become a bona fide Cuban superstar by 1921. He won two consecutive Cuban League batting titles in the late 1920s while fashioning a thirty-game hitting streak during the winter of 1928–29.

A five-foot-nine, 190-pound man with impeccable manners, Oms was blessed with superb speed and glided across the spacious outfields of Almendares Park and La Tropical in Cuba where fences were 498 feet away from home plate. During one game, Oms is said to have tracked down a fly ball 460 feet away from the plate, and the runner at second base tagged up and scored. He also played with a signature flair, credited with perfecting in lopsided games the basket catch that later made Willie Mays famous—only Oms caught the ball behind his back.

Oms's average arm strength was his lone deficiency, though he was very accurate with his throws. He made up for it in all other phases of baseball, including the legendary power stroke to all fields that routinely sent tape-measure home runs over the four-hundred-foot marker in right field at Almendares Park. Oms, whose career lasted from 1917 to 1935, is considered one of the best players ever to come out of Cuba.

Equally impressive was left fielder Pablo "Champion" Mesa, who teamed with Oms and Oscar Charleston to form Santa Clara's outfield during the 1922–23 Cuban League season, considered among some historians to be the greatest outfield ever assembled. When the trio returned the next season to play with a star-studded infield, the 1923–24 Santa Clara team became a legendary group revered by historians as much as the 1927 New York Yankees. Mesa, six foot and 175 pounds, was a colorful and multitalented rookie in 1921 on his way to a seven-year career.

Though Charleston was not in Bristol with the Stars, right fielder Isidro Fabré brought his own impressive credentials.

During the previous October when Babe Ruth came to Cuba to play with the New York Giants, Fabré, a left-hander, pitched a three-hitter against New York in a 5–0 win. No Giants reached third base, and John McGraw fielded a talented team, though Ruth did not arrive on the island until two days later. The Giants lineup included George Burns, Ross Young, Vern Spencer, George Kelly, Larry Doyle, Dave Bancroft, Frankie Frisch, Jesse Barnes, Lee King, Pol Perritt, Patrick "Rosy" Ryan, Frank Snyder, Earl Smith, and Johnny Evers as coach. Fabré also was known in the Cuban League ranks as a fine hitter.

Left-hander Luis Padrón was the starter in Bristol, and his battery mate was a player named Borroto, also known as Borselo, whose scant biographical information compiled by James A. Riley reveals that he spent just the 1921 season with the Stars.

The pitcher, who was among the most talented Cuban League players for two decades, actually had a connection to Bristol and the New Departure club. Padrón was one of four Cuban players signed by New Britain of the Connecticut State League in 1908. Members of this quartet, which included Armando Marsans, Rafael Almeida, and Alfredo Cabrera, made baseball history, and all of them but Padrón played in the major leagues. All four men spent considerable time with a player who enjoyed a short-lived career with the Cincinnati Reds, New Departure right fielder Swat McCabe.

Marsans and Almeida became the first Latinos in the National League when they debuted on July 4, 1911, with the Reds and enjoyed an eight-year and three-year career, respectively; Cabrera broke in with the St. Louis Cardinals in 1913 and played in just one game.

Padrón bounced around the American Negro Leagues with the Chicago American Giants, New York Lincoln Stars, New York Lincoln Giants, Birmingham Black Barons, and Indianapolis ABCs, and he was known for his devastating changeup and good hitting ability. He left his mark on Cuban baseball, becoming the first player to lead the Cuban League in hits (thirty-one) and wins (thirteen) when he accomplished the feat in 1900.

Padrón was the first of five from this Cuban Stars team elected into the Cuban Baseball Hall of Fame when he earned the distinction in 1943, followed by Oms (1944), Chacón (1949), Fabré (1957), and Mesa (1964).

The talent possessed by the Cuban Stars lineup outclassed many clubs, and they were one of the premiere teams ever to play at Muzzy Field. Along with being one of the first black aggregations to visit Bristol, the importance of their appearance cannot be overstated.

Eddie Goodridge bore the task of subduing five future Hall of Famers, and he was duly impressed when he scouted the Stars' 6–2 victory in Hartford against the Brooklyn Royal Giants of New York, another talented black club with a connection to Muzzy Field.

"Everybody who is in the least responsive to baseball thrills will miss something big if they don't go to Muzzy Field tomorrow afternoon," Goodridge said to a *Bristol Press* reporter. "If the Cubans put up anything like the game they did in Hartford, our people will see the fastest team that ever came to Bristol, bar none."

The New Departure-Cuban Stars contest was scheduled for four o'clock Friday, and the advance notice of the August 26 game allowed shopkeepers to close early and downtown workers to punch out in time to catch the game. On Thursday, the *Bristol Press* announced that New Departure bolstered their lineup with Joe Gaudette, a hard-hitting right fielder from the Massachusetts semipro circuit, an addition that forced Jim Green to shortstop for Joe Holcomb, who did not play.

On game day, local youth Donald "Peanuts" Funk, a student at Choate School, started at short for Green, who was nursing a bad back and boils.

The Stars lineup radiated brilliance and refined acumen. For New Departure no better potential conqueror of the Cuban bats existed than left-hander Goodridge, steely competitor and undisputed staff ace.

Goodridge collected twelve victories leading up to the game against the Stars, six of them against Massachusetts' finest clubs, and was the big-game pitcher for a team that stood at 20–9. He was as hot as a sultry summer from June to August with five shutouts and four other victories in which he allowed two or fewer runs. He knew exactly what to expect from the Cuban lineup, and he was poised for a magnificent afternoon against the likes of Oms and Mesa.

The subplot to this and every game featuring notable power hitters involved the battle between man and wall. Muzzy Field was an egotist's passionate desire. To clear its distant barriers with one swing of the bat was to be celebrated for a prowess displayed only by Babe Ruth, the world's most feared hitter. When Alejandro Oms stepped into the batter's box, he might have known about Ruth's rare feat and maybe vowed to match it.

Fans and reporters certainly anticipated that matchup.

"Oms, the Babe Ruth of Cuba, nearly broke his back trying in vain to knock the pellet out of the lot," said the game report in the *Bristol Press*. "His one terrific high wallop to deep right, which Gaudette pocketed, was his nearest approach to a hit."

On any other day Oms probably would have succeeded, but Goodridge was firing a stingy shutout, and his "baffling delivery held the heavy-slugging Cubans powerless."

In a fantastic duel, Padrón kept New Departure off the bases through the first three innings before the locals started the fourth with singles from Eddie Goeb and Smoke Halbach. Eddie Zielke then lifted a pitch to center that Oms tracked down before doubling up a runner. Where run production was lacking, the Stars' defense never waned: "Oms and Fabré by marvelous stops of line clouts helped materially to hold down the New Departurites."

New Departure threatened again in the fifth with a double by Gaudette and a sacrifice bunt by Gus Forslund, but the runner was stranded and the game remained scoreless.

The shuffling of players at shortstop placed local youngster Peanuts Funk in a difficult position. He had been with the team less than a month and found himself in the middle of a game that was fast becoming a classic. The locals were scrapping with some of Cuba's finest baseball players ever and threatening to secure one of the greatest victories in what is now a long history of Bristol baseball.

But in August 1921 during the sixth inning, Peanuts Funk just wanted an out.

Tatica Campos led off the frame by smacking a pitch in Funk's direction. It took a bad hop in front of the youth and Campos reached first. Julián Fabelo followed with a crisp single to set the table for Oms. His dribbler to Goodridge gave the southpaw time to cut off Campos at third, but Halbach could not hang on to the throw and the ball escaped him as the Stars took a 1–0 lead.

With runners at the corners, Pelayo Chacón popped up high behind his counterpart at short while left fielder George Scott charged in.

"The sun evidently got in Funk's eye and the pill fell between him and Scotty, letting in another run," the *Bristol Press* reported, and Oms moved to third.

After Pablo Mesa popped out in foul territory for the first out, Julián Terán shot a hard grounder in Funk's direction with enough power that he had a chance to nab the speedy Oms who was running on contact. Funk fumbled momentarily and his only play was at first, Oms scoring for the 3–0 lead.

Isidro Fabré grounded out to Forslund at second for the final out.

It was a defensive meltdown for New Departure, and the injured Green replaced Peanuts Funk, who made an ignominious exit from an otherwise sharp game.

For Padrón, the lead was more than enough. He pitched a shutout for 8$^1/_3$ innings before a Goeb single, a Halbach double, and a Zielke sac fly completed the scoring in the 3–1 Stars victory. Padrón allowed his defense to do the work as he struck out four and walked one while surrendering nine hits.

Goodridge surrendered two singles to Chacón and one to Fabelo while walking a batter in one of the finest pitching performances in Muzzy Field's history. The *Bristol Press* trumpeted New Departure's nine hits compared to the Stars' three, and visiting manager Nat C. Strong told the paper, "That Goodridge is sure some pitcher. It is mighty seldom that we meet a man that can tame our boys like that."

But New Departure had only plaudits and visions of what might have been as twilight descended on the ballpark.

Two weeks later, the Brooklyn Royal Giants paid a Saturday afternoon visit to Muzzy Field, bringing with them a lineup of considerable talent. This was the first of four appearances in Bristol by the Royal Giants between 1921 and 1925, and each visit brought more spectacular players and stories.

In 1921, Brooklyn played as an independent Negro League team whose major attraction was first baseman Eddie Douglass, considered the best at his position from the post–World War I era to the mid-1920s. He combined great defense and base running with his knack for collecting hits when they mattered most. The Texas native also carved out a remarkable career in Cuba and batted .336 for the juggernaut Santa Clara club of 1923–24. At Muzzy Field, Douglass batted fifth.

Brooklyn's leadoff hitter was right fielder Ralph Jefferson, a right-handed batter whose fifteen-year career began in 1918.

Lee "Red" Miller batted second and played third base. He was two years away from the end of a long and solid career, and his life ended tragically due to his drinking problem. Someone killed Miller by pounding his head on a concrete sidewalk while he was intoxicated, according to author James A. Riley.

Robert Scott, a small and speedy left fielder, was playing his second year at the highest level of the Negro Leagues and set the table for cleanup hitter Chester "Irvin" Brooks, the center fielder and versatile player from the Bahamas. An underpublicized star, Brooks was considered one of the best all-around players of the 1920s and the most lethal utility man in the East. He was discovered in the Florida Keys by Rube Foster, former player and pioneering Negro League executive and team owner, and started as a pitcher before arm problems relegated him to the outfield and infield.

Second baseman John Cason, another versatile utility man, batted behind Douglass. Catcher Charles Spearman hit seventh, and rookie shortstop Bill Wagner followed. Wagner, a rather light hitter who usually batted in the bottom of the order, brought considerable defensive talents to Brooklyn and later became a manager.

Wayne Carr was at the beginning of a journeyman's career and became one of the best pitchers in the East by 1924. He started against New Departure and batted ninth. Tony Welch got the nod for New Departure.

The *Bristol Press* announced that legendary fireball pitcher "Cyclone Joe" Williams, also known as "Smokey Joe," would start for Brooklyn, but a hand injury prevented his appearance, much to the fans' chagrin.

Nevertheless, the Royal Giants arrived with sturdy bats and hitting feats that enticed the Bristol fans.

"Never has Bristol seen a team which swung as hard after the old apple," the local paper reported.

Welch, however, pitched a scoreless one-hit game through three innings before a walk and a sacrifice bunt placed Scott at second for Douglass, who drove him in with a single, his first of two on the day. In the seventh inning, Welch passed two batters who eventually scored on a two-run single by Jefferson with two outs. A fielding and throwing error by Halbach on the same play allowed Jefferson to score for a 4–0 Brooklyn lead.

New Departure failed to score at the hands of Carr. The Royal Giants hurler scattered eight hits and struck out four while superb defensive plays by Brooks and Douglass squelched any potential rallies. Goeb, Waters, and Goodridge collected seven of the hits for New Departure in a game Brooklyn controlled from the start.

The Royal Giants' first Muzzy Field appearance was the last for black ball clubs during the season and set the stage for significant games against legendary players in the future. While the significance of these games stands out when considering the history of Muzzy Field, the more immediate concern and interest in 1921 involved Manchester.

Prior to 1921, Torrington served as New Departure's chief in-state rival, but three straight victories over Torrington early in the season and five wins in the seven-game season series deflated the excitement of 1920 when the teams split eight games.

Warm weather holidays always meant a home-and-home doubleheader with Torrington, but New Departure sought another competitive rivalry and looked to an old foe.

For the Fourth of July weekend, they found willing participants in Manchester, featuring former St. Louis Brown and town native Herman Bronkie as player-coach, and the teams worked out a deal during mid-May negotiations. Like the Torrington series, the teams would play a morning-afternoon doubleheader on each other's turf. New Departure hosted the first game on July 4.

The teams played each other once the previous season, a 7–1 road win for New Departure, but Manchester fielded an impressive team in 1921. Bronkie's boys won their first sixteen games of the season coming into the doubleheader against the Endees, who were 13–7 at the time, and emotions were running high for the holiday.

Art Johnson, the familiar face of 1920, opposed Goodridge on the hill and the two dueled artfully into the eighth inning with Manchester leading, 2–1.

With the bases loaded for New Departure, Gus Forslund hit a grounder to short and the throw beat him to the bag by a half step. During the close play at first, Forslund "bumped (Manchester first baseman) Fay in his excitement" and the ball squirted free after McCarthy, an umpire from Manchester, called Forslund out, according to the *Bristol Press*.

McCarthy reconsidered the play and overturned his ruling. Bob Coughlin, the home plate umpire from Bristol, accepted McCarthy's explanation that Forslund unintentionally collided with Fay. Forslund had been standing on second and the deliberations resulted in counting the two runs for New Departure, giving them a 3–2 lead.

In protest, Manchester refused to finish the game, and Coughlin announced the forfeit. Outraged by the egregious violation of sportsmanship, New Departure management cancelled the afternoon game, and one of the most acrimonious rivalries in Connecticut baseball emerged.

Newspapers in both cities weighed in on the decision, and even the *Manchester Herald* called its hometown team "poor losers." The *Bristol Press* described it as "doubtful sportsmanship" and completed its game report with the following: "It is most regretable [*sic*] that Manchester did not see fit to finish the game and take the chance of winning in the ninth, as it would have at least given them the record of losing their first game of the season like good sports."

After two months of bickering through their hometown newspapers, Manchester and New Departure announced a five-game series to determine supremacy, one game per weekend. The series lasted more than a month from September 11 to October 16 and comprised some of the most hotly contested games ever played between the two clubs. Thousands of fans packed Muzzy Field and Mount Nebo Grounds in South Manchester in vocal support of their teams.

Goodridge was called upon to pitch every game for New Departure and performed some of his best work. Manchester hosted the opener and started Sammy Hyman, the former Georgetown star who had pitched a shutout for Meriden over New Departure in 1919.

Neither pitcher budged, surrendering five hits apiece. The Endees notched a quick run in the first inning on a sac fly by recent signee Chet Waite that scored George Scott. After Manchester tied the game in their first at-bat, Clyde Waters drove home Scott in the fifth for what proved to be the game-winning run in a 2–1 decision. Goodridge struck out four and walked three while Hyman struggled with control, striking out seven but walking six and hitting two more.

Game two the next Sunday afternoon at Muzzy attracted two thousand fans who witnessed a game that matched the first for tension and well-played baseball. The pitching matchup was the same as the ugly affair in July and followed nearly the same pattern.

Goodridge and Johnson battled for nine innings as both teams squeezed out only one run against them. Tied in the tenth inning, two Bristol veterans decided the game. Scott rapped a leadoff double, and Waters punched the game-winning two-out hit to score him for a 2–1 victory. Again Goodridge sparkled, allowing three hits, striking out four, and walking two. Johnson gave up eights hits and walked three as Manchester dropped the first two games of the series.

New Departure and their fans were thinking sweep when they hosted game three the following Saturday. A reprise of Goodridge-Hyman promised another nail-biting affair, which it was, but New Departure's defense betrayed their pitcher.

The Endees committed two errors in the game and fell behind 3–0 after the second inning in front of a large home crowd, many of whom came from the annual New Departure Club sheep barbecue that had been downsized considerably in recent years and attracted *only* four hundred people. The New Departure band joined the festive revelers in the stands and played loudly between innings.

New Departure scored two runs in the third inning and tied the game in the seventh when Goodridge scored from third on an error by Bronkie, who appointed himself cleanup hitter and third baseman in his first action of the series.

Goodridge subdued Manchester after the second inning until a Forslund error and a passed ball placed a runner at second with no outs in the ninth. A sacrifice bunt by Bronkie and a sac fly gave Manchester a 4–3 lead, and Hyman quieted the Bristol bats three more times for the victory.

The next weekend sent New Departure on the road for the fourth game, and Bronkie imported a pitcher named Anderson from Salem, Massachusetts, to oppose Goodridge. Manchester's new hurler gave up the game's first run in the fourth inning and displayed enough wildness to be pulled in favor of Art Johnson.

From then on, it was another classic Goodridge-Johnson battle. The *Bristol Press* described Goodridge's performance as "the most masterful game of his career" in "one of the most wonderful games ever staged in semipro baseball."

Manchester was one out from losing the series when Bronkie, batting cleanup and down to his last strike, belted an RBI triple under the automobiles that lined the outfield to tie the game at one. Two innings later with darkness settling in, Johnson hit a deep fly ball that glanced off of George Scott's glove for a double.

Jim Green fumbled a slow roller at shortstop two batters later, and Johnson scored the winning run. New Departure stranded eight runners and wasted an eleven-inning five-hitter from Goodridge, who struck out five.

Johnson scattered eight hits in relief and held New Departure scoreless in tying the series. The Bristol club never recovered, and Manchester soon capped their incredible comeback in the emotional series.

Rain postponed the fifth game until October 16, and in fairness to the two teams, the Eastern League field in Hartford served as neutral grounds. The wonderful performances in the first four games set up a potentially brilliant finale between Goodridge and Johnson. But the pitching and defense on both sides devolved into a malaise of sloppiness and an anticlimatic finish.

Neither side was sharp as Manchester took their third consecutive game and the series, 11–7, by battering Goodridge and Gaudette for thirteen hits. The teams combined for twenty-two hits and committed six errors; Bronkie scored three times, and Manchester center fielder Eddie Munson collected four hits.

The 1921 season left a lot to be desired by New Departure, and the final game was one they would not soon forget.

# 1922: Red Sox, Black Beards, and White-Hot Emotions

As the automobile became more widely available to Americans and the industry progressed rapidly, New Departure Manufacturing Company enjoyed steady job growth starting in January 1921. Eight hundred employees joined the company in the early spring of 1922, swelling the workforce to thirty-three hundred or nearly two-thirds of "our best (numbers) in the period of remarkable wartime activity," the local paper reported.

One of those new employees, Ben Reilly, turned out to be arguably the greatest hitter ever to wear the New Departure uniform. Reilly was a twenty-five-year-old center fielder and catcher known for his power hitting abilities in the Appalachian and Florida State Leagues during the 1919 and 1920 seasons. He moved north in 1921, playing for two teams in the Massachusetts Industrial League, Three Rivers and Ware, and hitting sixteen home runs against stiff competition. Reilly's and Ware's season reached their zenith when the Massachusetts team defeated the Eastern League champion Pittsfield club as Reilly collected three hits.

During his career with Bristol, Reilly was a baseball vagabond, playing games in Massachusetts on Wednesday and Saturday while suiting up for the Endees on Sunday.

He arrived in Bristol with Jack Ruckley, a twenty-three-year-old outfielder who teamed with Reilly in Massachusetts. But while Reilly set fields afire with his hitting for New Departure, Ruckley played but a handful of games before returning to his old club.

Shortstop Harold Horkheimer exhibited more staying power, and the Meriden shortstop of 1921 would become an important figure on the diamond for several years to come.

Another new face was pitcher Ralph Knight, a standout right-hander at Brown University the previous season. Knight commuted from Hartford, where he worked, to play for New Departure on the weekends. Though he was one of the top hurlers at the beginning of the 1922 campaign, he was gone by June.

Manager Eddie Goodridge could count on one steady pitcher who lasted the duration of the season, left-hander Les Lanning. He served as staff ace while posting commendable offensive numbers and playing the outfield after spending most of 1921 on the sick list.

Goodridge, however, could not keep himself healthy, and he lost more than two months of playing time suffering from rheumatism, which he reportedly contracted during the season opener in late April against the Hartford Senators. Joe Carroll, boxing promoter and New Departure women's basketball coach, assisted Goodridge as business manager and soon became the head of the baseball program.

The 1922 season provided intriguing games at Muzzy Field, most notably a return visit from the Boston Red Sox in July and the inaugural appearance in September by a quirky, yet talented, Michigan team/religious cult that lived on a commune, refused to shave or cut their hair, and defeated some of the best semi-pro teams in the country.

New Departure fashioned a 29–13–1 mark, one of their finest records during the era, and again disposed of a majority of the Massachusetts teams they played, winning seven of ten games against six teams. The Bristol club emerged as a state title contender against the likes of familiar powers Manchester and Torrington and a burgeoning aggregate in Winsted, which won the two-game series from New Departure the previous season.

At Muzzy Field, the home opener attracted one thousand fans on a cold, damp, and windy April Sunday to a pedestrian 3–1 loss to the Eastern League Hartford Senators, which followed a similar game played the day before on the Waterbury Brasscos' field.

Early May brought another visit from the Elm City Giants, and New Departure squeezed out an 8–6 win as Lanning pitched three scoreless innings of relief to hold Elm City at bay.

The Giants brought many familiar names in a lineup that included Golson in right field with two hits; Moore at catcher, hitless in four at-bats; Lawrence at shortstop with two hits and a run; Ching at second base, hitless in five at-bats with a run; Redmond in center field with a hit and a run; Twyman in left field, hitless in three at-bats with two runs; Stedwell at first base with two hits and a run; Adams at third base, hitless in three at-bats; and Logan and Conquest the pitchers, both hitless in two at-bats.

Ben Reilly infused New Departure's lineup with an offensive presence previously lacking, and his four hits against the Giants not only set the tone for his season individually but also for a team that would post stronger numbers at the plate.

When the contracts were finalized in June for the Red Sox game in mid-July, New Departure had won fifteen of their first twenty-three games with one tie. Boston, meanwhile, was in a tailspin that would send the club to a last-place finish with a 61–93 record in 1922. Despite the team's struggles, and minus the huge gate attraction of Babe Ruth, many expected a grand crowd at Muzzy Field when the Red Sox arrived on the 1:27 PM train with several regulars ready to suit up.

A clause in the contract required Boston to bring their top-flight players rather than just a collection of reserves, and the Red Sox management assured New Departure a strong lineup. Boston arrived in Bristol on a Sunday in the middle of a series with the Detroit Tigers—baseball on the Sabbath being outlawed in Boston—and traveled back to Massachusetts after the game.

"The whole town is at fever heat and advance indications point to one of the largest crowds that ever witnessed a game in Bristol," the *Bristol Press* reported.

For Bristol fans, ex-New Haven resident "Jumpin' Joe" Dugan was the most popular member of the Red Sox lineup. A former standout at New Haven High School and Holy Cross, Dugan played at Muzzy Field as an amateur in the first years of the ballpark and broke into the major leagues as a twenty-year-old shortstop right out of college for Connie Mack's 1917 Philadelphia A's team. His dissatisfaction with the losing organization and dislike of its reportedly abusive fans prompted him to leave the A's on numerous occasions, only to return. Sportswriters dubbed him "Jumpin' Joe" for his frequent defections. On two occasions in the summer of 1919, Dugan appeared at Muzzy Field with the New Haven Nutmegs, collecting three hits in eight at-bats.

Finally, Dugan convinced Mack to trade him and he landed with the Red Sox, the highest bidders, in January 1922. By the time the Red Sox arrived in Bristol, Dugan was being called the finest third baseman in baseball.

Also riding the 1:27 train were second baseman Del Pratt, outfielder and first baseman Joe Harris, outfielder Mike Menosky, and infielder Pinky Pittinger. The rest of the lineup included outfielders Elmer Smith and Nemo Leibold, infielder Eddie Foster, and catchers Jabber Lynch and Roxy Walters, the only Red Sox player who appeared at Muzzy Field with Babe Ruth three years earlier. Curt Fullerton and a left-hander named Irwin were the pitchers.

Hugh Duffy, a seventeen-year veteran who hit .324 for his career and entered the Hall of Fame in 1945, managed the Red Sox, but there is no proof that he accompanied his club on the trip.

Mired as a team, a few of the Red Sox players enjoyed successful individual seasons in 1922. Pratt batted .301 with eighty-six RBI, and his forty-four doubles were second only to Cleveland's Tris Speaker in the American League. Harris paced the team with a .316 average and nine triples while driving in fifty-four runs and hitting thirty doubles. Dugan hit .287 in eighty-four games but would prove to have a better season than all of the Red Sox in the end.

New Departure countered with their regular lineup: George Scott, left field; Harold Horkheimer, shortstop; Smoke Halbach, third base; Ben Reilly, center field; Eddie Zielke, first base; Gus Forslund, second base; Eddie Goodridge, right field, replaced early in the game by Joe Coughlin; Clyde Waters, catcher; and Les Lanning and Pete Condon, pitchers.

Waters Lifts One Toward the Fence.

Though he rarely hit above .300, Clyde Waters was known for his clutch hitting for New Departure. (Courtesy: Bristol Public Library)

The two-umpire system, implemented that year for all games at Muzzy Field, featured veteran Bob Coughlin behind the plate and Swat McCabe, out for the season with his back injury, on the base paths.

On Sunday, July 16, the Red Sox players disembarked the train and headed to Muzzy Field for the three o'clock start. While newspaper accounts never offered a firm number or even a guess at the attendance, they intimated that the crowd was smaller than anticipated.

As a sharp, well-played ball game, the second Red Sox affair did not meet the standard primarily because New Departure's defense betrayed Lanning throughout the contest. Regardless, fans who clamored for the appearance of a big league team at Muzzy Field must have been satisfied by factory management's ability to book the Red Sox.

Boston tallied immediately in the first inning after the normally sure-handed Zielke fumbled a throw from Forslund on Menosky's grounder before Harris slammed a triple to right field. A sac fly by Pratt staked the Sox to a 2–0 lead.

Pittinger smacked a two-out single to left in the second inning followed by another to right from Walters as Pittinger raced for third. Forslund's relay throw zoomed past Halbach, and Pittinger scored easily for a 3–0 advantage.

Irwin, meanwhile, was working out of trouble, stranding runners in scoring position after a Forslund triple in the second and a Scott double in the third. New Departure broke through in the fourth inning when Reilly led off with a long smash over Smith's head in right field. "The former Cleveland player loafed in going after the ball and attempted to catch Reilly at the plate," the *Bristol Press* reported, "but the center-fielder slid in ahead of the throw."

Lanning held the Red Sox scoreless for four innings before two more errors in the sixth salted away the game for Boston. After a Pratt triple, Dugan lifted a pitch toward left that Scott could not catch, and Dugan scored when Smith followed with a single.

Two more singles loaded the bases before Smith got caught in a rundown. Irwin struck out for the third time in the game, and New Departure could have closed out the inning without further damage. But Forslund misplayed Leibold's grounder and two runs scored for a 7–1 lead.

Zielke's third error of the game allowed another Red Sox run in the seventh, and New Departure countered with an RBI single from Scott, who finished the game 4-for-5. Three Red Sox singles in the eighth, including an RBI by Fullerton that scored Pittinger, accounted for the 9–2 Boston victory.

Irwin and Fullerton limited New Departure to eight hits while the locals committed five errors. Harris hit two triples for Boston, Pratt collected a triple as part of his two hits, and Smith and Walters also smacked two base hits. Pittinger scored three runs after reaching base on three singles in four at-bats. In the loss, Lanning surrendered thirteen hits and struck out seven batters while Condon retired the Sox in order in the ninth.

Dugan batted three times, reached on an error, and scored a run. He "hit a torrid grasser to short" in the first inning, but Horkheimer knocked it down and threw him out. In all, Dugan's day with his new team was nondescript in an exhibition game meaningless to the sinking big league club.

Within a week of the Bristol game, Dugan's season changed dramatically. The Babe Ruth transaction was the first of many between the Red Sox and Yankees that stockpiled the latter with former Sox who helped mold New York's dominant teams of the 1920s.

On July 24, the Yankees, locked in a heated pennant race with the St. Louis Browns, announced another trade with Boston that sent Dugan and Elmer Smith to New York for four players and fifty thousand dollars. Dugan's fortunes soared immediately from last place to first, and he became a vital component of five pennant-winning New York teams, three of which won world championships, including the vaunted 1927 Murderers' Row. Smith's stint with the Yankees was short and less dramatic.

The deal so incensed the Browns and other western clubs that their protests prompted baseball's new commissioner, Judge Kennesaw Mountain Landis, to impose a June 15 trading deadline, according to author Jim Langford.

After the game with New Departure, the Red Sox returned to Boston to finish their series with the Tigers, who coincidentally lost that same day, 9–2, to a team of collegiate all-stars in an exhibition game played in Windsor Locks, Connecticut. Boston dropped to 35–50 on Monday, Dugan finally would play for a winning team, and Duffy never managed another major league club after 1922.

Prior to Boston's arrival, New Departure once again had been carving out their niche among Connecticut's and Massachusetts's best teams.

Former Eastern Leaguer Pete Condon bolstered the pitching staff when he signed in June a week before New Departure played their first game against Winsted. With four former Torrington players in their lineup, the club from northwestern Connecticut posed a formidable challenge in the state championship race.

Condon's first start of the season resulted in a 9–5 win over Winsted, and the New Departure rookie emerged as the team's number two starter the rest of the summer.

Several players with New Departure ties gravitated to other teams for the 1922 season and returned to Muzzy Field amid much fanfare in the papers. Anticipation ran high for fast, tight games against the Hartford Coe-Bills and the Bigelow-Hartfords of Thompsonville, but New Departure hosted one-sided reunions.

Hal Justin, pitcher of 1921, suffered a rude encounter when his former team smacked him for eleven runs on fourteen hits, seven of them doubles and three of those from Harold Horkheimer. Ex-Bristol players Eddie Goeb and Squiz Pillion accomplished little against Lanning in an 11–2 New Departure victory.

Ralph Knight, winner of three games early in the 1922 season, jumped ship for the Thompsonville club in June and met the wrathful bat of Ben Reilly in July.

"Ben picked out one of Ralph's offerings to his liking and drove it far over the scoreboard in center field for the longest clout seen on Muzzy Field this season," the *Bristol Press* said of the triple. It was one of two on the day for Reilly, who added a double as New Departure won 17–0 on sixteen hits.

Though newspaper reports do not specify the identity, either Joe or Bill McCarthy caught that day at Muzzy Field and finished 0-for-4. The newspaper referred to McCarthy as a former major league player. Both enjoyed short stints as catchers in the major leagues between 1905 and 1907.

Series with the primary in-state rivals started out as heated affairs. New Departure won two of three games against Winsted and tied another before Winsted notched impressive wins over Torrington and Manchester in late summer. Emboldened by the feat, Winsted's manager challenged New Departure to a three-game championship series in September with the winner taking five hundred dollars.

On the second day of the month, "as exciting a ballgame as has been seen this season" in Winsted came down to a play at the plate in the bottom of the thirteenth. George Scott fielded a hit and fired to relay man Pete Condon, who cut down a runner at home to preserve a 12–11 New Departure victory.

Three weeks later, the Bristol club completed a home-and-home sweep to take the championship. Goodridge tossed a complete-game three-hitter, and Horkheimer homered for a 6–1 win at Winsted before Lanning threw a four-hitter at Muzzy Field in a 9–2 victory during which Halbach went 4-for-5 with a triple and a home run that rolled under the fence in left field.

New Departure left little doubt in determining supremacy with Winsted, and the same applied to the Torrington series of 1922. After dropping two of the first three games, New Departure outscored their rivals 20–4 in three games to turn a heated rivalry into an afterthought.

One notable moment occurred in early August when Torrington appeared at Muzzy Field with second baseman Leo Dowd, who played ten games and gathered six hits as a shortstop for Harry Wolverton's eighth-place New York Yankees of 1912. Dowd finished 0-for-3 that day as New Departure's Pete Condon scattered five hits in a 6–1 victory.

For a second year, fervor surrounded the Manchester series. The dramatic outcome of the 1921 series "has left its rancor on the souls of Bristol fans," according to the *Bristol Press*, and that sensibility captured the essence of what proved to be another thrilling set of games.

"On every corner, in lodges, smoke-shops and in fact everywhere real live members of the sporting fraternity congregate, this series is the chief topic of discussion," the paper reported in late June, more than two months before the official showdown began. The bravado, personal attacks, and general rabidity intensified throughout the summer.

In late July, managers of New Departure, Manchester, and Torrington discussed the possibility of a three-team championship series governed by rules restricting the use of ringers signed to play for the specific purpose of earning one team the one-thousand-dollar prize money or trophy.

At least, discussion was the goal.

When Eddie Goodridge and Torrington skipper Jack Miran arranged to meet with Manchester's Tom Chambers at the *Hartford Courant* newspaper offices, the group made no progress on account of Chambers's absence. Discord reportedly ran rampant within Manchester's ranks. Players cycled through, a team captain quit midseason, and New Departure had swept a home-and-home doubleheader from them on July 4.

There were questions about Manchester's willingness to ante up one thousand dollars for first place, and Chambers's actions prompted a *Bristol Press* headline, "What is the matter with Manchester?" before the reporter fired a harsh salvo to the eastern part of the state: "The thing that puzzles Bristol, however, is the fact that Manchester fans seem to be lying down and quitting."

Though a more formal championship series stalled immediately, Manchester soon bolstered their lineup in the second half of the season, and when the teams met again their fans showed no signs of the apathy of which they were accused. Those player transactions, which would have been illegal if the series rules had been agreed upon, simply added to the acrimony and sharpened a rivalry already defined by a distinct edge.

But New Departure had business to tend to before the ballyhooed Manchester series commenced in September.

Several newspaper accounts of the era promoted the arrival of teams whose players were considered among the finest in organized baseball. While reading glowing appraisals of unknown players who never reached the major leagues, one can imagine that their exploits might have been hyperbolized to increase gate receipts. However, the inability to ascertain this as fact, short of extensive biographical work on each player, leaves open the possibility that some of the ghosts of Muzzy Field might have become legendary had they traveled a path that is more lucrative and glamorous today.

Undoubtedly, playing baseball professionally in the 1920s was not a secure career, and several players who appeared at Muzzy Field reportedly chose semipro baseball because they could play the game on the weekend and hold down a respectable job Monday through Friday. Some players left minor league baseball for this reason, and some who might have had the talent to achieve sporting glory never ventured from their more comfortable life.

Maybe Buster Brown was one of the latter men. The third baseman for the General Motors team out of Tarrytown, New York, arrived at Muzzy Field in mid-August trumpeted as a sure bet for professional baseball and the best player at the "dizzy corner" in the New York area. Despite the contention that he piqued the interest of numerous teams, the *Bristol Press* said Brown had no intention of playing professionally because he "holds a responsible position with the General Motors Company."

If things had been different, Buster Brown might be a more prominent figure in baseball history. As it was, his mark on Muzzy Field is a quiet box score entry, a double in a 14–0 loss to New Departure.

Religious beliefs might have prohibited Paul Mooney from attaining stardom in professional baseball. As a standout pitcher, Mooney reportedly caught the eye of professional clubs when he pitched a no-hitter in October 1919, and the Chicago Cubs offered him twenty thousand dollars to join the team. Mooney refused the offer because the team required he cut his long, flowing hair.

One of the most unique attractions to play at Muzzy Field, the House of David traveling baseball team was known to challenge any team anywhere in the country. They made their first visit to Bristol in 1922. Members of the 1922 team in this photo are, from left, George Anderson, Doc Tally, Victor Smith, Horrace Hannaford, Artie Veritz, Francis Thorpe, Jerry Hansel, Charles Faulkenstein, Paul Mooney, Ezra Hannaford, Percy Walker, and Zeke Bauschke. (Courtesy: House of David Museum, Benton Harbor, Michigan)

The right-handed pitcher "has performed so brilliantly in the past few years that it is stated Ty Cobb offered to sign him up with his Bengal Tigers, but because of his religious scruples the crack flinger refused to become affiliated with professional baseball," the *Bristol Press* wrote.

Mooney was a member of the House of David, a religious colony established by Mary and Benjamin Purnell in Benton Harbor, Michigan, in 1903. The beliefs that ruled colony life forbade men from shaving or cutting their hair (a directive out of the Book of Leviticus), even for the members of the powerful baseball teams fielded under the watchful eye of Purnell, a sporting enthusiast. Their appearance made for a fascinating attraction when the team set out on grueling trips across America to play all comers of any color to raise money for the commune and spread the word of the gospel.

They were a quirky and cutting-edge group of barnstormers, playing with and against great teams like the Pittsburgh Crawfords, Kansas City Monarchs, and Satchel Paige and his All-Stars while earning a victory over the St. Louis Cardinals at Sportsman's Park in 1933. The colony team played in the first ever night game in Independence, Kansas, in 1930 and the first such game at Sportsman's Park in 1931. They traveled with their own portable lighting system advertised in 1933 as a forty-thousand-dollar unit. Former team members included Olympic champion Mildred "Babe" Didrikson and Virne Beatrice "Jackie" Mitchell, the female pitcher who struck out Babe Ruth and Lou Gehrig on seven pitches combined during a 1931 exhibition game in Chattanooga, Tennessee.

The *Bristol Press* and the *New Departure News* hailed House of David's appearance with headlines such as "Long Haired Baseball Team Coming Sunday" and described the team as "the bewhiskered gentlemen from the Michigan lake shore resort" that look like "a bunch of decrepit old men but … the majority of them are still in their twenties" and are "capable of displaying a snappy brand of baseball."

House of David's performances on the field were impressive. Entering the early September game at Muzzy Field, they carried a 65–28 record after a trip to the Northeast originally scheduled for three days kept them in the Boston area for six weeks. They motored into Bristol in a pair of twin-six Packards and a Cadillac Eight.

As successful as it was and would prove to be, their baseball program, formed in 1914, fell in line with other notable accomplishments that distinguished the small colony of pacifist vegetarians. House of David members developed one of the first cold storage facilities in the country, and they were the first to preserve jellies in jars and produce a sugar cone. As early as 1908, they operated an amusement park with miniature trains, a zoo, and an aviary. They also were credited with inventing an automatic pinsetter for their bowling alley, and their world-renowned orchestra and jazz band, featuring several of the baseball players, performed in a large amphitheater constructed solely for them.

Members of the order bottled water from their natural springs, built elaborate motor lodges and hotels in the area, and operated an on-site hospital. They farmed the land and also operated a logging community on High Island in northern Michigan.

In 1922, two of their baseball players, Walter "Dutch" Faust and Jesse Lee "Doc" Tally, started playing a game called "High/Low" that morphed into what is known now as "pepper." The choreography began as a complement to the House of David Band playing between innings.

"The Pepper Game was usually performed in the middle of the fifth inning, with the three performers lined up approximately 2 feet apart. A fourth player acted as a batter and hit to the group," House of David historians Joel Hawkins and Terry Bertolino wrote. "Each player had a repertoire of moves they performed. Perhaps a behind-the-back toss, a fake throw to one of the others, or a roll of the ball down their arms."

Their histrionics caught on, popularized on the big league level by the St. Louis Cardinals Gas House Gang of 1934 who played a version of the game called "flip."

This popular photograph was used as marketing for the House of David baseball team before their arrival in Bristol. Team members, from left, are: Hip Vaughn, Dutch Faust, and Horrace Hannaford. (Courtesy: House of David Museum, Benton Harbor, Michigan)

On Saturday, the day before the game against New Departure, Bristol's daily newspaper introduced the visitors with the following, accompanied with team photos:

Members of the House of David believe they are the nucleus for a reunion of the lost tribes of Israel, although they are not Hebrews and conform to the New Testament as much as the Old. There are no laws governing their community save the Golden Rule, and law and order is represented only by a night watchman, who keeps his eyes open for suspicious-looking characters. The sect has preachers as well as ball players touring the country, and believing that there is neither material nor spiritual death, is confidently looking forward to the millennium. They play Sunday ball because their interpretation of the scripture leads them to believe that a Scriptural Day is 1,000 years long. By the time the millennium rolls around the ball club expects to have a record string of victories.

The Corner Shop in Bristol received a barrage of calls for tickets as baseball fans learned of House of David's reputation. Two years prior, the Michigan club traveled through Connecticut playing in Bridgeport, New Haven, and Torrington, but New Departure officials could not book the team because of scheduling conflicts.

Expectations ran high in town not only because of the visitors' strange appearance but also because of their baseball talents, promising to provide an entertaining exhibition of "Whiskers and Baseball at Muzzy Field," as one headline read.

House of David had formed a farm team of junior players who graduated to the traveling team, and new talent infused the club in 1922. During their first visit to Bristol, fans watched the development of two young House of David infielders playing their first season away from the Benton Harbor commune.

Dutch Faust and Dwight "Zeke" Bauschke became two of the biggest stars in House of David history though neither had played baseball prior to joining the order. In 1922–23, the middle infielders earned the nickname "Diamond Cutters" for their ability to turn double plays, and their raw athletic abilities translated well to the baseball field.

At seventeen, Faust was a heralded attraction in Bristol and within the House of David compound. He had lived on High Island and worked in the lumber operation before the team summoned him to Benton Harbor to begin his baseball career in 1920. Faust progressed quickly and in March 1926 became the only true House of David member to sign a professional contract when he joined the Dallas Steers of the Texas Association. He lasted one season in Texas and one season in Ohio playing low minor league baseball before injuries ended his pro career, though he continued playing for the colony's teams upon his return to Michigan.

Bauschke and his family were original members of the House of David and donated land that the colony still uses. As a member of the traveling band, Bauschke's interests extended beyond baseball, and he too left the colony in 1926, moving to Detroit to become a professional musician.

Faust's life took a more mysterious turn. He played baseball for the colony until about 1935.

"Dutch then left, never to return. His whereabouts were never established, and rumors abound as to how he ended up" (Hawkins and Bertolino 2000).

Fans at Muzzy Field also saw Doc Tally, whose longevity with the colony's teams was a remarkable feat. Arriving from Mississippi as an eighteen-year-old in 1914, Tally played a key role in forming the first uniformed House of David nine, winning the county championship as a knuckleball pitcher, and he continued playing as a member of the City of David team after the colony split into two factions in 1930. Aside from pitching, he was known as a fine all-around hitter with plenty of power.

Upon his arrival in Bristol, "The Bearded Babe Ruth" was said to have smacked twenty-nine home runs in 1922, earning him the distinction of being the "bewhiskered behemoth of biff" by the local paper.

Interviewed in 1948, Tally estimated that he played in more than twenty-two hundred games as an outfielder and pitcher, according to Hawkins and Bertolino. As he prepared for his thirty-sixth season in 1950, he died suddenly at fifty-three years of age with no explanation ever given.

Two other colony members joined this trio at Muzzy Field: Ezra "Cookie" Hannaford and Art Vieritz.

Because of the taxing travel schedule, House of David's lineup at Muzzy Field included several players who were not true members of the order but had been hired by the team, a common practice in the club's history. These players included Charlie Falk, George "Lefty" Gilbert, Burnett Fish, Chick Buyesse, and Max Wolfe, who would pitch against New Departure despite newspaper advances that promised Mooney.

Les Lanning drew the start for the home team, responsible for keeping Tally's power in check and subduing a hot-hitting Faust who carried a .384 average into the game. New Departure countered with their own muscle as Ben Reilly's average stood at .402 while the first-year player had gathered ninety-one total bases through thirty-three games.

House of David's lineup was altered somewhat with Mooney starting at third base and Bauschke in center field.

Both pitchers performed admirably in a tight, low-scoring affair. New Departure scored three runs in the first five innings on a hit-and-run, a double steal, and an RBI single. Lanning cruised along through six innings before House of David scored in the seventh after Gus Forslund fumbled a grounder and threw wildly to set up first baseman Hannaford's RBI single to left.

Trailing 3–1 in the ninth, House of David threatened to take the game by scoring one run and loading the bases with one out before Lanning induced two pop-ups to seal the 3–2 victory. Lanning struck out eight and scattered six hits, two of them singles by second baseman Faust and left fielder Tally. Mooney and Bauschke finished 0-for-4.

Wolfe struck out six and gave seven hits, two each from George Scott and Smoke Halbach. Scott was 2-for-4 with a double, two runs, and two stolen bases while Halbach drove in two runs. With an 0-for-4 performance, Reilly's average dipped below .400.

Defensively, neither team was especially sharp, but where New Departure's three errors led to unearned runs, House of David's five miscues proved innocuous.

The first of several House of David visits was in the books, and New Departure and their hometown fans turned their attention to vaunted and reviled Manchester.

Entering the first game of the series, momentum sided with New Departure. Not only had the club won eight consecutive games at home since July 2, except the loss to the Red Sox, but they had swept Manchester in a Fourth of July doubleheader. Manchester, however, strengthened their lineup considerably from that point.

"The team that met the locals earlier in the season was only a shell of the one now banded together," the *Bristol Press* warned.

The first four games of the best-of-five series took place over consecutive September weekends, and the quest for a competitive advantage led to a bidding war for one pitcher believed capable of delivering the championship.

For game one, a "large army of rooters" traveled from Manchester to Muzzy Field where they cheered as a "rabid" throng among New Departure fans, the *New Departure News* reported. The frenzy was warranted. Saturday afternoon's matchup pitted Les Lanning against a familiar opponent in left-hander Pete Wilson, the former Yankee hurler who appeared at Muzzy Field with the 1920 Bridgeport Singers.

The two former major leaguers treated fans to a ball game befitting a championship series filled with tension and intrigue.

Neither pitcher surrendered much through the first three innings, but New Departure struck hard in the fourth. Three runs on an Eddie Zielke sacrifice fly, a Gus Forslund RBI double, and a Clyde Waters RBI single proved an insurmountable total as Lanning rendered Manchester bats impotent.

The former Philadelphia Athletic tossed a two-hitter with five strikeouts and two walks as the Bristol club took game one, 3–0, aided by a flawless defense that turned two double plays. Wilson remained untouched after the fourth inning, scattering nine hits and striking out two batters to match Lanning's complete-game effort.

Game two the next day at Mount Nebo Grounds in Manchester only intensified the excitement. Manchester imported a left-handed pitcher named Palmer who had played for New Britain and Orlando in the Florida State League while New Departure countered with Pete Condon, the former Eastern Leaguer who signed with the team in June.

At the hands of two highly capable flingers, the teams remained scoreless through the first five and a half innings, until New Departure's defense faltered for the only time in the game. A throwing error by shortstop Harold Horkheimer placed the go-ahead run on the bases ultimately to be driven in by Tommy Sipples on a sacrifice fly. The 1–0 lead held up as Palmer stymied New Departure's offense, countering Lanning's performance with a two-hitter of his own.

Horkheimer smacked a double as one of the lone base runners, but he was stranded as Palmer struck out four and walked two in nine innings. Condon pitched a gem that probably would net a victory on any other day, scattering five hits in the complete game, but Manchester's pitching and defense tied the series.

In the wake of stellar pitching performances in two games, Bristol fans chafed at Manchester's ability to emasculate their team's offense so completely.

"The New Departure team as a whole rates 100 percent higher than Manchester's crew," the *Bristol Press* snipped in an article leading up to the next weekend, "but it is easy to see how new and imported stars on the mound can more than equalize this advantage."

On September 16, the series returned to Mount Nebo Grounds where Lanning made his second start and opposed Mike Hogan, described as a "well-known" pitcher by the *New Departure News*. Again, the finer details decided the outcome.

Game three's scoring began quickly when George Underhill walked in the bottom of the first before attempting to steal second. On a close play, Underhill slid in under the tag and then raced home on a base hit. Manchester would not score again as Lanning allowed only three more hits the rest of the way.

Hogan, posting zeros on the scoreboard at a rapid pace, found trouble in the top of the eighth when Zielke pasted his pitch for a triple. An ensuing squeeze play failed, however, and Zielke was erased as New Departure's best scoring chance in the game. Manchester again locked down New Departure's offense in a 1–0 win as Hogan pitched a four-hitter with ten strikeouts for the series lead.

Facing elimination, New Departure returned to Muzzy Field the next day where their two-month home winning streak collided with Palmer's mound wizardry. Condon returned to the hill in what promised to be another pitching classic.

The fourth game, however, featured none of the flawless pitching and defense from the previous battles as the teams combined for twenty-three hits and seven errors. Still, the momentum swings and wild plays were enough to exhaust the fans after a memorable tilt.

New Departure scored more runs in the first four innings against Palmer than they had in the previous three games as the Bearing Makers staked Condon to a 6–0 lead and chased the left-hander they could not touch in game two.

Refusing to go quietly, Manchester chipped away. Condon departed for Goodridge after allowing three runs in the seventh as the visitors pulled to 6–4. Needing a clutch hit in the ninth inning, Manchester shortstop Billy Dwyer stepped to the plate with two out and the tying run on base.

Already with two hits on the day, Dwyer blasted a Goodridge offering for a triple that tied the game and surely ignited "the hostile crowd of about 500 rooters" for Manchester.

The teams played into the eleventh inning when Goodridge ended up on third with two outs. Condon, who had moved to right field after pitching, came to the plate and slapped a grounder to Dwyer at short. With Goodridge and Condon racing down the lines, Dwyer fielded and fired to first. Condon's foot thumped the bag a split second before Dwyer's throw arrived, and Goodridge scored the winning run to tie the series and cap another gut-wrenching weekend of baseball.

New Departure and Manchester took the next weekend off as the Bristol club finished their season sweep of Winsted before preparing for their deciding bout. After four games of heady elation and sinking disappointment, the newspapers were buzzing with emotion.

"The coming game has been marked by the display of much animosity on the part of both clubs," the *Bristol Press* wrote, adding that "relations are anything but cordial" as the "belligerent pair" ready themselves for "one of the most bitter contests of the year."

Things then got personal. As in 1921, the teams played to a draw on each other's home fields, and a site was needed for the title game. The *New Departure News* reported that Manchester refused to play the fifth game at Muzzy Field, and

New Departure officials said the team was accustomed to "cavorting on a diamond—not a mudhole—and therefore could not even consider (Mount) Nebo Grounds." The teams agreed to play in Hartford.

New Departure's company newspaper further reported that Manchester manager Tom Chambers refused to submit his roster because two of the players' availability for the game was in question. Goodridge told him to leave the spots open, adding that Chambers "could get any player in the country provided he was a member of the semipro ranks, and the Bristolites would not worry for a moment."

Bristling at the directive, Chambers shot back saying he would employ any player he pleased and "guaranteed that (former St. Louis Brown) Herman Bronkie was as good as signed." Bronkie, who starred in the teams' series the previous season, had not appeared in 1922.

The debate surrounding the use of semipros versus ringers had been roiling not only for the entire month of September but also earlier in the summer when the issue prohibited the creation of a formal three-team championship series with Winsted.

Now at the threshold of the deciding game, Bristol's badgering became insufferable.

The *Manchester Herald*, in announcing championship game Saturday an official holiday, criticized Bristol officials for "domineering tactics" in attempting to dictate which Manchester players would be eligible.

Though previously taking a self-righteous stance on the subject, New Departure countered Manchester's tactics by entering a bidding war for Frank Woodward, a pitcher from the Eastern League champion New Haven team who from 1918 to 1922 played for Philadelphia and St. Louis in the National League and Washington in the American League. His major league career ended the next season after he pitched two games for the Chicago White Sox.

"In securing Woodward, the locals are simply beating Chambers at his own game as the pilot had the former Philadelphia National twirler all signed up when Goodridge offered inducements that took Woodie right out of their grasp," the *Bristol Press* reported in an article both rationalizing and boastful.

Manchester countered by signing Georgetown pitching ace Art "Specs" Reynolds. Herman Bronkie did not appear in the lineup.

All of the bombast and gamesmanship swirled around three thousand fans who bet the game heavily and watched Woodward and Reynolds engage in a solid contest. The college star got the best of the veteran when Dwyer launched a two-run triple in the fifth inning for the game-winning runs in a 4–2 Manchester victory.

Reynolds scattered seven hits and walked four while Woodward's performance was less than New Departure desired as he allowed eleven hits and a walk.

As Manchester celebrated another championship, Bristol and its club endured more disappointment that tainted an otherwise fine season.

"Perhaps the sad event of the season was the loss of the series with Manchester, but (when) the mistake made in getting foreign players for the windup is considered, there should have been no tears shed in that direction," the *Bristol Press* intoned in the season's postmortem. "The only mistake made was that the local outfit was not played in its entirety. There might have been a different story to tell."

It is difficult to imagine Bristol's newspaper and fans apologizing for signing a ringer had he won them the championship as expected.

As for the regulars, Ben Reilly set a new benchmark for New Departure offense, hitting .386 with 66 hits in 43 games, 110 total bases, and 41 runs scored—all numbers that paced the club. The table-setters were George Scott, who hit .301 with fifteen stolen bases and thirty-two runs, and Smoke Halbach, who hit .299 with seventeen steals and thirty-four runs. Collectively, New Departure continued winning games in familiar fashion, batting .277 with seventy-nine stolen bases and seventy-five sacrifices, in support of leading pitchers Lanning (twelve wins, .280 batting average) and Condon (eight wins).

An important addendum to the season occurred in June when a news item said New Departure's Meriden plant would be operational in the fall of 1922, around the time that DeWitt Page treated his New Departure baseball players to a weekend in New York to take in the Giants-Yankees World Series.

The factory expansion eventually would alter the future of New Departure's team.

# 1923: "This Clash Will Be for Blood"

The new year was in its infancy when Adrian J. Muzzy died shortly after midnight on January 2 at the age of seventy-two, the result of suffering nervous shock from a minor car accident on South Street in December, according to newspaper accounts.

The man who shaped Bristol through politics and philanthropy maintains a strong presence with the ballpark that bears his name and the granite arch entryway inscribed with a dedication to his two sons and him.

For all of his accomplishments and contributions, the athletic field has become Muzzy's most lasting impression on the city.

"It was through his great liberality that Bristol has enjoyed one of the finest baseball, football, and track fields in the state," the *Bristol Press* reported in his obituary.

Muzzy would have been filled with civic pride to see the baseball team that represented his city in 1923.

New Departure completed one of their most successful campaigns of the 1920s with an era-best thirty-six wins against fourteen losses. Considering the changes to the roster, such a season seems improbable on its face. Before opening day, New Departure lost infield stalwarts Smoke Halbach and Eddie Zielke, both of whom earned promotions to the Meriden plant. Their schedules prohibited their participation with the team in Bristol. Zielke's departure forced Eddie Goodridge to become a mainstay at first base and severely limited his appearances on the mound; and team spark plug George Scott missed nearly half of the season after wrenching his knee in July.

New Departure and their new field manager, Clyde Waters, adapted by re-signing third baseman Bill Tamm from Albany of the Eastern League to replace Halbach. Tamm appeared briefly in 1921 when Gus Forslund landed on the disabled list. Goodridge proved more than capable defensively at first base and reawakened his bat after an injury-plagued 1922 campaign. Swat McCabe also returned from injury, relinquishing his duties as base umpire to don once again the white and blue duds for New Departure as an outfielder.

To add a little spice to the season, Halbach and Zielke later appeared in uniform with Manchester as that fantastic rivalry reached new heights in histrionics in 1923. Torrington again challenged Bristol's club in a six-game series, and other talented teams in the state such as Norwich, New Milford, Quono Athletic Club of Guilford, the All-Collegians of Windsor Locks, and Fuller Brush of Hartford all salivated at the chance to trump New Departure. In the end, the mythical state championship remained just that; no team could definitively claim supremacy in Connecticut.

New Departure won six of ten games against Massachusetts teams but failed to capture a pivotal five-game series against Ware. Against four General Motors teams, New Departure finished with a 5–0 record and claimed the company title, at least in the Northeast region.

From outside the state came another impressive collection of black ball clubs such as the Cuban Giants, Brooklyn Royal Giants, and the annual appearance by the Elm City Giants, all of which fielded historically important baseball stars.

As was traditionally the case during the time, the New Departure Athletic Club announced in March after a meeting with the city's park commissioners that the company would incur all expenses for maintaining Muzzy Field with no expense to the taxpayers. At the same time, however, the ballpark would remain under city control as it always has during its history.

With the ballpark in fine shape for the season opener, so too was New Departure. The locals welcomed Bridgeport and former ND shortstop Tommy Bowden in late April and subsequently pasted former Yankee pitcher Pete Wilson, 15–6, as "an unusually large throng looked on," according to the *New Departure News*.

A torrent of offense followed as New Departure rattled off eight straight victories to start the season, scoring 86 runs, pounding 103 hits, and batting a collective .364.

Included in that stretch were three wins in the General Motors series, a 7–6 win over Ware in which a relay throw from Harry Horkheimer cut down the potential tying run at the plate in the ninth inning, and an 8–0 conquest of Fisk when right-hander Pete Condon tossed a three-hitter with six strikeouts in front of twelve hundred fans.

"Seldom has the veteran … looked so sweetly as he did on this day," the *New Departure News* gushed.

The next week, Condon opposed spitballer Cannonball Smith and the Elm City Giants in a matchup of two teams that usually entertained with competitive games. But the New Departure juggernaut was running in high gear, exploding for eight runs on six hits in the fourth inning to chase Smith en route to a 14–2 victory. Condon scattered seven hits and struck out five, and Ben Reilly provided some of the fireworks with an inside-the-park blast "to the far corner of the pasture for one of the longest clouts seen in many a moon," the *New Departure News* wrote.

Elm City fielded Golson in right field, hitless in four at-bats; Moore behind the plate, hitless in three at-bats; Lawrence at first base with two hits and a run; Ching at first base with a hit and a run; Redmond in center field with two hits; Twyman in left field, hitless in four at-bats; Pettiway at third base, hitless in three at-bats; West at shortstop with a hit; Smith the starting pitcher; and Logan in relief with one hit.

Ware ended New Departure's winning streak on a Wednesday afternoon in late May, 5–4. Tragedy struck the New Departure family that weekend when Goodridge's two-year-old son, John Coates Goodridge, died of an illness, and Goodridge missed two games before returning for the traditional Memorial Day doubleheader against Torrington, which New Departure split.

Condon continued to sparkle on the mound in early June as he limited Tarrytown Chevrolet to four hits in a 5–1 victory, the team's first after losing three games to the New York club in 1920. Left-hander Les Lanning took a backseat to no one, and on June 10 he was pitted against the Schenectady Red Sox of New York, a team that posted a 37–9 record the previous year. In response, Lanning pitched a three-hitter with six strikeouts, and Goodridge exploded with a 5-for-5 performance with two triples and five runs scored as New Departure cruised, 14–0, leading into the first game against Manchester.

No game on the New Departure schedule elicited a more fiery reaction from the fans than a meeting with Manchester.

"Because of the intense rivalry between the teams one victory over Manchester would have made a bigger hit with the spectators than perhaps a dozen over some other club," the *Bristol Press* reported. "To say that a keen contest is expected is almost unnecessary ... a seething struggle always ensues."

A red-hot start offensively and on the mound imbued New Departure followers with great confidence for the Saturday afternoon melee at Muzzy on June 16. The visitors imported former Eastern League southpaw Lefty Thompson to oppose Condon, and the battle started hot and heavy thanks to a couple of ex-New Departurites.

After Smoke Halbach singled in the second inning, a hit-and-run with Eddie Zielke worked to perfection as Zielke blasted an RBI double to center for a quick 1–0 Manchester advantage. Swat McCabe notched the equalizer in the third when his RBI double scored Condon after Halbach's relay throw to home sailed high, preventing what would have been a close play at the plate.

Manchester struck again in the fifth with a runner on third and one out. An inning-ending double play for New Departure evaporated when second baseman Gus Forslund threw wildly on the pivot, allowing the run to score for a 2–1 Manchester lead.

In their next five innings at the plate, New Departure failed to find the hitting groove they carried into the game, wasting leadoff doubles in the seventh and eighth innings. Thompson continually worked out of jams and held New Departure scoreless the rest of the way to take the first meeting of the young season.

After a 14–3 win over Hyatt the next day, New Departure stood at 16–3 with a .320 team batting average. Horkheimer paced the team with a .425 average and thirty-one hits, Scott was batting .375 with twenty-seven hits, and Reilly had smacked twenty-five hits at a .347 clip.

A stern test arrived with great fanfare on the first of July when the Cuban Giants from Havana appeared at Muzzy Field, bringing along another slugger who threatened to conquer the distant walls of the Bristol ballpark. Jesús "Lico" Mederos reportedly bashed twenty-one home runs in forty games for the Marianao Baseball Club in Cuba, and the wallop packed in the lanky outfielder's swing excited newspapermen who wrote of his heroics.

Though not possessing the legendary talent of the 1921 Cuban Stars, the Cuban Giants probably fielded several players who were among the top performers in the Cuban League. Because of misspellings in the newspapers, it is difficult to ascertain the Giants lineup. Undoubtedly, José Junco pitched against New Departure. His catcher, A. Abren, might have been Eufemio Abreu, a notable backstop on the island; E. Jiménez could have been Eugenio, though historically that man is considered a Cuban baseball impresario rather than a player. The *Bristol Press* refers to him as "Eusbeesio." D. Jiménez is unknown.

The rest of the lineup included J. Villar in center field, R. Martínez at shortstop, F. Rivas at third base, and Angel Dominguez in right field. Mederos clearly was the big-ticket attraction. Amid the excitement, newspapers introduced the Cuban team to readers with the casual racism of the day, pointing out that the Cuban players were "darker and heavier" than average American semipro players.

"How they will compare in team work, which requires brains as well as brawn, remains to be seen," the *Bristol Press* reported, though they recognized the athletic ability of the players, "many of whom would be in the big league if it were not for their color."

The Giants arrived in Bristol in three large, high-powered cars on Saturday night, and were received as guests at the Endee Inn, which featured high-end accommodations and amenities.

"Undoubtedly (they) will attract a great number of curiosity seekers," the *Bristol Press* wrote. "It is only natural that the public would want to see such a strange people who speak very little English and yet can play the great national pastime with such skill. As an attraction, the Giants should go big in most any of the cities in this section."

The game, however, proved less exhilarating than advertised. George Scott and Ben Reilly both hit triples in the first with Reilly driving in Bill Tamm, who had singled in Scott, for a 2–0 lead. Two singles and a double steal notched another run for the locals in the third before the Cuban Giants melted down defensively with three errors late in the game that led to four runs.

New Departure cruised to an 8–1 victory. As promised, Mederos provided the fireworks for the Giants, crushing a pitch from Les Lanning toward the oak tree in left-center and circling the bases for an inside-the-park home run. Though he failed to clear the walls, Mederos kept his team from suffering an embarrassing shutout loss.

Lanning scattered eight hits and struck out seven while Junco went the distance and collected three hits in three at-bats.

New Departure carried that momentum into a pivotal holiday doubleheader played in Bristol and Manchester with control of the season series on the line. In the morning game at Muzzy Field, Pete Condon opposed Rube Patten, whose start was brief. Patten could not throw strikes, as he walked five batters in $1^2/3$ innings, forcing in a run in the second. Eddie Zielke muffed a pickoff throw for another New Departure run, and former New Departurite Eddie Goeb walked in a third run in relief of Patten.

After an RBI double by Zielke in the top of the third, Horkheimer answered with his own RBI double and a 4–1 New Departure lead. In the fourth, Manchester pulled within 4–3, and Goeb allowed no more hits for the locals. With Bristol's offense stagnant, Manchester was poised to make a comeback in the seventh when Halbach and Zielke reached base; however, snappy catcher Clyde Waters caught Halbach off the bag, and his throw erased him to end the threat as New Departure won, 4–3, with just three hits.

The second game at Manchester's new stadium was just as exciting as left-handers Les Lanning and Lefty Thompson dueled while the defenses played fine ball behind them. Lanning escaped with a sharp 2–1 win sealed by Horkheimer's RBI double in the seventh, his second game-winning RBI of the day.

New Departure had taken two of three games on the season, and they were priming themselves for the knockout blow the following month. But first, the locals had to complete a challenging stretch in their schedule that invited the talented Brooklyn Royal Giants, members of the newly formed Eastern Colored League, to Muzzy Field two days after their doubleheader sweep of Manchester.

Always a powerful ball club, the Royal Giants again brought slugging first baseman Eddie Douglass to Bristol along with several other veterans such as Robert Scott, Chester Brooks, John Cason, and Bill Wagner. Center fielder Tom Fiall, a solid contributor to the Royal Giants in the late 1910s and early 1920s, was making his first appearance at Muzzy Field along with third baseman Johnson Hill.

Two other notable men were right fielder Connie "Broadway" Rector and pitcher Jesse "Pud" Flournoy. James A. Riley's research fills in their biographies.

Rector, all five foot eight and 165 pounds of him, played baseball for twenty-five years with such teams as the New York Lincoln Giants and the New York Black Yankees. Known for his pitching exploits, Rector had great control with his changeup, curve, slider, and knuckleball, and his intelligence allowed him to get by with an average fastball. The Texas native loved the New York nightlife, which earned him the nickname, and he was a sharp dresser always ready to entertain the ladies. He became the third starting pitcher behind Cyclone Williams and "Cannonball" Dick Redding for the 1924 Brooklyn Royal Giants.

Flournoy, a stocky pitcher and outfielder who batted and threw left-handed, had zip on his fastball and good control of a variety of curves, and he also enjoyed a long career in the Negro Leagues. Flournoy played frequently in exhibitions against white major leaguers and is credited with striking out Babe Ruth three consecutive times.

Flournoy and the Royal Giants were a difficult matchup, but New Departure put up a stronger fight than their shutout loss two years earlier. When Condon came back to pitch on one day's rest, Brooklyn shocked him for three runs on five hits in the first inning as he gave way to Lanning.

Lanning surrendered another run for a 4–0 New Departure deficit before settling into a groove with the help of a superb defensive performance behind him. After scoring three runs in the fifth, New Departure entered the ninth inning searching for a run against Brooklyn's southpaw. After a Horkheimer single and Forslund sacrifice, Waters's penchant for clutch hits revealed itself again as his RBI single tied the game and sent it to extra innings.

Despite Lanning's gritty relief effort of $9^2/_3$ innings, the Royal Giants batters reached base in the eleventh and scored on a sacrifice fly to left field that held up in Brooklyn's 5–4 conquest. Douglass finished 2-for-6 with a triple and a run scored. Scott set the table as the leadoff man with three hits; Fiall sacrificed three times; and Brooks, Cason, Wagner, and Hill all collected one hit. Rector and Flournoy had two hits apiece with Flournoy scoring a run.

A New Departure victory would have capped an incredible four victories in six days against three of their toughest opponents, but taking three of four proved their worthiness as state title contenders.

One of Connecticut's upstart teams in 1923 hailed from New Milford, and a mid-July meeting at Muzzy Field provided a notable game historically when the visitors arrived with shortstop Neal Ball in their lineup. Ball spent seven quiet years in the major leagues from 1907 to 1913 with the New York Yankees, Cleveland Indians, and Boston Red Sox, but it was a game on July 19, 1909, that etched his name in history.

Playing for the Indians against the Red Sox with Cy Young pitching and runners on first and second, Amby McConnell smashed a line drive at Ball who snagged the shot, stepped on second base, and tagged Jake Stahl who was running from first, thereby registering what has been called the first triple play of the twentieth century.

That same inning, Ball smacked an inside-the-park home run, one of only four that he hit in a career that included a strikeout in his only World Series at-bat for the world champion Red Sox of 1912.

Ball arrived at Muzzy Field dubbed "the triple play hero," and New Milford fielded a good team. On a hot and humid July afternoon, New Departure jumped on top quickly when Eddie Goodridge hit a two-run single in the first inning. Bristol's club added another run in the fourth when Gus Forslund hit a double and scored on an outfield error.

Ball had his chance to be the hero when Lanning hit a wild streak and walked four batters in the eighth inning. A double play prior to Ball's at-bat kept New Milford off the scoreboard, but with the bases loaded, Ball delivered a two-run single to cut the lead to 3–2.

The next batter, Ray Holden, hit a grounder that forced Ball at second, and New Departure added an insurance run in the bottom of the eighth on Forslund's RBI single for the 4–2 victory. Lanning survived an uncharacteristic six walks with the help of three double plays in the win.

New Departure closed out the month with an impressive sweep of Torrington the following weekend in which Ben Reilly drove in seven of his team's nineteen runs and captured a scintillating 5–4 win over Fisk in twelve innings. Harold Horkheimer hit a game-winning sacrifice fly following Pete Wood's pinch-hit bloop single in the ninth inning.

But the team incurred significant losses. For the second time in the month, Schatz Athletic Club of Poughkeepsie soundly defeated the Bristol club to take the season series, and in an 11–5 win at Ware, New Departure lost George Scott for the season when he either wrenched his knee going after a ball in left field or injured it sliding into a base. Newspaper reports differed.

None of those factors prohibited Bristol fans from making a spectacle for the next Manchester game in early August. Ten New Departure buses carried the company band, a special booster club of singing fans called the Royal Rooters, and other fans to Manchester where the New Departure band and team supporters marched around the field before the game.

Formed in 1923 and ostensibly named after the famous Boston Red Sox fan club, the New Departure Royal Rooters were a group of singing, ebullient fans who traveled throughout the state to watch their team play. (Courtesy: Bristol Public Library)

In another duel of left-handers, Lanning bested Thompson, 2–1, as he scattered seven hits and struck out eight while Goodridge and Waters hit RBI singles in the second inning that held up, despite Manchester threatening with a run on two errors in the ninth. After the game, the New Departure supporters again marched around the field and then rode to the center of town where they proclaimed loudly their supremacy over Manchester.

The good times failed to return to Bristol the next day when Norwich, the self-proclaimed champions of downstate Connecticut for three years running, stuck it to the local team that they said had snubbed them in trying to schedule games in previous years. Norwich posted six runs in the third inning and knocked around Pete Condon in a 6–3 victory, bolstering their argument that they were the best team in the state.

Neal Ball made a return visit to Muzzy Field with the All-Collegians of Windsor Locks featuring players from Holy Cross and Penn State. With reported wins over the Boston Red Sox, Detroit Tigers, and Pittsburgh Pirates in previous years, the All-Collegians seemed to pose a stiff challenge but apparently fielded a weaker than normal lineup, bowing 5–3 to Les Lanning and committing three costly errors. Ball again went 2-for-4 with an RBI single, two runs scored, and a triple.

New Departure stood at 26–9 and another monumental clash with Manchester loomed the following weekend. For all of the feverish commotion surrounding all previous games in this series, the August 18, 1923, contest might reign supreme for its theater and gamesmanship among the towns' fans.

In response to New Departure's Royal Rooters, Manchester formed the Centennial Celebration Committee, headed by the board of selectmen, and traveled to Muzzy Field five hundred strong in a one-hundred-car caravan with a twenty-five-piece band, according to the *Bristol Press*. The newspaper ensured all fans were whipped into a frenzy for the game that "should be about the wildest affair of its kind that has been staged" in Muzzy Field's history. "The rivalry ... has broken out anew and with an intensity that is at white heat" creating what promised to be "one of the hottest baseball fights ever seen" in the state.

As Manchester's retinue traveled westward, New Departure supporters turned out in kind; the Royal Rooters led a mammoth street parade that left the Endee Inn at 2:00 PM and marched to the field with a goat wearing a sweater that read, appropriately, "We've copped Manchester's goat."

Intercity rivalries were heated affairs at Muzzy Field, especially when Manchester was involved. In this undated photo, a group leads a goat across the field. It could be the goat that New Departure supporters led to the field in August 1923 wearing a sweater that read, "We've copped Manchester's goat," before the teams played a game that the local newspaper said would be "for blood." (Courtesy: Bristol Public Library)

"The streets of Bristol will be practically empty between three and five o'clock," the newspaper reported. "This clash will be for blood."

Apparently, the bombast also came from the dugout.

"We're going to trim (Manchester) so decisively that next year we'll be crossed off their schedule as being too tough," manager Joe Carroll told the Bristol newspaper.

Despite winning three of the first four games of the series, these were confident words coming from a team that had nearly pinned Manchester in previous years yet failed to win the championship. With two games to play, Manchester certainly had an opportunity to emerge with an even draw.

The fans who arrived at the park were "the largest gathering that has been seen at Muzzy Field in some years, and amid the most colorful scenes that have taken place in a decade," the *New Departure News* reported.

Dueling bands set up on the first and third base lines outblaring each other with songs like "Barney Google" and "Down in Tennessee."

Pitcher Tommy Sipples entered the game for Manchester with a lengthy scoreless streak of either twenty-seven innings, according to the *Bristol Press*, or thirty-four innings, according to the *New Departure News*, and the youngster opposed Les Lanning in the fifth game. On paper, the matchup promised to be spectacular, but New Departure jumped on Sipples from the beginning with three runs on four hits in three innings.

Sipples departed for Lefty Thompson.

Meanwhile, Lanning was in a pitching groove the likes of which rarely had been seen at Muzzy Field. Inning after inning, the left-hander defied Manchester's lineup, and after New Departure's offense scored five runs in the fourth inning for an 8–0 lead, victory seemed imminent.

Lanning finished the day by tossing a two-hitter and allowing only four base runners in what the *New Departure News* called "one of the most brilliant games of his career" and "a masterful exhibition and the best seen on the lot since Nixie Carney turned in his no-hit, no-run game in 1920." No runners reached second base, and Lanning struck out three, denying visiting players a new pair of shoes offered by a Manchester merchant to the player who scored first.

Condon's two-run double, Reilly's three hits, and the RBI from Goodridge and Waters provided the offense, but the truly inflammatory actions occurred after the game.

Undeniably supercharged from the victory, the Royal Rooters staged a mock burial by carrying a black box representing Manchester's coffin. "One thousand silent sympathizers followed the funeral to center field as the band played the funeral procession," the *New Departure News* reported. In the outfield, the box was lowered to its final resting place with "due ceremony."

The offensive mockery must have galled Manchester players and fans, but the entire ordeal underscored not only the bitterness of the rivalry but also New Departure fans' deep wounds from watching their team fold in key games the previous two years.

With Manchester out of the way, New Departure defeated the All-Collegians, 4–3, the next day and arranged to face another upstart state team in Fuller Brush of Hartford.

Left fielder George Scott had injured his knee enough that he would miss the rest of the season, and New Departure brought in Mike Lynch from New Britain as his replacement. Another back injury forced Swat McCabe to sit for a little more than a week, and the Bristol club plugged in different players to man the outfield spots.

Lynch proved his worth quickly by swatting a two-run single to center field to tie the Fuller Brush game at five in the bottom of the ninth inning. When Reilly followed with a hit to score Lynch, New Departure had captured the first game, 6–5, in dramatic fashion to improve to 29–9 as Lanning picked up another victory.

Labor Day weekend started with an 11–0 road win over a strong Connecticut Light & Power team from Waterbury followed by a 9–2 conquest of Norwich in which McCabe collected three hits.

The traditional doubleheader with Torrington nearly cost New Departure a precious series. After Torrington drubbed them 10–3 at Muzzy Field, New Departure needed four runs in the tenth inning to steal a 7–3 win on the road in the second game.

New Departure came out flat the next weekend, dropping a 3–2 decision at Manchester after newly signed Neal Ball hit the game-winning single to right field in the eighth inning and a 3–1 decision at home against Fuller Brush, which brought four hundred fans to Bristol. The skid extended through the next two weekends with losses to Ware in the series clincher and a shutout loss in Meriden to Quono A.C. of Guilford.

Having lost four of five, New Departure could lay claim neither to the New England championship nor the outright state championship, but they had a score to settle with Fuller Brush in the third game of that series played in late September.

On a cold and breezy day, Lanning took the mound and scattered eight hits in a complete-game effort as New Departure rolled, 12–2, with fourteen hits and assistance from five Fuller Brush errors. Gus Forslund launched an RBI triple to the track in right-center, Goodridge added a two-run single, and Reilly smashed an RBI double in the victory.

Reilly won the team batting title for the second consecutive year with a .337 mark, fifty-nine hits, and forty-seven runs in forty-nine games as New Departure finished with an impressive 36–14 mark. George Scott hit .331 before the knee injury cost him two months; Harold Horkheimer collected a team-high sixty hits in fifty games and batted .313 with fourteen sacrifices, the latter total matched by Bill Tamm who batted .305 with fifty-three hits and fifteen stolen bases in forty-five games. Eddie Goodridge belted out a .324 average with fifty-seven hits and forty-nine runs in forty-eight games as the team posted an average of .290 and averaged more than six runs per contest.

Les Lanning dominated on the mound with a 17-4 mark. He struck out 112, walked 40, and allowed 165 hits in 183 innings. Pete Condon finished 15–8, and though incomplete, his stats show that he struck out 56, walked 18, and surrendered 187 hits in 187 innings in his last season with the team during this era.

For Scott, his knee injury caused lingering effects into 1924 for both himself and the team. While he struggled to get back into playing condition, his absence allowed New Departure to sign a youngster who would be the only player to catapult into the major leagues after playing for the Bristol club.

# 1924: A Star in the Making

Johnny Moore never played in an historically high-profile game for New Departure, but he became arguably the highest-profile athlete to don the royal blue and white uniform after twenty-six games in 1924.

The twenty-two-year-old outfielder, who had no high school or college baseball experience, joined the team in the spring after honing his game in the sandlots of Waterbury, Connecticut, and with semipro teams in that city and Torrington. In 1923, Moore played against New Departure for Connecticut Light & Power and Torrington, smacking a double for the latter.

With New Departure, he joined a talented mix of outfielders that included veterans Ben Reilly, Swat McCabe, and George Scott, who seemed to surprise reporters with his return to the lineup in mid-May. Moore arrived during a season in which the scope of state championship competition changed.

No longer relying on mythical titles, at least among familiar foes, New Departure formed the Connecticut State Semipro League with Manchester, Meriden, New Britain, Torrington, and Willimantic. Each team posted a five-hundred-dollar security bond to enter into competition, and teams played a thirty-game schedule on Saturdays, Sundays, and holidays in the quest for the silver championship cup.

Because some of the teams played against each other in non-league competitions that limited the number of available dates, New Departure and Muzzy Field did not host the big-name teams and players that they had in the past. Excitement swirled around the tightly formatted league operated by league president and Bristolite William J. Tracy, who had experience running the previous incarnation of the Connecticut State League, a professional version.

Along with Moore, New Departure brought three right-handers into spring camp with college and minor league experience; none, however, lasted beyond a couple of weeks. Les Lanning and Eddie Goodridge, who could pitch more often while Moore covered first base, handled the bulk of the pitching duties along with Tommy Tracy, a recent Dartmouth graduate and captain of its baseball team.

By the end of the season, the main contributors all were familiar.

Several ex-New Departurites appeared on other rosters in the league. Eddie Goeb, Eddie Zielke, Joe Holcomb, and Jimmy Greene suited up for New Britain while Smoke Halbach played for Meriden. Zielke reportedly refused another contract from Manchester, his employer the previous year, because he would have been required to move there.

With well-known players and spirited rivalries among league members, the 1924 script played out in wonderful drama, despite the lack of superstar names.

A wet spring, which led to the Pequabuck River flooding part of town in early April, pushed back opening day at Muzzy Field and cancelled two of the first four games before New Departure opened league play with a 9–5 win over Meriden, George Scott's first home game back in the lineup. The anticlimactic victory mirrored the first month of the season in which the Bristol club went 7–4 but failed to sweep any weekend doubleheaders, splitting with New Britain and Willimantic.

The New Britain game offered a bit of side entertainment at Muzzy Field when bicyclists Amandus Carlson and Fred "Flying Dutchman" Foster raced for five miles around the cinder track with Carlson emerging victorious.

Willimantic, meanwhile, promised to threaten New Departure all season. After a 10–5 road loss to Manchester, again featuring player-coach Herman Bronkie, things looked grim, and New Departure sat near the bottom of the standings in early June.

But wins over two teams based in central New York kick-started the club, and New Departure returned home to sweep Meriden during the weekend of June 21. Newcomer Johnny Moore accomplished an historic feat in the first game against Meriden when in the eighth inning he blasted a pitch over the right field wall for a "Herculean wallop ... about the same spot" as one of Babe Ruth's home runs several years prior, the *Bristol Press* reported.

In the second game, New Departure scored four runs in the ninth before winning 10–9 in thirteen innings.

At 11–5 and on a four-game winning streak, New Departure soon grabbed a foothold atop the CSL standings. In fact, New Departure stretched their winning streak to eleven games before losing the second game of a weekend series against Torrington on July 13.

During the streak, Moore, Bill Tamm, and the rest of the Bristol lineup continued driving the ball while Lanning and Goodridge remained nearly unhittable.

One of the more interesting teams of the season, the Detroit Clowns, appeared at Muzzy Field in late June. The *Bristol Press* buzzed about a group of talented ballplayers who dressed in full clown regalia and grease paint and finished 68–8 in 1923 against some of the top semipro teams in the country.

Managed by Harry Howlett, the Clowns were a white ball club that looked like a traveling circus promising fans an afternoon of comedic antics and fine play.

When the Clowns arrived in Bristol, their pregame ritual included some comedy, but overall, "fans were disappointed when the Clowns failed to perform" in their signature style, according to the *Bristol Press*.

The visitors certainly were not jovial during the game. New Departure took an early lead entering the fifth inning, which was "particularly disastrous to the Clown cause," before scoring eight runs en route to an easy 11–2 victory.

A blowout victory and no true clown performances provided little excitement for the fans, many of whom watched New Departure dismantle New Britain, 6–1, the day before on a complete-game effort by Lanning.

By Fourth of July weekend, shouts of "Beat Bristol" and "Massacre Manchester" rang out in preparation for another chapter in that saga, and New Departure continued playing a sharp brand of baseball. A home-and-home doubleheader with Manchester resulted in Goodridge's three-hitter in a 4–1 victory at Muzzy Field and Lanning's six-hitter in a 1–0 road victory that ended when Goodridge scored in the ninth on a wild throw by center fielder Tommy Sipples.

A shutout win at New Britain the next day behind left-hander Gerald Woodruff, an Amherst alum and Plantsville, Connecticut, resident signed for one game, pushed New Departure into first place in the league. Despite the winning streak, New Departure never pulled away in the standings as Willimantic nearly matched each victory.

The split with Torrington maintained a one-game lead for the Bristol club entering a pivotal weekend series with Willimantic, whose top pitcher, Pete Wood, was 4–1 and whose top hitter, Ray Holden, was batting .404. Johnny Moore paced New Departure with a .326 average, 15-for-46.

On the cusp of what should have been a fantastic duel, Willimantic surprisingly voted to withdraw from the league and discontinue their baseball team two days before the game. The *Bristol Press* reported that Willimantic's high-priced team had lost three thousand dollars since May 17 due to anemic attendance, and sixteen hundred members of its athletic association supported the team's dissolution by an overwhelming majority.

After their closest competition folded, New Departure scrambled to fill their weekend with a home game against American Chain of Bridgeport, a 9–5 win in which mauling outfielders Ben Reilly (4-for-5, triple, and inside-the-park home run) and Moore (3-for-4 and triple) provided most of the runs, and George Scott stole home to break a tie in the fourth inning.

The situation in Willimantic caused the Bristol daily newspaper to examine New Departure's overall economic health, recognizing that they, too, fielded a team with a high payroll.

"The attendance at the past few games has certainly been far from that expected to greet a league-leading aggregation, and there is absolutely no reason for such ragged support on the part of the fans," the *Bristol Press* chastened. The paper further presented its case by saying the action at Muzzy Field was "far superior" to anywhere else in the state where fans "turn out en masse to see nothing but a parody of the national game."

With New Departure winning consistently, observers might have wondered if fans were becoming spoiled by success, as they were certainly bold and cocksure. Meanwhile, fans had rallied in Willimantic and promised more support for their team, and the second-place club was reinstated after a week's absence.

The hot pennant chase was back on.

New Departure gained no ground after splitting with New Britain, though Moore continued his torrid hitting with an inside-the-park home run in the second game of the late-July series. After that, New Departure ripped off eight straight wins through the month of August.

Triples by Reilly and Moore and a two-run double from Swat McCabe supported an Eddie Goodridge six-hitter against Meriden. Lanning and a balanced offense combined to defeat the Dilboy Post VFW of Somerville, Massachusetts, 8–4, with the visitors' lineup featuring Harold "Pie" Traynor's older brother, Edward, a shortstop who hit an RBI single and scored a run.

Prior to a home game with Meriden, the newspaper reported New Departure's number three starter Tommy Tracy had been signed by Meriden, though he was not used in the contest. New Departure ran away with an 11–2 victory in front of only 238 fans who razzed the home team for unknown reasons, according to the *Bristol Press*. Moore blasted another inside-the-park home run, and Meriden's lineup included former Yale second baseman Foon Kai Kee (a.k.a "Mike" of China), who played first base and went 2-for-3 with a double.

A 9–4 win at Torrington the next day frosted the losers so much that they challenged New Departure to a five-game series after the CSL season with one thousand dollars on the line for the winner. But New Departure and Manager

Carroll had other business to tend to before then. Torrington returned to Muzzy Field the next weekend, and Moore's bases loaded triple in the first inning staked Goodridge to an early lead and an ultimate 7–4 triumph.

Firing on all cylinders, New Departure knocked off Willimantic, 2–0, the next day on a three-hitter by Lanning and RBI singles by Reilly and Moore off of Rube Richards. By Sunday evening, August 17, Bristol's club held a three-and-a-half-game lead over second-place Willimantic.

It seemed as if no one could cool down the team or Johnny Moore, who was attracting attention with his consistent performances. One man who took notice was Neal Ball, former pro and three-time opponent of New Departure in 1923. Ball attended the Torrington game at Muzzy Field as a representative of New Haven of the Eastern League and saw Moore crush his first-inning triple. After the Willimantic contest, Ball signed Moore to a contract with New Haven where the youngster suited up within a couple of days and went 7-for-17 in his first four games.

The loss of a top hitter and run-producer had little effect on the team as they entered a series with Manchester, which had dropped off in the standings at 13–12. Unlike previously riotous years, there would be "no bands or burial proceedings" accompanying the game, the *Bristol Press* noted.

New Departure stole five bases and Lanning scattered six hits in an economical 4–2 win at Manchester the day after rain postponed the game at Muzzy Field, which was made up during the week at Manchester and won by the home team.

The split made little difference as New Departure picked up another game in the standings and stood poised to secure the CSL title with four games over Labor Day weekend to close league play.

Following a win at Meriden, Swat McCabe pitched fourteen innings in his first start of the season, and Bill Tamm went 3-for-6 in a 3–2 win at Manchester. The next morning in Bristol, McCabe climbed the hill again and pitched seven innings before Goodridge relieved in a 2–1 win over Willimantic. In the return engagement, McCabe capped a fantastic weekend with three hits as Lanning shut down the home team, 5–2.

Four wins in four games for New Departure clinched the silver cup with a 22–7 league mark and a six-game cushion over second-place New Britain. But the season was not over, and arguably the best games of 1924 remained to be played.

SCOTTIE SCORES RUN THAT TIES.
Thrilling Moment in Hyatt Game That Sent the Throng Into Fenzy of Joy

There was no shortage of fans at Muzzy Field during the halcyon days of
New Departure baseball in the 1920s. (Courtesy: Bristol Public Library)

New Departure accepted Torrington's challenge to a separate championship series, agreeing to a whittled down best-of-three format for one thousand dollars and 60 percent of gate receipts. If either team won the first two games, to be played in Torrington, the third game at Muzzy Field still would be played.

The series began on Sunday, September 7, and nothing changed for New Departure, which took four of six games against Torrington in league play. Reilly hit two triples, and Tamm and Lanning smacked one apiece in the 9–5 win; the main loss came when Gus Forslund either tore a ligament in his right knee or fractured his kneecap. Newspaper reports differed. Regardless, the injury forced him to miss the rest of the dwindling season.

The following Saturday offered an anticlimactic conclusion as Lanning pitched his team to a 5–2 victory to sweep the series as New Departure improved to 33–8.

On Sunday, the meaningless third game turned out to be an unforgettable classic for the 425 fans who witnessed it. Goodridge opposed pitcher Joe Mulville, a sixteen-year-old right-hander from Waterbury whose most important games probably had been played in high school.

Against a veteran of Goodridge's ability, the outcome seemed obvious, and for eight innings the left-hander pitched shutout ball. Mulville, however, had been nearly as effective, limiting the home team to two runs. In the top of the ninth inning, Torrington scored twice to tie the game, and Mulville surrendered nothing.

In the eleventh inning, both teams traded single runs. Goodridge and Mulville continued to battle, dueling against each other as the game stretched into the twenty-first inning. At that point, Torrington loaded the bases for Bill Sheehy, who hit a two-out single for a 5–3 lead. Mulville came out to the mound for the bottom of the twenty-first and slammed the door on one of the longest games in Muzzy Field's history.

Amazingly, both Goodridge and Mulville pitched complete games; Torrington collected seventeen hits off Goodridge while Mulville surrendered only six—quite a performance for a high schooler.

Torrington's club became so excited by the performance that the teams agreed to meet the following Sunday, September 21, in Torrington with the winner taking 75 percent of the gate receipts. Johnny Moore, whose season at New Haven was finished, suited up for New Departure.

Again, Goodridge and Mulville took the mound. This time, the teams combined for twenty runs, thirty hits, and nine errors. Torrington led 5–1 after two innings and 8–3 after seven, but a five-run eighth inning from New Departure tied the game. Again, the game went to extra innings, and the teams traded two runs in the tenth. Neither Goodridge nor Mulville budged, and both pitched into the fifteenth inning before darkness ended the affair.

After thirty-six tense innings of baseball in two games and two complete games on both sides, the teams decided a third game was necessary. Because the West End Athletic Club's football season opener was scheduled for Sunday at Muzzy Field, the baseball game was played again in Torrington. Mulville drew his third assignment, and the *Bristol Press* reported that Eastern League scouts would be in attendance after learning of the youngster's recent performances.

But instead of Goodridge, New Departure started Les Lanning in front of one thousand fans. Mulville pitched another solid game, surrendering four runs on ten hits with five strikeouts, but Lanning outlasted him by scattering seven hits and striking out ten in a 4–0 New Departure victory. Moore notched a hit and scored once for New Departure while Reilly went 2-for-3 with a double and a run scored.

New Departure won the season series, league games included, 7–4–1 as the Torrington rivalry rekindled in 1924. At the postseason dinner at Judd's Fall

Mountain Fish and Game Preserve, the team presented the CSL silver cup to company president DeWitt Page.

Despite a season that was "not successful financially," according to the *Bristol Press*, New Departure posted a 34–10–1 record. One last game was scheduled against Fuller Brush to be played in Hartford for the county championship, but the 1–0 New Departure loss hardly registered as everyone in Bristol seemed focused on football and the World Series by October 5.

Though he batted just .162 for the season, Les Lanning proved again to be a team leader and the pitching staff ace with a 14–4 record while Eddie Goodridge finished 10–3–1 and batted .314. Tommy Tracy went 6–2 before signing with Meriden, and Swat McCabe's two fabulous outings against Manchester and Willimantic resulted in wins. Short-lived starters Gerald Woodruff and Ray Paradis earned the other two victories.

Bill Tamm broke Ben Reilly's monopoly on the team batting title by hitting .361 with sixty-six hits and eighteen stolen bases. Reilly's average dropped precipitously to .254, though he scored a team-high thirty-four runs. In just twenty-eight games with New Departure, Johnny Moore hit .327 with thirty-seven hits and three home runs before hitting .323 in thirty-one games at New Haven. Veteran captain Clyde Waters (.278) and fellow leaders George Scott (.264 and ten sacrifices) and Gus Forslund (.259 and eleven sacrifices) completed a solid lineup that collectively batted .279, averaged about five runs, stole sixty-seven bases, and sacrificed fifty-nine times.

McCabe hit .260, collected forty hits in thirty-seven games, and scored eighteen runs. For the forty-three-year-old former Cincinnati Reds outfielder, the 1924 season was his last with the powerful New Departure teams, but he remained in the game as a base umpire starting in 1925.

McCABE

It was a Mighty Swat into the High
Heavens.

Arthur "Swat" McCabe instantly became the most feared hitter in the New Departure lineup when he joined the team in 1919. He previously spent parts of 1909 and 1910 with the Cincinnati Reds. (Courtesy: Bristol Public Library)

# 1925: "El Immortal"

After winning the Connecticut State Semipro League pennant, New Departure returned to old scheduling practices and filled their slate with the best teams from Massachusetts, New York, and beyond. Outside of games against Manchester and Torrington, New Departure spent little time playing against in-state teams; the CSL did not exist in 1925, and manager Joe Carroll opted to play teams with great reputations rather than Connecticut teams that attracted small crowds the previous season. But even that plan backfired, and New Departure suffered at the gate throughout the season, especially for twilight games played during the week.

As a result, one of the greatest players in the history of the game, and arguably the most versatile, played as an unheralded twenty-year-old in front of a sparse weeknight crowd at Muzzy Field. He arrived in early June with his highly touted teammates from Cuba, many of whom appeared in 1921, but for whatever reason, fans simply stayed away from the ballpark.

It had nothing to do with the home team's record. New Departure's early season schedule was impressive and difficult, but the Bristol club added two players who would make significant positive impacts.

Outfielder Albert Harlowe, the leading hitter in the CSL with a .368 average for New Britain, signed on to replace McCabe in the outfield, and Howard Delaney arrived from Vermont as a right-handed pitcher to bolster the staff. Both carried impressive resumes.

After playing semipro ball in Meriden in 1918, Harlowe worked his way through the New York State League with Oneonta (managed by former Chicago White Sox pitcher "Big Ed" Walsh) and into a position with the powerful Baltimore Orioles of the International League, where he pitched in eleven games. During batting practice, Jack Bentley, who played for three teams in nine major league seasons, hit Harlowe with a pitch that fractured his elbow, and Harlowe never was the same pitcher, the *New Departure News* reported. After bouncing around the South and New York State, Harlowe ended up in Connecticut.

Delaney pitched in the Green Mountain League under the tutelage of Ray Fisher, who pitched two games for the Cincinnati Reds in the 1919 World Series during his ten-year career, and soon became New Departure's winningest pitcher in 1925.

Local player Steg Zetarski, an outfielder and first baseman, joined the club "in his first attempt with a team of this caliber," the *Bristol Press* reported. He might have been added to spell Eddie Goodridge at first base and give the left-hander more starts on the mound, but Zetarski ended up playing only nine games and collecting three hits.

On April 28, several people from Bristol and New Departure traveled to Waterbury for an Eastern League game against New Haven, featuring rising star Johnny Moore. In honor of the Waterbury native, "Johnny Moore Day" was celebrated, and the former New Departure slugger received three hundred dollars in liberty bonds and a new bat while the celebration committee, which included Clyde Waters, presented Moore's wife with a large bouquet of flowers. Though New Haven lost 3–2 in ten innings, Moore tied the game in the fifth with a single.

His former teammates opened their season on the road against the Brooklyn Bushwicks, a powerful semipro club that featured two ex-Brooklyn Robins, pitcher Leon Cadore and catcher Otto Miller. After absorbing a 12–6 loss, the Bristol club notched a home-opening win over Torrington followed by a victory over Gardner, Massachusetts, the next weekend, both in front of small crowds. Gardner's lineup at Muzzy included Ivan Bigler, who played one game for the 1917 St. Louis Browns. He went 0-for-4 against Delaney and made a couple of stellar plays at third.

At some point during this time, Gus Forslund reinjured his knee and missed the next several weeks as New Departure used a platoon system at second base starting with Chick Bowen, a former Holy Cross player.

After a one-year absence, the Brooklyn Royal Giants returned to Muzzy on Wednesday evening, May 20, with another powerful lineup and blasted New Departure, 11–4, on the strength of a seven-run fourth inning against Les Lanning.

Brooklyn's lineup included Johnson Hill, Eddie Douglass, Chester Brooks, Robert Scott, and John Cason, all paying return visits to Muzzy Field.

McKinley "Bunny" Downs, a five-foot-five, 158-pound second baseman, was the prototypical leadoff hitter with great bunting and hit-and-run skills. He was a sharp man—a Morehouse College grad—who formed a fine double-play combination with Dick Lundy during their days with the Atlantic City Bacharach

Giants. In 1923, an incident in Philadelphia in which Downs shot and killed a woman who supposedly tried to shoot him forced Downs to leave the city and its hometown team, the Hilldale Daisies, and he signed with Brooklyn, according to author James A. Riley. Considered one of black baseball's smoothest second basemen, Downs later became business manager of the Indianapolis Clowns where he scouted and helped develop a young Hank Aaron.

William Watson also played for the Royal Giants at Muzzy Field, but little is known of his short career on the highest level of the Negro Leagues. He hit .234 for the 1925 Royal Giants.

Bill Holland, on the other hand, spent parts of three decades in the Negro Leagues. A five-foot-nine, 180-pound switch-hitter and right-handed pitcher, Holland threw five pitches for strikes and became by 1930 one of the most successful moundsmen for the New York Lincoln Giants. On July 10 of that year, Holland was the first black pitcher to pitch in Yankee Stadium. Wins were harder to come by with Brooklyn, however, and he finished with a 7–13 record and a losing record in each of his three seasons there.

Like many minority players of that era, their stories and accomplishments are not evident in the white newspapers of the day. Brief play-by-play accounts do not reveal the magnificence that graced Muzzy Field during this incredible time when fans paid to watch some of the best.

Charlie "Chino" Smith, a twenty-two-year-old rookie with the Royal Giants in 1925, may have been better than all of them. Many former Negro Leaguers said the dynamic Smith was the finest hitter ever to play the game.

He batted second behind Downs against New Departure and finished the 1925 campaign with a .325 average at the start of a mercurial career.

Dramatic, cocksure, and controversial, Smith had more pure hitting ability coiled inside his five-foot-six, 168-pound frame than many players before or since. He was a scrappy, left-handed line-drive hitter with power to all fields, especially later in his career, and had a knack for laying down a drag bunt. He played fine defense in the outfield and at second base with good base-running skills, and while he played with intensity and was unafraid of confrontation, many players said he was not as combative as some believe.

He rarely struck out, and his bat control was superb and scary. "He could hit those line drives back through the box just like you were throwing a ball over to first," pitcher Jesse "Mountain" Hubbard, a teammate of Smith on the Royal Giants, told author John B. Holway.

Smith loved playing to the crowd as much as he enjoyed needling opposing pitchers. Watching a pitcher warm up, he would yell, "Is that all you got?" and when he stepped into the batter's box, Smith often spat at the pitcher's best offerings to rile the fans and the opponents. He would step out, absorb some heckling from the crowd, taunt them, and then rip the cover off the next pitch. Nothing pleased him more than taking off a pitcher's head with a sharp line drive up the middle, and he rarely missed a chance to warn the pitcher right before it happened.

"That was the best man I ever faced," William "Sug" Cornelius, a Negro League pitcher from 1928 to 1946, told Holway. "Smith hit me just like he knew what I was going to throw him. He hit to all fields, and he would spit at the first two pitches then tell me, 'Young man, you've got yourself in trouble.'"

Smith came from Greenwood, South Carolina, and worked at New York's Penn Station while playing for its baseball team, the Pennsylvania Red Caps, prior to joining Brooklyn. It did not take long for him to introduce himself to the big time.

Satchel Paige said that Smith, Josh Gibson, and Ted Page were the best three hitters he ever faced. Ted Page deferred and called Smith the greatest Negro League hitter of all time. Laymon Yokely, a Baltimore Black Sox pitcher, faced Gibson, Jimmie Foxx and Oscar Charleston, and said Smith was better than any of them.

The numbers support him. Smith owns a .423 or .434 lifetime average (depending on the source) in the Negro Leagues and a .423 or .405 average (again, depending on the source) in exhibitions against major leaguers including Dolph Luque, Ed Rommel, and Johnny Ogden. In the Cuban Winter League, Smith fashioned a .335 lifetime mark.

As he refined his hitting skills, his power stroke emerged. In 1929 with the New York Lincoln Giants, he hit .461 with 28 doubles and 23 home runs in 245 at-bats, according to author William F. McNeil. Author James A. Riley credits him with a .464 average in 1929. Either way, Smith's mark was the highest in Negro League history.

In 1930, Smith was a teammate of Holland with the New York Lincoln Giants during the first all-black game at Yankee Stadium against the Baltimore Black Sox. He became the first black man to hit a home run when he blasted a pitch into the right-field seats, the first of two home runs that he hit while also rapping a triple. Smith finished that season with a .429 average.

Seemingly on his way to assuring his legacy as one of the all-time greats and most recognized players, Smith ventured to Cuba to play winter ball as he always did. Sometime during his stay, he fell ill. Many believe he contracted yellow fever. Not yet thirty years old and entering his prime, Chino Smith was dead.

Among casual baseball fans, his name has not lived on as that of Paige or Gibson, and unfortunately, he is as relatively unknown today as he was in 1925 when he appeared at Muzzy Field.

A skeleton game report and box score exist for the Royal Giants' win over New Departure. Douglass socked a triple and Holland earned the victory. Smith's contributions are unknown.

On Memorial Day weekend, the usual excitement preceded the doubleheader against Torrington, and the usual outcome resulted as it had more times than not since 1919; the teams split, only this time New Departure finally won at home. Delaney and Lanning pitched well, though Lanning lost a tough ten-inning decision, and New Departure added a win against a New Haven team during the weekend to improve to 4–3.

The following game remains one of the most important moments in Muzzy Field history for the sheer amount of talent assembled on the field. Continuing with the twilight game tradition of 1925, New Departure booked the Cuban Stars (East) for a Wednesday evening, June 3, contest with hopes that the visitors would attract a large crowd as they had in 1921. The visitors had dropped their independent status and became charter members of the Eastern Colored League in 1923.

There was no question that the Stars were bringing a squad even more talented. Many of the same names from 1921 appeared in the lineup: future Cuban Hall of Famers Pelayo Chacón, Pablo Mesa, and Alejandro Oms. But a versatile teenager who played with style, grace, and fluidity, and who some argue never has been matched in baseball, most impressed the "unusually small crowd" that turned out in Bristol that evening.

At just twenty years of age, Martín Dihigo had been playing professional baseball for three seasons, still a raw player discovering his vast talents when he stepped onto Muzzy Field. By the time he died in 1971, Dihigo was beyond a Cuban legend, a highly revered symbol of a country whose people referred to him as "El Immortal" and descended in great numbers upon open-air cafés in Havana to listen to him talk baseball.

Arguably the most versatile player in baseball history, Martín Dihigo was a raw youngster at the beginning of an unprecedented career when he played for the Cuban Stars of 1925. Nicknamed "El Immortal" and "El Maestro," Dihigo is the only player enshrined in halls of fame in four countries. (Courtesy: Getty Images)

Author Roberto Gonzalez Echevarria described him as "a tall black man with the physique of ... Dave Winfield, but with the grace of movement and agility of a Roberto Clemente, and just as proud," a player who remains an icon decades after his death.

Dihigo's legacy is that of an unusually gifted ballplayer who mastered nearly every position he played, and he played everywhere. When former Negro Leaguers named the all-time best players at each position, Dihigo earned the nomination for second base. Incredibly, he also received votes as the best-ever third baseman and outfielder. He carved out an impressive career as a right-handed pitching wizard with a devastating three-quarter arm curve, and he threw the first no-hitter in the Mexican League, where he was known as "El Maestro." He is the only player enshrined in halls of fame in four countries: the United States, Cuba, Mexico, and Venezuela.

The National Baseball Hall of Fame in Cooperstown called him "perhaps the most versatile player in baseball history." Only "Bullet Joe" Rogan and Babe Ruth rivaled Dihigo as a threat both on the mound and in the batter's box, author John B. Holway contends.

Players marveled at his arm strength. In Holway's research, Judy Johnson said Dihigo and a jai alai player once squared off in a throwing contest from home plate. The jai alai player one-hopped the center-field wall "using his long basketlike *cesto*." Dihigo stepped up with his powerful right arm and hit the wall on the fly. Many base runners fell victim to that same arm, especially at home plate, which amused Dihigo endlessly, and his defensive range was remarkable.

"He'd just fall down and laugh," Johnson said. "'You no run on me, boy, you no run on me.'"

Negro League history books are filled with tales of prodigious home runs in the United States and Cuba.

"Neither before his appearance on the baseball horizon, nor since his departure from the scene, has the multitude of talents afield ever been approached by a single player," James A. Riley wrote. "Hall of Famer Johnny Mize called him the best player he ever saw and remembered that when they were teammates in the Dominican Republic, opponents would intentionally walk Dihigo to pitch to him."

Buck Leonard said of Dihigo, "He was the greatest all-around player I know. I say he was the best player of all time, black or white. He could do it all. If he's not the greatest I don't know who is. You take your Ruths, Cobbs and DiMaggios. Give me Dihigo and I bet I would beat you almost every time."

Roy Campanella echoed those sentiments, according to author Roberto Gonzalez Echevarria, and when Dihigo filled out at six foot three and two hundred pounds he cut a striking profile as a personable, funny, and well-spoken man who always dressed in classy suits and endeared himself to Americans by quickly learning the English language.

"Those who played with Dihigo or who saw him play say that he had it all: coordination, speed, power, arm, good hands, batting eye, intelligence and poise," Gonzalez Echevarria wrote, adding that his gracefulness was something akin not to the diamond but to the bullfighting ring.

And he could slay pitchers. Dihigo is credited with a .319 batting average and sixty-two home runs in twelve years in the U.S. with a 27–21 record on the mound. In Mexico, he hit .317 with fifty-five home runs in eleven years and finished with a 119–57 pitching mark and 2.84 ERA. In Cuba, he hit .295 with twenty home runs in twenty-three years playing in those mammoth yards and went 106–57 on the mound. Historians argue that his Negro League numbers are incomplete and Dihigo could be credited with more than 350 wins in his career.

"It does not matter," Gonzalez Echevarria stated. "Dihigo's consummate mastery of the game was something that could not be quantified. He seemed to belong in a league of his own in everything he did ... Dihigo shone in the Mexican Leagues, the Negro Leagues, and the Cuban League, not to mention countless independent games and transient tournaments."

He later became a successful manager, too, as well as the Minister of Sports under Fidel Castro.

It is unfortunate that so few people braved the threatening skies at Muzzy Field on June 3, 1925, when the young Dihigo and his teammates squared off against New Departure.

Those who did show up witnessed a fine game.

The Cuban Stars lineup included Dihigo leading off and playing first base; Bernardo Baró in right field; Alejandro Oms in center field; Pelayo Chacón at shortstop; Armando Massip in left field, replaced late in the game by Pablo Mesa; P. Cardenas behind the plate, replaced early by José María Fernández; Bartolo Portuondo at second base; light-hitting reserve infielder Pedro Ferrer at third base; and two pitchers, Oscar Levis and Juanelo Mirabal.

Baró was a regular with the Almendares clubs during the winter season and played in the notable game against the New York Giants in 1920. Vastly talented, quick-tempered, and contentious, Baró was a superb left-handed hitting and throwing outfielder who could do everything on the field and do it with speed. Historians write that he could make any play in the outfield but often showed off too much.

In 1925 at Muzzy Field, Baró was coming off a compound fracture of his leg—suffered the year prior while chasing a foul ball into the stands—that required surgery and was initially believed to be career-ending. He worked his way back into the lineup, playing with a limp said to be the result of the surgery that left one leg shorter than the other. His speed was not the same, but he remained a dangerous presence.

Four years after his Muzzy Field appearance, Baró suffered a mental breakdown that forced doctors to restrain him in a straitjacket. He finished his eighteen-year baseball career in 1930 and died suddenly in June of that same year.

Massip hit .208 in limited appearances for the Cuban Stars in 1925, and Cardenas was a talented catcher whose predicted stardom never materialized. Injured during his 1924 rookie campaign, Cardenas finished with a .239 average in 1925 and played two more seasons with the Cuban Stars.

Fernández was the Stars manager and "an accomplished catcher with some power and much intelligence," Gonzalez Echevarria wrote. A veteran of the Marianao club during the winter, he became a player-manager for the New York Cubans in 1938 and led the team to the Negro World Series championship in 1947. At the time of his appearance in Bristol, Fernández was considered one of the best catchers around.

Portuondo was an Alemendares infielder who played for the Kansas City Monarchs earlier in the decade.

Levis, a southpaw spitball ace, was the leading pitcher for the Stars in the 1920s but played on teams that often finished at the bottom of the Eastern Colored League. Mirabal was a five-foot-eight, 150-pound right-hander with a three-quarter arm delivery and excellent control of his curveball and sinking fastball. In 1925, he struggled to a 2–9 record but by 1928, he was the ace of a Stars team that finished 93–22.

Mirabal also was instrumental in Dihigo's development as a hitter. In the beginning of his career, Dihigo struggled with curveballs until he started taking batting practice off of Mirabal, who would throw nothing but his breaking pitch.

Delaney drew the pitching assignment for New Departure and surrendered triples to Baró and Oms for a quick 1–0 Cuban Stars lead in the first inning. He settled down after that until the Stars scored again in the sixth on a Chacón single and Fernandez triple. New Departure answered when Eddie Goodridge scored a run in the bottom of the sixth after Ben Reilly left the game when he was struck in the head with a pitch.

New Departure got to Juanelo again in the seventh after George Scott singled, advanced on a Tamm single, and scored when Chacón threw wildly on Goodridge's ground ball, tying the game at two.

Despite Chacón's error, Dihigo was impressing Bristol fans with his defensive play on a day when it seemed the infielders were erratic.

"An elongated chap by the name of Dehigo [sic], built on the lines of George Kelly of the Giants, covering first for the Stars, provided the big hit of the tilt with the crowd because of the apparent ease with which he fielded seemingly impossible thrown balls," the Bristol Press reported.

Locked in a tight duel entering the eighth, the Stars grabbed a 5–2 lead with two singles, two walks, two sacrifices, and an error, but New Departure still had life in the ninth inning. Scott, on his way to a 3-for-5 evening, socked a double before Goodridge drove him in with an RBI single.

Juanelo allowed nothing more, however, and the Stars capped a 5–3 victory. Baró, Oms and Fernández combined for five hits, three triples, and three runs as the Stars' offensive catalysts. As for the young legend in the making, Dihigo went 0-for-4 with eleven putouts at first. He finished the year batting .295.

Four days later on Sunday afternoon, New Departure battled a team from Pittsfield, Massachusetts, in an exciting, ten-inning contest significant for one play by Ben Reilly, who seemed to recover fully from the beaning against the Cuban Stars. With runners on the corners in the tenth inning and the game tied at two runs apiece, Reilly worked the count to 2-and-1 before he hammered a pitch high and deep to right-center field. The titanic shot to the opposite field cleared the wall—with room to spare as reports later measured it at four hundred feet—and whipped the fans into a frenzy at the sight of the game-winning blast.

"It was a sure-enough homer and was propelled a greater distance than either of the socks from the bats of Babe Ruth or Johnny Moore, the only other two personages to accomplish the feat," the Bristol Press opined.

The home run was maybe the most impressive singular moment for the speedy, power-hitting outfielder who was one of New Departure's all-time greats.

Taking in the fantastic atmosphere at Muzzy Field that day was Paul Berlenbach, a former Olympic gold medal wrestler who had usurped from Mike McTigue the title of light-heavyweight boxing champion of the world after their fight in May. Berlenbach was inducted into the International Boxing Hall of Fame in 2001.

During the rest of June and through the Fourth of July, New Departure played a little better than break-even baseball, extending their record to 11–7. A four-game split with Manchester in some tight games and victories over Fuller

Brush and the Troy (NY) Grogans left the team in decent shape. The fill-in second baseman, Peanuts Funk, who was now at Wesleyan University, played great baseball before Gus Forslund returned in late June.

The problem, however, remained in the stands, and attendance, when reported, was as low as five hundred on a Sunday afternoon at Muzzy Field. Even the Manchester series failed to attract large crowds as it had in the past, and no one could offer an explanation.

"The fact remains that management is taking an awful licking at the box office every game of late," the *Bristol Press* intoned. "Criticism is all right in its place—but support, both financial as well as vocal is necessary if these games are to continue."

New Departure tried to lure fans with a game on July 12 against the Twin Cities club of Fonda, New York, featuring Jake "Bugs" Reisigl, a former teammate of Clyde Waters in the Eastern League. Between innings during one game with New Haven, Reisigl was warming up on the mound with Waters catching when Waters crouched down to await the first batter. Reisigl, however, was in the middle of throwing one more pitch when he beaned the oblivious Waters and knocked him out. Waters was revived at the end of game.

The *Bristol Press* wrote repeatedly about the incident leading up the game, which New Departure won, 3–2, despite Reisigl's 3-for-4 performance from his first-base position. But again, the crowd did not impress with its size.

No better way to create a buzz than with some juicy controversy with Manchester, team management thought. New Departure got just that during a Wednesday evening road game that ended deadlocked at two runs apiece after Manchester scored in the bottom of the ninth.

As usual, Art Johnson pitched well against the Bristol club, scattering hits and allowing few scoring opportunities. But during the game, Waters and Goodridge protested angrily to umpire Mike Lynch that Johnson was using an illegal, slimy substance to doctor the ball. The New Departure representatives remained vehement that the ball be removed from play, and Manchester's players and fans became incensed. Lynch stood his ground in the middle.

Frustrated that his arguments progressed nowhere, Goodridge, who always seemed in newspaper accounts to be a studious, even-keeled player-coach, made an executive decision. He grabbed the ball in question and heaved it over the short fence that extended down the base lines at Manchester, forcing a new ball to be used. The fans roared, and the incident provided new ammunition for the rivalry.

Meanwhile, Lynch ejected no one, which further angered Manchester. Its newspaper said such behavior never would be tolerated in the big leagues.

"It shows the calibre [sic] of the men when they take advantage of independent [baseball] conditions to make rowdies of themselves," wrote the *Manchester Herald*, charging that Waters collaborated in the controversy by sticking chewing gum on the ball before Goodridge threw it out, ensuring that it could not be used again.

"That alibi … is a lot of blah and is simply a sample of cry-baby methods that those Manchester boys will use," the *Bristol Press* retorted. "It seems as though they'll never grow up."

The Bristol newspaper never condemned the players' actions but instead attacked Manchester's decision to prohibit Lynch from umpiring any of their future games.

"While we do not wish to be unduly severe with our criticism," the *Bristol Press* wrote, "Umpire Lynch was … a vast improvement over the alleged arbiters we have seen officiate [at Manchester] in previous years."

After a season and a half of tameness, the war was back on.

Suddenly, the teams' "quarrel this season is more intensified than ever," the *Bristol Press* wrote.

Art Johnson took the mound for Manchester at Muzzy Field against Delaney, but even the newest controversy could not pack the stands as it would have in 1922 or 1923. Eight hundred people split evenly in their allegiances cheered frantically on July 26.

"Rooting seems to be a lost art these days," according to the Bristol paper, but the fans who were in attendance "added spice and pepper to the game."

Delaney survived four walks and eight hits by stranding thirteen Manchester base runners. Albert Harlowe and Goodridge hit RBI doubles, and Reilly finished 3-for-4 with two runs and two RBI as New Departure jumped out to a 4–0 lead and won, 7–2.

The following Sunday, Delaney topped himself in "unquestionably the best played ballgame of the season," according to the local daily paper.

Against Norwich and ex-Baltimore Oriole hurler Tony West, Delaney allowed one hit and a walk while hitting a batter. Those runners were erased in a double play, a pickoff, and an assist by the outfield. He faced the minimum twenty-seven batters but received no offensive support as West allowed only three hits through eight innings.

In the ninth, the Norwich left-hander finally cracked and gave up three hits, including the game-winner by George Scott on a two-out screamer into center field. The 1–0 win sealed a two-game season sweep for New Departure.

The remainder of August played out with more highs than lows for the home team. Victories over Fisk and New Process Gear of Syracuse, New York, were two of the highlights, but North Adams, Massachusetts, dealt a severe blow to New Departure's ego when left-hander Joe LaPlante shut them down in a 9–0 win at Muzzy Field, dubbed "the most humiliating loss in years" by the *New Departure News*.

In three games against Manchester, the teams split and tied once, forcing a definitive championship game in September. In the scoreless tie at Manchester, the *Bristol Press* complained of poor umpiring that prohibited New Departure from scoring before darkness fell.

The 7–4 win at Manchester on August 20 was scheduled for seven innings, and New Departure scored five runs in the second for a quick 6–0 lead. As Manchester clawed back to within 7–4, manager Breck Breckridge of Manchester requested the game go the full nine innings, and the *Bristol Press* wrote that New Departure players were miffed that manager Joe Carroll obliged him. When New Departure scored three more times in the eighth, the *Bristol Press* reported that Breckridge called mercy and the final score reverted to the official tally.

Ferdie Steinhilber pitched both of these games for Manchester, and on August 30, he was slated against Delaney at Muzzy Field in front of eight hundred fans. After George Scott hit an inside-the-park home run in the first, Steinhilber scattered seven hits the rest of the way as Manchester won, 6–1.

Four days prior to that loss, New Departure engaged the Brooklyn Royal Giants on a Wednesday evening at home and performed admirably in front of a "few hundred" fans.

Brooklyn fielded the same lineup as in May with the exception of pitcher Jesse "Mountain" Hubbard.

At six foot two and two hundred pounds, the right-hander towered over many hitters of his day, and like many of his teammates and fellow Negro Leaguers, possessed major-league ability. With part American Indian blood, Hubbard nearly passed for a white player to earn his shot. The New York Giants sent him to a farm team in Massena, New York, and the Detroit Tigers expressed interest but neither team took the risk of signing him.

Hubbard started playing baseball at sixteen while working in a Texas sawmill. After serving in the war, he joined Brooklyn's pitching staff of 1919, featuring

Cyclone Joe Williams and Cannonball Dick Redding, and pitched two shutouts against the New York Giants.

In 1925, he suffered an arm injury that forced him to develop a sidearm and underhand delivery. He mostly threw junkballs but could sneak a fastball or cutball past a lot of batters. During his stint with Brooklyn, Hubbard sometimes pitched batting practice for Lou Gehrig and the Columbia University baseball team.

Always a crowd favorite, Hubbard was a sharp dresser and handsome ladies' man who "loved big cigars and bigger Cadillacs," James A. Riley wrote.

In Bristol, Hubbard hurled one inning of relief, collected a single, and scored a run.

Les Lanning started against Broadway Rector, and the Royal Giants tagged the lefty early for three runs in the first inning. New Departure answered in the second with three runs on RBI singles from Waters and Tamm and a sac fly from Harold Horkheimer.

The Bristolites continued swinging the bats against Rector in the third. A throwing error and Forslund's RBI double staked the team to a 5–3 lead, and Lanning helped his cause in the fifth with an RBI single. Another error and a sac fly by Reilly made it 8–3, a surprising development against the talented Royal Giants.

Lanning, meanwhile, settled down after the first inning and allowed no base runners from the second to the eighth innings. Though he allowed a single run in the ninth, Lanning completed one of the most impressive victories of his career with three strikeouts and six hits surrendered in the 8–4 win.

For the Royal Giants, right fielder William Watson went 2-for-4 with a run; shortstop Bill Wagner was 0-for-4; second baseman Chino Smith was 1-for-3 with a triple and a run scored; first baseman Eddie Douglass was 0-for-3 with a run; center fielder Chester Brooks hit a double in four at-bats; left fielder Robert Scott was 0-for-4; catcher John Cason collected a single; and Rector was hitless at the plate and gave up eight runs on ten hits in seven innings.

Captain Lanning.

Les Lanning was a multithreat talent during his playing days in Bristol, hitting .336 in 1919 and posting a 17–4 mark in 1923. His most impressive victory came in 1925 when he tossed a six-hitter against the Brooklyn Royal Giants at Muzzy Field, whose lineup included Negro League greats Broadway Rector and Charlie "Chino" Smith. (Courtesy: Bristol Public Library)

In terms of the opposition's talent, the win over the Brooklyn Royal Giants ranked as the notable one-game accomplishment for the 1925 New Departure team. But resolving the feud with Manchester provided more satisfaction for fans and players.

Rainy weather over Labor Day weekend postponed the game until September 20 when New Departure entered the contest with twenty-three wins, the latest two against Winsted and an all-star team from Meriden, featuring old friends Eddie Zielke, Smoke Halbach, and Tommy Tracy.

In the season series, New Departure held four wins compared to Manchester's three, but the two draws necessitated another game for either a convincing series conquest or the continuation of festivities.

In his first mound action in nearly a month since the Royal Giants win, Lanning took the hill against mainstay Steinhilber in what played out as another tight ball game.

At the end, the pitchers' numbers looked nearly identical. Both struck out five and walked five. Lanning scattered four hits and Steinhilber five.

Manchester scored the first run on a bloop single in the fourth before New Departure tied it when Manchester's catcher dropped a pop-up in front of home plate and Waters, running all the way, scored from second. It was Manchester's lone error of the game, but it cost the team more than New Departure's two misplays.

In the sixth, Harlowe and Horkheimer smacked run-scoring singles for a 3–1 lead, and Lanning allowed nothing the rest of the way.

With victories over the main Connecticut competition in multiple-game series, New Departure proclaimed themselves 1925 state champions. Against Massachusetts teams, they finished a respectable 5–3 with splits against Gardner and Fisk, and they won five of nine games against New York teams, despite losing the last two games of the season to New Process Gear.

New Departure teams from the Elmwood and Meriden plants also fared well in their respective leagues, and the company claimed three championships with the Bristol team finishing 24–13–2.

Goodridge paced the club with a .320 average and eight doubles while finishing 6–0 on the mound. Harlowe (.311) and Reilly (.301) were consistently heavy hitters and Tamm (.290), Waters (.290), and Scott (.252, thirty runs, seventeen stolen bases, twenty walks) remained table-setters with a penchant for clutch hits. Tamm retired from New Departure after the season and moved to New York City to enter the printing business with his brother.

At 11–6, Delaney was the winningest pitcher, and Lanning recovered from a 1–4 start to finish 7–6 while hitting .250 in eighteen games.

In December, Edward D. Rockwell, cofounder of the New Departure Bell Company with his brother Albert F. Rockwell, died in the hospital at age seventy-one as the last original organizer of the company.

Another era was passing at the town's ballpark. Because of lagging attendance, Muzzy Field saw a decline in star-studded baseball teams from out of state after the 1925 season. But the golden era of New Departure baseball was to end with a bang the next season.

# 1926: The Greatest Game in Bristol History

Decreasing interest in New Departure baseball was palpable in 1926. Evidence of such did not come strictly from the season's schedule, which notably lacked some of the traditional powerhouse teams of previous years probably due to losing money at the gates. Nor did it come primarily from the numerous references to sagging attendance at Muzzy Field in 1925. It came in the presentation of news reports.

The newspapers wrote shorter stories about New Departure and dedicated increasing space to grammar school, high school, and interfactory games played at Muzzy Field during the week and sometimes on the weekend when New Departure was out of town.

In previous years, these school and amateur game reports warranted only a brief mention in a multiparagraph roundup, but in 1926, box scores and detailed descriptions started to appear. More than anything, this hinted at the fans' shifting attitude toward baseball—that they would rather watch a game featuring local teams and players they knew well.

Had the defending World Series champion appeared at Muzzy Field four or five years before, the coverage leading up to and following the game would have been far greater than it was when the Pittsburgh Pirates came to town in June.

On the field, however, these things hardly affected New Departure as their familiar nucleus carried them to a twenty-win season. For the first time during the era, though, the team's top pitchers were not Eddie Goodridge and Les Lanning.

Two right-handers, Armand "Jack" Brooks and the sidearm twirler Ed Thorpe, pitched the bulk of the games as Goodridge concentrated more on playing the field. Lanning, meanwhile, won his first two starts in May and June before leaving the team to play with Middletown of the Middlesex County League.

Pregame ceremonies. (Courtesy: Bristol Public Library)

Thorpe brought minor league experience from Canada and the Eastern League, and Brooks had been a star semipro pitcher around western Connecticut.

Bill Tamm's departure left a void at third base, which was filled by former Torrington star Bob Christie and newcomer Jimmy Malcolm, who had played for some teams in Massachusetts. Malcolm was known more for his exploits on the basketball court with New Departure where the forward performed admirably for coach Joe Carroll's state championship team of 1925. Carroll expected similar results as he managed the baseball team for yet another season.

A harsh winter of heavy winds and snow delayed New Departure's home opener at Muzzy Field because the outfield fence required significant repairs before it was suitable for play. After a season-opening loss at Wilton, New Departure returned home against Haverhill, Massachusetts, and defeated the New England League members, 5–2, behind Ben Reilly's three-run, inside-the-park home run against the wind in left-center field and Thorpe's six strikeouts. Eight hundred fans attended the home opener in blustery conditions.

Bristol's club finished the rest of the month 3–0–2 with three games at Muzzy Field. One of the tied contests came against the Philadelphia Giants in a six-inning affair halted by rain on May 16.

The Giants were inferior in talent compared to Negro League teams such as the Cuban Stars and Brooklyn Royal Giants, or even the first incarnation of the Philadelphia Giants from 1902 to 1916; however, the 1926 Philadelphia club included an interesting mix of players passing each other at different points in their careers.

Jess Barbour was Philadelphia's notable veteran in center field. He spent sixteen years on the highest level of the Negro Leagues and played most of his career on Rube Foster's Chicago American Giants during the glory years of the 1910s. The left-handed hitter used his blinding speed to collect many infield hits throughout his career, but he also was an all-around good hitter and bunter. Defensively, his versatility led him to play every position but pitcher and catcher.

Barbour's albatross was the bottle. As a member of the Detroit Stars, he showed up drunk at the ballpark and was removed from the lineup and eventually the team. After starting his career with the top-notch Philadelphia Giants, Barbour ended his career with the low-level team of the same name. He retired after the 1926 season (Riley 1994).

Philadelphia's two up-and-comers were twenty-two-year-old shortstop Bill Yancey and twenty-eight-year-old pitcher Will Jackman.

Yancey was in his last season with the Giants before moving up to the Hilldale Daisies. Only 165 pounds, he was a solid hitter with good speed and a strong, accurate arm. In the off-season, Yancey was a star guard for the New York Renaissance basketball team, which was inducted into the Basketball Hall of Fame in 1963.

Yancey ended up with the New York Lincoln Giants in 1929 and honed his skills at shortstop under the tutelage of the legendary John Henry Lloyd. He also spent the 1930 season with the Lincoln Giants, playing in the all-black game at Yankee Stadium with Bill Holland and Chino Smith.

When the team arrived for the game, Yancey ran out and took phantom swings at the plate and pretended to catch fly balls, thereby becoming the first black man ever to set foot on the field at Yankee Stadium. Later in life, he managed a team in Latin America and scouted for the Yankees and Phillies, but he said his experience in Yankee Stadium was one of his biggest thrills in baseball, James A. Riley wrote.

Jackman, a six-foot-three, 225-pound right-hander, was in his prime years when he arrived at Muzzy Field. Sometime during his days with the Philadelphia Giants from 1925 to 1927, Jackman suffered an arm injury that required changing his delivery from overhand to underhand.

It certainly occurred prior to the game against New Departure because the newspaper referred to him as "Submarine."

Jackman was a certified flamethrower. His fastball exploded out of large hands that enveloped the ball and was described as being faster than Satchel Paige's or Bob Feller's. Except for four seasons, the Texas native with a "gap-toothed, boyish smile to complement his easy-going temperament" made his living playing in the lower Negro Leagues (Riley 1994).

After adjusting his delivery with the Giants, Jackman is credited with posting a 52–2 record in one season, including two victories in two outings against a young Paige. In the peak of his career, Jackman commanded $175 per game and $10 per strikeout; and like Paige, Jackman continued pitching into his fifties, only with semipro teams.

Other Giants in the lineup included right fielder Ralph Jefferson, second baseman Clay Carpenter, third baseman and manager Burlin White, left fielder Goldie Cephus, catcher Barney Jenkins, and a first baseman named Ricks, possibly Pender Ricks although James A. Riley did not link the player to the 1926 Philadelphia Giants in his research.

New Departure's Brooks allowed three hits, two to Jefferson and one to Yancey, and Jackman fanned eight before the rain came. The disappointed fans would see the Giants later in the season.

After dropping the first two games of June, including another loss to ex-Baltimore Oriole left-hander Tony West of Norwich, New Departure's record stood at an unimpressive 4–3–2.

Certainly, it was nothing to concern a major league team visiting for an exhibition game. But by the time the Pittsburgh Pirates arrived at Muzzy Field, their season already was in trouble.

The defending world champions were an offensive juggernaut that overcame a 3–1 deficit in the 1925 World Series to defeat mighty Walter Johnson and the Washington Senators. Pittsburgh boasted four future Hall of Famers in their everyday lineup along with a manager, Bill McKechnie, who would be inducted into Cooperstown as the only man to win National League pennants with three different clubs.

The 1926 Pirates returned nearly every player from the previous season, and expectations soared with Max Carey, Kiki Cuyler, Pie Traynor, and rookie Paul "Big Poison" Waner, who would lead the league with twenty-two triples, swinging the bats.

On June 13, however, none of them could reverse a downward spiral that was accelerated by New Departure.

John Gunshanan, a former ballplayer with Bristol of the Connecticut State League, had been responsible for arranging such exhibitions throughout the state in previous years. He coaxed the Pirates to Bristol during a long road trip that featured an open date between their series in Philadelphia and Boston. The exhibition game benefited a firefighter's pension fund, and Muzzy Field braced itself for a projected crowd of several thousand people. Temporary bleacher seats were added in the outfield to handle the crowds.

Approximately three thousand people showed up, spilling out of the grandstand, and they awaited the Pirates' arrival by car from the Hartford train station.

Pittsburgh maintained a respectable 28–21 record in mid-June. Despite splitting four games with the lowly Philadelphia Phillies prior to their trip to Bristol, the Pirates were playing good baseball after stumbling to a 2–7 start.

But their main problems were internal and irrevocable in 1926. Former manager Fred Clarke, himself a future Hall of Famer with four pennant-winning clubs and a World Series ring in Pittsburgh, was a team stockholder and self-appointed assistant coach to McKechnie. The two men rarely agreed on baseball strategy, and the smoldering tension imploded the team after a doubleheader loss to Boston in August.

"Clarke's meddling led to dissension within the clubhouse," John Bennett wrote in his Max Carey biography. "Carey called a team meeting and attempted to pass a resolution banning Clarke from the bench. [He] felt that he should represent the players in their dispute, and his stand resulted in his becoming the fall guy for the whole ugly affair. In what would be known as the 'great Pirate mutiny,' Pirate owner Barney Dreyfuss foiled Carey's uprising by first suspending and then waiving … his team captain."

This was the baggage the Pirates carried when their motorcade reached Muzzy Field. Pittsburgh used sixteen players, including the four Hall of Famers, against New Departure and named forty-four-year-old Babe Adams their starting pitcher.

Adams was a relief pitcher in 1926, appearing in nineteen games, but he was a hero in Pittsburgh after earning three victories as a starter and stymieing Ty Cobb's Detroit Tigers in the 1909 World Series. Known as a control pitcher with a sharp curveball, Adams won 194 games in 19 seasons and became part of the Clarke-McKechnie fallout when he, Carey, and Carson Bigbee were cut from the team in 1926.

New Departure countered with Ed Thorpe on the mound.

Jimmy
Malcolm

Known more for his play on the basketball court, Jimmy Malcolm joined the New Departure baseball team as an infielder in 1926. He scored the first run in that season's historic game at Muzzy Field against the Pittsburgh Pirates, defending World Series champions. (Courtesy: Bristol Historical Society)

The two pitched scoreless ball for the first three innings before New Departure got to Adams in the fourth. Jimmy Malcolm led off with a hot smash off of Pirates third baseman Traynor and moved to second on a single by Reilly. After a sacrifice bunt, Clyde Waters drove in Malcolm with a single.

When shortstop Harold Horkheimer hit a fly ball to Waner in right field, Reilly scored from third for a 2–0 New Departure lead. Bud Culloton replaced Adams after that inning.

Thorpe scattered three hits through five frames before giving way to Ed Vargus, a Boston Braves rookie and former Boston College star, who nursed the two-run lead into the ninth.

"Most of the Pirate attempts were either infield grassers that were quickly gobbled up or outfield flies that were captured with alacrity," Carleton Beckwith wrote in the *New Departure News*.

At the risk of losing to a group of ex-minor leaguers and unknown semiprofessionals, the Pirates staged a two-out rally in the ninth inning.

With Eddie Moore on third and George Grantham on first, catcher Jack Onslow came to the plate. Onslow was not a member of the 1926 Pirates but was a notable ballplayer who logged forty-five games combined for the 1912 Detroit Tigers and 1917 New York Giants.

During Onslow's at-bat, Grantham bolted for second, and a low throw by Waters skipped away, allowing Moore to score easily. Onslow followed with a double to tie the game before Culloton hit a fly ball to George Scott in left field to end their inning.

"The Pirates probably felt pretty sure they could finish the job in another inning and the fans thought along the same lines," a staff reporter wrote in the *Hartford Courant*.

Even Beckwith, an unapologetic homer, conceded, "At this juncture most of the fans would not have given even a plugged nickel for the local chances."

Culloton had allowed only a walk in his four innings of relief, and he started the ninth by inducing a pop-up from Gus Forslund. Waters, a consistently clutch hitter, broke through with a single to right field with Horkheimer coming to the plate.

The shortstop connected with a Culloton offering and lifted it into the gap in right-center field "while Carson Bigbee and Paul Waner made a valiant but futile effort to pull down the horsehide, and the ball game was over," Beckwith wrote.

Waters scored easily and New Departure sealed an improbable victory over the defending champions who "suffered the ignominy of a defeat," according to the *Hartford Courant,* to a team of part-time ballplayers. And it took fewer than ninety minutes.

Oddly, Pittsburgh's star players affected the game minimally. Center fielder Carey, left fielder Cuyler, and third baseman Traynor garnered two singles in five at-bats before giving way to replacements. Waner, who finished his career with 3,152 hits, played all 9 innings in right field and hit 2 singles in 4 plate appearances.

It is possible the Pirates gave less effort than they would have against a National League team, maybe because the Clarke-McKechnie fiasco was such a distraction. Pittsburgh finished in third place at 84–69 that season in a tight race with St. Louis and Cincinnati.

In October, McKechnie was relieved of his duties, a move he described as "very expected" in an Associated Press story. Owner Barney Dreyfuss said fans "had lost confidence in McKechnie and there was only one thing to do."

McKechnie reemerged in 1928 when he led the Cardinals to the National League pennant. Donie Bush took over the Pirates in 1927 and guided them to the World Series behind "Big Poison" Waner and his rookie brother and future Hall of Famer, Lloyd "Little Poison" Waner.

The turmoil of 1926 shook up the Pittsburgh franchise, but led to one of the most important moments in Bristol baseball history.

The remainder of June's schedule at Muzzy Field featured no games that matched the thrills of the Pirates' visit. An 8–3 road win against Manchester on a Thursday evening nearly escalated into something ugly when catcher Clyde Waters caught a foul pop-up and bumped a Manchester fan who refused to make room for an easier play. Police stepped in as emotions started to flare.

Otherwise, early summer lacked definitive moments. A burgeoning rivalry with Norwich provided some excitement as Tony West took the hill on two occasions at Muzzy Field and earned a split, his victory coming on July 4 when Norwich got the best of Ed Thorpe, 5–3.

The following day, the Meriden Endees, a new team spawned from the company's factory that opened in that town in 1922, swept a home-and-home doubleheader from New Departure on the strength of former Bristol players Eddie Zielke and Smoke Halbach. In the second game at Hanover Park in Meriden, Halbach tied the game in the ninth inning with a bloop single, and Meriden scored once more for a 6–5 victory in front of "the largest crowd of the season," according to the *New Departure News.*

The team found themselves at 8–8–2 on a four-game losing streak, and the sweep dealt a severe blow to their state title aspirations.

In response, New Departure reeled off two wins against a factory team from New London before entertaining Manchester during a Wednesday twilight game on July 14. The home team exploded with ten runs in the opening three innings, but Thorpe gave up three runs in the first before settling down. Manchester struck again with four runs in the seventh and one in the eighth before Eddie Goodridge slammed the door in the ninth for a wild 10–8 victory.

Meanwhile, the Philadelphia Giants had been playing great baseball since visiting Muzzy Field in mid-May. With a 42–8–6 mark, the Giants returned to Bristol three days after the Manchester game touting their lineup of second baseman Charles "Babe" Lewis (thirty home runs, according to the *Bristol Press*) and pitcher Submarine Jackman, who reportedly carried a 20–3–3 record and pitched two no-hitters and eight one-hitters during the season after neutralizing Bristol's bats.

Philadelphia's lineup mainly was unchanged with Jefferson, White, Ricks, Cephus, Yancey, and Jackman. White replaced Jenkins at catcher, and A.J. Lockhardt, a former Morris Brown University star and Washington Potomac, filled in at third base. Lewis made his Muzzy Field debut along with right fielder Leonard Pierce, another former Washington Potomac.

Jackman got the nod for the three o'clock start and lived up to all expectations. Thorpe opposed him in a battle of pitchers with funky deliveries, but Bristol's right-hander did nothing to fool the Giants.

Lewis started with an RBI single in the first inning before a two-out flurry of hits chased Thorpe in the third. A two-run triple by Cephus preceded RBI singles from Yancey and Pierce, and Thorpe lasted just $2^2/_3$ innings before giving way to Goodridge.

Jackman, on the other hand, induced easy grounders and pop-ups with his "hooks, slants, fast ones and underhand shoots," the *New Departure News* reported. The right-hander fired a three-hitter, allowing two singles to Goodridge and one to Christie, but two errors by the defense contributed to New Departure's one run.

Lewis tacked on another RBI single in the seventh for the 6–1 victory. Though the power hitter failed to clear Muzzy's walls, he smashed a towering fly ball to left that George Scott caught on the track and finished 3-for-5. Lockhardt scored twice with two hits, and White scored once while "the talkative catcher … made a hit with the spectators as a result of his continual chatter and loud war whoops, while the entire infield injected a lot of comedy into their practice workout that also received a big hand from the fans," the *New Departure News* reported.

As an intense heat wave gripped Bristol in mid-July, New Departure went about disposing of familiar teams whose financial problems rendered them less competitive than in years past. Torrington went down 5–1 in the face of Armand Brooks's three-hitter on July 23 before Thorpe bested Fisk and Rube Richards, 3–2, in a game in which Bob Christie's sacrifice fly with the bases loaded in the sixth inning completed New Departure's comeback from an early 2–0 hole. Always a compelling series between proud and feisty teams, the Fisk game provided some of the season's greatest excitement but attracted only five hundred fans to Muzzy Field.

A split with teams from Westfield, Massachusetts, and Syracuse led into an important fourth and final game against Norwich at Muzzy Field. Already trailing the series 2–1, New Departure needed a victory to save face. Again, the visitors trotted out ex-Baltimore Oriole Tony West against Armand Brooks.

The Sunday afternoon contest on August 8 quickly became a tight pitchers' duel. Norwich posted two runs on two hits in the first inning, normally a large deficit to overcome against West, who pitched a shutout into the fifth.

Though unable to score, New Departure collected a few hits against West before Ben Reilly finally broke through with an RBI single in the fifth inning, cutting the deficit to 2–1 as Brooks was finding a groove after the shaky first.

New Departure attacked again in the sixth inning with four bunt singles, pushing across two runs and taking a 3–2 lead. Brooks continued to post zeroes though he struggled with wildness in walking five batters in the game. But he allowed only two hits after the first inning, four for the game, and Norwich never pushed across another run.

West gave up nine hits and four walks as he took the loss, and the teams settled on splitting the four-game series.

The victory kick-started New Departure for the final month and a half of the season as the team dusted teams from New York and Massachusetts in August and took care of Manchester, 11–5, at home with sixteen hits.

After rain postponed all Labor Day games, New Departure knocked off the Meriden Endees, 6–1, while Goodridge scattered twelve hits and Meriden stranded thirteen runners on September 11.

The next day, Thorpe shut out Ivoryton, the Middlesex County League champions, 3–0, in ten innings on the road in a tight battle against Colgate star Paul Hopkins. Harold Horkheimer's two-run single and Steg Zetarski's RBI hit sealed the victory in the first of a three-game series.

The following Sunday, Ivoryton traveled to Muzzy Field, again using Paul Hopkins. The college star pitched well, allowing three runs on five hits, but

Armand Brooks pitched even better and caught a break in the ninth when an Ivoryton base runner wrenched his knee rounding third and was tagged out. New Departure, scoring one run on Reilly's triple and two unearned runs on an error during an eighth-inning squeeze play, emerged with a 3–1 victory and the sweep in front of nine hundred fans.

Hopkins would see better days as he went on to pitch eleven games for the Washington Senators and St. Louis Browns in 1927 and 1929.

New Departure closed out their season on a tear the next weekend against the Meriden Endees. Former New Departure star Johnny Moore returned to the Bristol lineup after completing his Eastern League season and played center field in the September 25 game.

Like the final Norwich game, New Departure needed a win to salvage a split with Meriden. Moore and Ben Reilly, the hard-hitting duo from 1924, provided the offensive fireworks. Reilly smacked a two-run single as New Departure took a 4–0 lead in the first inning. In the second, Moore singled and moved to third on Reilly's single before the two attempted a double steal during which both runners were safe.

Eddie Goodridge scattered eleven Meriden hits, though former teammate Eddie Zielke drove in a run with two hits, and New Departure's five runs stood up in a 5–1 victory. Moore finished 2-for-4 with two runs scored and a bunt single.

The Bristol club whitewashed an overmatched local team from the Ingraham Clock Company, 7–0, as Thorpe pitched a one-hitter. New Departure scored six times in the seventh and smashed four triples among their six total hits.

New Departure finished with a seven-game winning streak and won ten of their final twelve games to post a 23–12–2 mark. They took three of four from Manchester but split a four-game series with Norwich and Meriden. A fifth game against Meriden was scheduled for October 10 but was cancelled because everyone was more interested in the World Series and football, according to the *New Departure News*.

Thorpe's one-hitter against Ingraham improved his record to 11–4 while Brooks finished 6–4 and Goodridge won three games.

Ben Reilly led all New Departure hitters for the third time in five seasons with his .355 average. He stayed hot all year, never dipping below .350 and reaching a high of .395 in August, the company's newspaper reported. He collected seventy-four total bases with seven triples and two home runs. Goodridge matched the latter total, though his batting average sank to .274. First-year player Jimmy Malcolm posted a .316 average, and George Scott batted .304 with twelve steals, thirty-two walks, and thirty-eight runs scored.

Though lacking numerous special moments, the 1926 season at Muzzy Field remains etched in the history books for New Departure's historic win over the Pittsburgh Pirates. Never again would Bristol fans witness such incredible exploits by their semipro team.

# Closing an Era

At the end of the New Departure era, fans separated themselves from the traditional semipro teams stocked with paid players and focused their cheering efforts instead on homegrown clubs filled with local guys who worked at the factory.

In June 1927, the first stirrings of the Bristol Twilight League emerged when nearly a dozen would-be managers attended a planning meeting, "and the good spirit shown by them without question shows that there is a demand by the young men for such an organization," the *Bristol Press* reported. Later in the summer, the City League started play, too, with weekend games that often drew more attention than New Departure's.

Fans wanted rivalries between teams and players they knew well off the field, and New Departure's regional significance dwindled, though the team won twenty games in 1927 with many of the same names such as Reilly, Goodridge, Waters, and Scott. Norwich ousted New Departure from the state championship race with four wins in five games, three consecutive by beguiling and bespectacled left-hander Tony West.

Muzzy Field underwent significant changes with the early-spring construction of the Muzzy Memorial Gate that stands sentry today between wrought iron fences off of Park Street at the entrance of the ballpark. Made of Concord granite, the arch was a gift from the Muzzy family with an inscription honoring the deceased sons of Adrian James and Florence Muzzy. Prior to its completion, the local newspaper wrote that the structure would "add materially to the attractiveness [of] the field."

The field hosted a noteworthy ball game early in the season when the Philadelphia Giants attracted twelve hundred fans in a late-May contest.

Philadelphia had declined further in talent and featured none of the players from the previous year. New Departure blew an early 4–0 lead and the Giants scored two runs off of errors to win 6–5 behind the pitching of left-hander Dazzy Monroe.

None of Philadelphia's players can be traced back to James A. Riley's extensive *Biographical Encyclopedia of the Negro Baseball Leagues.* The Giants lineup included Johnson in left field with two hits and a run; F. Scott at first base and catcher with two triples and three RBI; Forrist in center field; Newson at catcher and right field; Norman at shortstop; Allen at second base; Dillworth playing right field and first base and hitting the game-winning inside-the-park home run to left-center field in the eighth inning; and Silvers at third base with two hits and a run scored.

Many of the biggest sports stories around Bristol in 1927 had nothing to do with New Departure baseball. Town leagues and local teams soaked up the spotlight, and Col. Charles Lindbergh's transatlantic flight turned everyone's attention to aviation. In July, Muzzy Field introduced its wildly popular Friday Night Fights amateur boxing matches as the newspaper devoted more space to local, regional, and national fights. And in August, Tommy Armour, the recent U.S. Open champion, paid a visit to Bristol to play in a foursome at Chippanee Country Club. Weary from a day and night spent on the rails between a tournament in Toronto and Bristol, Armour shot a six-over par but pleased the hundreds in the gallery by signing many of their scorecards, the local daily reported.

New Departure entered into the Connecticut State Baseball League in 1928 with hopes of reviving their fan base but only "after many weeks of indecision during which it appeared as though New Departure Manufacturing Company would sever its relations with baseball," according to the *New Departure News.*

The CSBL failed to excite the masses and many of New Departure's stars from earlier in the decade defected to the factory's entry in the Twilight League, which was managed by Swat McCabe. The low point came after a 16–0 loss by the CSBL team in August did not even appear on the sports page but rather among the social notes.

New Departure's semipro program finished 13–12–1 in the disorganized CSBL though it won the city championship over the new local favorites from the Maple End Athletic Club. By the next season, New Departure had become a local team finishing 7–5 to defend their city championship.

Meanwhile, a former New Departure toolmaker-turned-young-baseball-star, Johnny Moore, continued his ascent in the professional ranks. After more than three years with New Haven of the Eastern League, the club sold Moore to Reading of the International League in 1928 for four thousand dollars, and Moore ended up hitting .326 with fourteen triples.

He earned a late-season call-up from the Chicago Cubs, going hitless in four at-bats. In May 1929, Moore filled in for Hack Wilson against the Boston Braves and collected a single and a double, drove in three runs, and made two notable defensive plays. From there, his career took off, and in 846 games spanning 10 seasons, Moore hit .307 with 73 home runs, 452 RBI, 155 doubles, and 26 triples for the Cubs, Cincinnati Reds, and Philadelphia Phillies.

"The idea of making a living at the game never entered my head," Moore said in a 1932 interview.

He might have had even more staying power in the big leagues if he had been consistent at the plate, opined *Bristol Press* sports columnist Charles McCarthy in 1934.

"He's a very good outfielder, but as far as his hitting is concerned—well, you know the rest," McCarthy wrote as he reported Moore's tenuous position with the Reds in spring training. "Johnny will hit like a Ruth one day and then look like a semipro player the next afternoon."

Moore's historically crowning achievement came in the 1932 World Series against the New York Yankees. During Game 3 on Saturday afternoon, October 1, fans at Wrigley Field razzed Babe Ruth and threw lemons on the field when he came to bat, newspaper reports indicate. In the fifth inning, a lemon rolled to the plate as Ruth came up in a game tied at four.

"... In no mistaken motions the Babe notified the crowd that the nature of his retaliation would be a wallop right out of the confines of the park," John Drebinger wrote in the *New York Times* the day after the game. "... Ruth signaled with his fingers after each pitch to let the spectators know exactly how the situation stood. Then the mightiest blow of all fell."

Ruth's magnificent blast to center field became one of his most famous, a controversial moment whose veracity has been debated for decades. Eleven years after the game, Cubs pitcher Charlie Root addressed a high school assembly in Los Angeles: "When I got the first strike on Ruth, he held up one finger. When I got the second strike, he held up two fingers," Root said, according to a 1943 wire story. "When he held up those two fingers, the press box thought he was pointing to the scoreboard. Maybe it thought so only after he had hit the home run. I do not believe he called his shot."

Regardless, when Ruth hammered the pitch from Root, even Cub fans had to cheer the legend's theatrics. Not only did New York Governor Theodore Roosevelt watch the ball soar into the bleachers from his seat, so too did Moore, playing center field on that warm, windy autumn day, forever linked to one of baseball's legendary moments.

Later in life, Moore told author Richard Westcott that his view of Ruth's famous at-bat was inconclusive. "I can't say whether Ruth pointed or not,"

Moore recalled. "I know both teams were really razzing each other. Our bench was really riding Ruth, and he was answering them right back."

It was a moment that added to Ruth's aura.

Back home in 1930s Connecticut where Moore spent his winters working in a bowling alley and coaching high school basketball, Muzzy Field was adding different chapters to its history.

# 1930–1939: Of Football, Fire, and Females

The luminous history of Muzzy Field dimmed slightly in the wake of the stock market crash that precipitated the Great Depression.

No longer willing to plunk down extra money to watch a baseball game even if they had it to spend, Bristol residents watched the sport fade into irrelevancy inside the walls of Muzzy Field, or at least observed the continuation of the game played on an informal basis among townsfolk for a while.

One of the last hurrahs came in the summer of 1930 when the City League brought in $1,174 and paid out a 40 percent share to its champion, the Maple Ends.

In early June 1931, officials of the City League voted to discontinue its money-losing operation as disinterest among fans became a chronic problem. The local newspaper marked the era as the low point in Bristol's history for support of the game. Even the popular Friday Night Fights suffered, and Hartford promoter Tex DeNino followed suit with City League officials by announcing he was discontinuing boxing matches at Muzzy Field due to lost revenue.

At the same time, however, interest had been growing in the high school baseball program.

Guided by Thomas A. Monahan, the baseball team enjoyed a fruitful period during the Depression as two of their most decorated athletes were passing through. Albie Gurske and Andy Palau not only formed one of the most talented batteries in the state during their high school careers but they also infused the old West End ballpark with the type of excitement it enjoyed in the previous decade.

A multiple-sport star at Bristol High School, Andy Palau made a name for himself as quarterback of the Fordham Rams behind the famed Seven Blocks of Granite before signing a contract with the New York Yankees and spending several years in minor league baseball. (Courtesy: Bristol Public Library)

The town's most popular diversion soon became the BHS Maroons as the baseball and football teams both ascended to the top of the state rankings by the time Gurske and Palau graduated.

The spring of 1931 was the first instance. Monahan's boys posted a 13–1 record and won the Central Connecticut Interscholastic League championship. In the process of compiling the best record in school history, Palau's .371 average and twenty-three hits paced the team, and he never struck out in sixty-two at-bats. Gurske finished 9–1 on the mound with 7 complete games, 73 strikeouts, and 17 walks in $79^{1}/_{3}$ innings. The team avenged their lone loss to South Manchester by taking the second game of the doubleheader.

Joseph "Sugar" Hugret was one of Bristol's most notable athletes. He
attended New York University after high school and played end for the
powerful Violet teams under head coach Chick Meehan in the late 1920s
and early 1930s. He later returned to the Bristol area and became
involved in West End Athletic Club football and other semipro teams.
(Courtesy: Bristol Public Library)

After spending the summer with area baseball teams in amateur leagues, Gurske and Palau came together in August for the start of football workouts. The Maroons' gridiron season proved as successful as their baseball campaign, and football in general caught hold of Bristol's sporting public like never before.

By the start of the 1931 season, the city boasted nine teams in addition to the high school squad and some junior league teams that were supported by the major athletic clubs such as the North Sides, West Ends, and Maple Ends. If the local programs failed to satiate the football appetite, plenty of stories in the *Bristol Press* updated everyone on Joseph "Sugar" Hugret, a six-foot-two, 184-pound standout end at New York University who predated Gurske and Palau at BHS and brought accolades to the high school for his exploits on the football field and basketball court.

At this point, football was becoming Muzzy Field's most popular sport in the 1930s and would offer more historically significant moments in the decade than any other sport. Fans' willingness to support the game allowed promoters to bring in several higher-priced attractions, and one of the most memorable games played during the time was a result of Palau's personal connections in college.

But Palau was just beginning his high school career, working hard to become the regular starting quarterback in 1931. Gurske staked his claim as a young, reliable running back. His four touchdowns in the opening game set the tone for an undefeated season in which the Maroons outscored opponents 250–36 in nine games, which included two exhibition contests, and clinched the CCIL championship.

Culmination came in November against Torrington, a game that was played to benefit a community relief fund for the unemployed of Bristol. A reported crowd of twenty-five hundred jammed into Muzzy Field to watch the hometown school score a 26–0 win, and the fans raised seven hundred dollars in the process.

Meanwhile, the West End, North Side, and Maple End football teams emerged as the class of the city, but the Westies, who had a long history of playing football in Bristol, maintained their stranglehold on the city title by knocking off the other two clubs by 13–0 scores in November and attracting approximately fifteen hundred in the process.

The focus on local attractions continued to sharpen as several athletic clubs emerged in the city during the Depression, and the baseball season soon spread to other facilities including the East Bristol Recreation Grounds and Page Park.

◆    ◆    ◆

Muzzy Field remained the high school's domain, and the 1932 baseball team did not disappoint their growing legion of fans. The team racked up victories of 11–1, 22–0, and 22–6 en route to defending their CCIL crown and finishing as the state's only undefeated team at 14–0.

Palau and Gurske, who the newspaper was calling perhaps the best all-around athlete produced by BHS, again led the charge and scattered to local teams for summer play. While Palau enjoyed a successful campaign with a team in nearby Southington, Gurske continued his torrid pitching pace.

Suiting up for a team from Terryville, located a few miles from Muzzy Field, Gurske extended his 1932 winning streak to twenty-four games between the high school and summer seasons by the time he entered his senior year. His fastball, curveball, and changeup baffled batters as he posted double-digit strikeout figures on a regular basis—including sixteen in one game at the end of the summer—and tossed a no-hitter. In the championship game of the Central Connecticut League, which governed the association of local teams, Gurske pitched a four-hitter in front of twelve hundred fans as Terryville defeated New Britain for the title.

The struggling citizens of Bristol not only received a lift from escaping to the ballpark at times during the summer but they were treated to free baseball hosted by the Bristol City Twilight League.

New and interesting forms of entertainment arrived at Muzzy Field in early June when the Red Horse Ranch Rodeo hosted a three-day performance to benefit the city's unemployed. Horses and cattle were set up in temporary stables several days before opening night on June 2, and the rodeo attracted its share of superstars in the sports of bronco bustin', trick riding, and championship roping.

Fog Horn Clancy was the manager in charge of the event and also served as announcer and later as rodeo historian. He brought with him to Bristol cowboy Tex Slocum, Pearl Biron of Chandler, Arizona—called "the sweetheart of the rodeo"—along with world champion all-around cowgirl Claire Thompson of Fort Worth, Texas, Ted Harmon, Thelma Warner, Candy Hammer, Ed Harney, Boo LeDeaux, Ray Larson, Poncho Villa, Cletes McCoy, and Art Mix.

Albie Gurske, a powerful running back, followed Andy Palau to Fordham after a year of prep school. His prowess on the pitching mound, however, etched him into Muzzy Field's rich history. (Courtesy: Bristol Public Library)

Decades later, Clancy and Slocum were inducted into the Rodeo Hall of Fame of the National Cowboy & Western Heritage Museum in Oklahoma City.

By all accounts, the rodeo was a success, though no firm attendance figures were published in the newspaper.

Football season again arrived with fanfare.

In 1932, Muzzy Field offered a different fan experience when the goalposts were relocated behind third base with the gridiron extending into right field as opposed to goalposts behind first base and the gridiron stretching into left-center field. The change was enacted to allow fans the opportunity to stay dry in the grandstands while watching games played in the rain and snow, the newspaper reported.

Hugret remained in the local football mix by lending his coaching services to both the high school and West End Athletic Club teams before he departed for Farmingdale, New York, site of NYU's fall camp.

His input obviously did not hurt. WEAC opened their campaign with a 52–0 drubbing of Terryville at Muzzy Field.

The Maple End club attracted the first notable opponent when the Hartford Colored Giants, financed by the Dunbar Athletic Club, arrived with a team of collegians and semipro players in early October. Featuring end Ed "Snowball" Glover, an all-city performer in Washington, D.C., and a "rangy, deadly tackler," and fullback Dave Donaldson from Livingston College, who "hits the line with tremendous force and uses his head as a battering ram," the Giants were to provide a stern test for the Maple Ends.

But coach John "Quinnie" McLaughlin had the Bristol club ready for action, and two of his star players, Bob Greene and Jim Kane, scored two touchdowns apiece as the Maple End passing attack overwhelmed the Giants, 38–0.

The game was not the only excitement in town. In East Bristol, Pons Field on King Street was christened in a Northside Athletic Club-Meriden Trunkline game. The event was notable mainly because Meriden resident and future Hall of Fame pitcher Big Ed Walsh, who won two games for the Chicago White Sox 1906 World Series championship team, traveled with the team and stayed briefly. Several years later, Walsh made it over to Muzzy Field.

With local teams faring well, an early October game between the Northsides and West Ends attracted twenty-five hundred fans at Muzzy Field. The Northsiders were considered the class of Bristol, but the venerable Westies disposed of them, 19–0, behind two touchdowns from halfback Ben "Twirler" Phelps.

WEAC followed it up the next weekend with a 12–0 road win against the Middletown Sons of Italy, a game marred by fistfights among players and female spectators.

The Maple Ends and high school also continued their winning ways. By the end of October, the high schoolers, captained by Gurske, won their third consecutive conference championship and had only one tie during that span. The title-clinching game, a 31–6 win at Muzzy Field, featured three touchdowns from Gurske and four conversion kicks from Palau. The team's winning streak reached fourteen games before a loss in November at Torrington in Palau's and Gurske's final game.

More attention, however, was focused on the WEAC club. A game against the Thomaston Ponies on October 23 provided Bristol fans the first opportunity to see a team that long had been considered the class semipro football club of Connecticut, having secured six consecutive state championships entering the 1932 season.

Their coach was Francis T. "Fay" Vincent, former Yale standout and team captain at his tackle position. When Vincent was not coaching linemen for the Yale junior varsity, he worked at the Meriden branch of Connecticut Light & Power Company. Fresh from his college days in New Haven, he was six years away from the birth of his son, Fay Jr., who became Major League Baseball's eighth commissioner in 1989 after many years as an entertainment lawyer and corporate executive.

Thomaston also featured 6–1 end Leo "Special Delivery" Smith, who had been a three-sport performer at Providence College. With Thomaston's tradition and WEAC's early-season success, the game attracted statewide attention.

Everything lived up to the hype. In front of twenty-five hundred "wild and wooly" fans at Muzzy Field, WEAC and Thomaston battled valiantly for four quarters, and Thomaston eventually suffered the losses of Smith to a knee injury and other key players, Joe Sevigny and Louie Bristol. Before he left the game, Smith caught a forty-yard touchdown pass from Mickey Fill for a 6–0 lead in the first quarter but the conversion failed.

Phelps led WEAC down the field in the second quarter and tied the game with a two-yard touchdown plunge. A delay of game penalty, however, pushed back the conversion attempt five yards and also failed, leaving the game tied at six.

The final two quarters netted points for neither side. WEAC, which was lighter than their opponent, gained a certain amount of pride for their performance against the powerful Ponies, which newspaper accounts admitted "appeared to be weak" due to losing players to injury.

In the end, Vincent never took a snap in the game.

The members of the semipro teams that filtered through Bristol were talented in their own ways. Some were former college stars who desired some extra money on the side; others were former high school players who wished to play the game on the weekends as long as possible.

Johnny Grip was a two-hundred-pound halfback who signed with the Maple Ends in late October. A standout at New Britain (CT) High School and later at Fordham, Grip played one season with the New York Giants football team, "but he soon got out of the pro game to get established in business," the local newspaper declared. Grip was the type of player who, in the early days of professional football, could make a better living in the business world than on the football field and so found his niche with the countless town teams and athletic clubs that existed in Connecticut, New England, and throughout the country.

As WEAC continued their steady and, at times, noteworthy season—including a scoreless tie in front of fifty-five hundred fans at Torrington in mid-November—excitement built rapidly as fans anticipated a second meeting against Thomaston.

On November 20, WEAC and Thomaston battled again on the Muzzy Field grass, this time in front of four thousand fans. WEAC's defense displayed a supreme resistance to Thomaston's line plunges and passes and held the Ponies to just two first downs in the game. Meanwhile, running back George Alexander provided WEAC all necessary scoring with two touchdowns in the 12–0 victory, staking the Bristol club to their claim at the top of the state.

The championship was elusive, however. After a Thanksgiving Day win in the mud on November 24, WEAC turned around on Sunday, November 27, and played at Torrington, where they fell, 16–0. That same day, the Maple Ends rounded out their season with a 7–0 win at Muzzy Field against Middletown as Hugret, who had injured his knee for NYU earlier in the season, returned home to log time at right halfback for the victors.

WEAC's season ended in brighter spirits. On December 4, the New Haven Annex—a team that had won all nine games against semipro competition, outscored their opposition 159–0, and lost their only game on Thanksgiving against the Providence Steam Roller—showed up at Muzzy Field with a dominating track record and star players from Michigan, Villanova, and Providence, only to be thwarted, 12–0, by a WEAC team that triumphed with second-quarter touchdown runs from Phil Alexander and Albert Mastrobattisto, the latter of whom added a fifty-yard interception return.

Football had exploded in popularity among Bristol fans during the 1932 season, and Muzzy Field had only begun the initial chapters of its impressive historical relationship with the sport.

◆      ◆      ◆

The spring of 1933 provided a continuation of story lines involving Gurske and Palau. After the duo led the high school basketball team to state and New England championships, they returned to the diamond where they again captured the conference championship. Gurske ran his winning streak on the mound to twenty-nine games while the team won thirty-two straight.

On Memorial Day weekend, a stellar matchup at Muzzy Field pitted the high school team against Hillhouse High School of New Haven, featuring Joe Frank Wood, son of Smoky Joe Wood. The senior Wood spent 11 seasons in the major leagues, winning 117 games from 1908 to 1920 and contributing mightily to World Series championship teams from the Boston Red Sox (1912) and Cleveland Indians (1920).

The younger Wood debuted in the major leagues during World War II, pitching in three games for the 1944 Red Sox with no wins and one loss.

As a high school pitcher in 1933, Wood reportedly wore his father's red-striped stockings from the 1912 World Series in the game against Bristol. Hillhouse also had a Major League Baseball connection through their coach, Emmons "Chick" Bowen, who appeared in three games with the 1919 New York Giants after a notable career at Holy Cross.

With Gurske and his team riding high for several years, the eagerly anticipated encounter against Hillhouse proved its worth to the fans. Bristol's defense, however, played sloppily and committed five errors. Though Gurske struck out fourteen batters and scattered five hits, Hillhouse posted three quick runs in the first inning off of two errors.

From there, Wood turned in a solid performance with eight strikeouts and seven hits surrendered, one of them an Andy Palau home run to the cinder track in right-center field. Bristol never crossed the plate again, and Hillhouse ended all winning streaks with a 4–1 triumph.

Because the game was received so well by the fans, the teams agreed to meet seventeen days later at Muzzy Field with proceeds going toward Bristol mayor Joe Dutton's Relief Fund for struggling families. Between the Hillhouse games, Gurske remained his dominating self, crafting a no-hitter with thirteen strikeouts in front of five thousand fans at New Britain and then tossing a two-hitter with fifteen strikeouts against the same team at Muzzy Field, where fifteen hundred fans showed up for the high school baseball game.

On June 17, a wet and muddy field at Muzzy greeted the rematch between Bristol and Hillhouse, Gurske and Wood, in the final game of the high school season. Gurske pitched another strong game with ten strikeouts and six hits allowed while Wood struggled with his control and walked five batters in just four innings of work. Bristol exacted a measure of revenge with a 3–1 triumph, and the two Bristol stars entered the summer season as members of the WEAC baseball team.

Palau had recently announced his intentions to matriculate at Fordham University to play football, basketball, and baseball with the hopes of catching a professional baseball scout's eye in New York City. Gurske would join Palau in the Bronx after a year spent at Iona Prep School.

Summertime baseball at Muzzy Field concentrated on two clubs: WEAC and a team sponsored by the Fraternal Order of Eagles. While the list of visiting opponents never mirrored those brought in by the 1920s-era New Departure teams, local teams started enticing a stronger caliber of out-of-town club, which led to more appealing matchups and increased gates. The Gurske-Palau factor also helped.

Off the top, F.O.E. contracted with a Hartford club whose roster included one Connecticut high school pitcher more impressive and dominating than Gurske. Seventeen years old in 1933, John Arthur Taylor was a recent graduate of Bulkeley High School in Hartford where he first played baseball during his senior year. At five foot eleven and 164 pounds, Taylor was a gifted athlete with a nimble and curious mind. His sporting interests focused on track in high school and later golf and bowling, but it was on the baseball field that he made a name for himself.

In his first baseball season, Taylor racked up 8 wins and struck out 102 batters, including an incredible one-hitter against New Britain in the last game of the year in which he struck out 25 batters and walked 9. He also hit .428 on the season and crushed a home run at Bulkeley Stadium that reportedly was the longest schoolboy home run ever hit at the now-demolished Hartford ballpark.

It was on the heels of that spectacular spring that Taylor arrived at Muzzy Field on June 24. Yet, Taylor never pitched in the game, a 10–9 victory for his Hartford-based club. The youngster was positioned in right field and finished a modest 1-for-2.

When he returned to Bristol in early August, however, nothing was modest about Taylor's performance. WEAC and F.O.E. had emerged as the top teams in the city, and WEAC signed Taylor as a pitcher for their matchup to decide the city championship. With his zippy fastball, a devastating overhand curveball, and changeup, Taylor toyed with F.O.E. for nine innings as he struck out sixteen batters, allowing just three hits, while working with Palau, his battery mate. Taylor also added a double in WEAC's 5–0 triumph for city supremacy.

Taylor never again played at Muzzy Field. With several months of spectacular pitching behind him, some teams were ready to invest in many years of similar performances in the future. The New York Yankees and Philadelphia Athletics both kept a close watch on him during his high school and semipro days in the Hartford area.

After a victory over House of David, Dan Jessee, head coach of Trinity College in Hartford, proclaimed that Taylor was worth one hundred thousand dollars to any club.

As the first black player in the venerable Hartford Twilight League, Taylor often was the only black player on Connecticut teams full of whites, but newspaper stories and discussions in 2006 with his widow, Estelle, never indicated any tension in those clubs.

As interested as the Yankees and A's might have been, the culture of the time kept Taylor in the Negro Leagues, and he joined the New York Cubans after owner Alex Pompez signed him. He finished 4–3 in the Negro National League as the Cubans captured the second-half title of the split season before losing to the Pittsburgh Crawfords in seven games in the championship play-offs.

"I remember [former Yankee general manager] George Weiss saying it was too bad Johnny Taylor was a black man because he would have signed him right away to be on the Yankees," the great Monte Irvin recalled in a 1997 interview with the *Hartford Courant*. "Yes, I can remember hearing Weiss say how it was just too bad."

It was not for lack of trying, however. Teams attempted to convince the light-skinned Taylor to change his name to reflect an ersatz Spanish heritage, but he refused. So in the Negro National League, which he joined as a nineteen-year-old and thus earned the nickname "Schoolboy," Taylor became a star.

He received $185 a month in 1935 and earned extra money in barnstorming games against all-white teams. In one such exhibition at Yankee Stadium, Taylor squared off against Dizzy Dean's All-Stars and pitched against Dean. A bloop single by New York Giant Jim Ripple provided the winning runs in the 2–1 decision against Taylor.

By 1937, Taylor was earning two hundred dollars a month and receiving two dollars a day in meal money. Off the field, Estelle described him as a trim, outgoing gentleman, classy in everything he did.

On the field, his shining moment came on September 24, pitching for a team of Negro National League All-Stars in the Polo Grounds against the inestimable Satchel Paige and his Santo Domingo Stars. In front of reported crowds ranging from ten thousand to twenty-two thousand, Taylor was fighting not only for personal validation in Paige's shadow but also for respect for his teammates' league, whose talent was considered inferior to Paige's team's.

Taylor responded to the situation with deadly precision. Working with his catcher Raleigh "Biz" Mackey, Taylor threw an historic no-hitter against Paige, inducing the final out on a grounder by James "Cool Papa" Bell, in a magnificent 2–0 victory.

"Johnny Taylor did more than achieve fame for himself—he performed a service for the Negro National League which is hard to estimate in any material way," gushed St. Clair Bourne of the *New York Amsterdam News* after the game. "With that right arm, he picked up the prestige of the league and hurled it higher than it ever had been."

During the 1937 Cuban Winter League when he won twenty-two games and fans called him "El Rey de Hartford" (the Sun of Hartford), Taylor suffered a costly back injury when he was accidentally hit by a streetcar in Havana. He never was able to maintain a level of dominance, though his career stretched into several more seasons. He joined the Pittsburgh Crawfords for four hundred dollars a month in 1938, earning a coveted spot in the East-West All-Star game.

He then jumped to the Mexican League where he earned six hundred dollars a month and from his team's millionaire owner, received a new suit for every shutout he pitched.

"I came home with 15 new suits," Taylor had said.

Pitching for Cordoba in his first Mexican League season in 1939, Taylor fashioned an 11–1 record with a 1.19 ERA and 92 strikeouts in 105 innings. He split the 1940 campaign between the New York Cubans and Vera Cruz in Mexico, posting a combined record of 4–8. He pitched exclusively for Vera Cruz in 1941, crafting a 14–10 record with a 4.40 ERA as the team won the championship; he did, however, suffer control problems with 150 walks in 190 innings.

From 1942 to 1944, Taylor served in the military.

Eventually, Taylor returned to Connecticut and pitched for the Savitt Gems, operated by Hartford jewelry store owner Bill Savitt. In another memorable game, Taylor toed the rubber against the Philadelphia Colored Giants and their ace Will Jackman. During a magnificent twenty-inning affair, Taylor got the better end of the outcome after striking out twenty-two batters and walking one, said to have been intentional, in a 6–5 win. He also notched a no-hitter against Jackman and the Giants.

By the time Jackie Robinson had broken the color barrier in Major League Baseball, Taylor was thirty-one years old and pitching with a bad back for the Hartford Chiefs.

"During his career he had all the skills necessary for stardom, but his lack of stamina inhibited him from pitching complete games," opined James A. Riley in his *Biographical Encyclopedia of the Negro Baseball Leagues*. "Consequently he consistently tired in late innings, with a correlating loss in sharpness."

Estelle suggested that he try to sign with a major league club as a relief pitcher, but her husband was ready to give up the game. He had various other interests in his life aside from his leisure sports. He went into the construction business with his father after baseball and helped build Hartford Hospital. Estelle left her own impact on the Hartford region health community, becoming the first black nurse at New Britain General Hospital.

"His joy was in refurbishing big homes and fireplaces," Estelle said. "He was such a perfectionist. He took us [with their four children] around to see his work. He was like an artist."

And though he relinquished his baseball dreams without any outward anger or bitterness about the opportunities withheld from him, Taylor carried in his wallet a small newspaper story that reported on the Yankees and A's scouting him during his high school days.

Like many of the black players who appeared at Muzzy Field in the days before Major League Baseball integrated, there was only so far that Taylor could go in the game. But before he passed away in 1988 at the age of seventy-one, he told a newspaper reporter that he was at peace with his baseball career and that the games he played, such as the ones in Bristol, contributed to the evolution of the sport.

"It's no good to dwell on the past," he told the *Hartford Courant*. "I like to think that what we did in the 1930s and 1940s by barnstorming with the white teams paved the way for the next generation."

What Taylor did on the mound established him as arguably the finest pitcher in Connecticut's history.

◆   ◆   ◆

In the spring of 1934, Bristol sports fans chirped more about the high school team winning their fifth state basketball championship than anything featured on the diamond of Muzzy Field. In fact, for the majority of the 1934 baseball season, there were few memorable highlights to withstand historical scrutiny many decades later.

As adopted hometown hero Johnny Moore reportedly was losing his Reds outfield job in spring training to former University of Georgia football and baseball standout Ivey Shiver, the WEAC nine were starting up another season in their old ballpark with news that the Bristol Polish American club also was throwing their hat in the ring.

Come mid-May, the difficult financial times and the proliferation of batters not hitting pitches squarely were precipitating local discussions about making it a felony offense for fans to keep foul balls that were hit outside Muzzy Field.

Though the situation never became that desperate, clearly there was no budget available to do much more than schedule games among local teams and rivals in the immediate area, with a couple of exceptions.

On the first day of June, the Bristol Polish Americans brought to town a team called the New Haven Chevies that were led by outfielder Albie Booth. The diminutive visitor, at five foot seven and 144 pounds, had earned quite a name for himself in the state and throughout the country for his fleet-footed elusiveness as a ball carrier for the fine Yale football teams of the late 1920s and early 1930s. Nicknamed "Little Boy Blue," Booth was somewhat of a local celebrity among the legion of Yale faithful in the Bristol area, and his arrival garnered much attention in the days leading up to the game.

Though he finished 0-for-3 with a run scored in his team's 6–1 victory, local fans cheered Booth's presence and asked for numerous autographs in his brief stay at Muzzy Field, the game itself lasting only sixty-five minutes.

Meanwhile, new athletic facilities constructed by New Departure off North Main Street were christened in early June and represented a shift in focus away from Muzzy Field. With one baseball field, two softball fields, and two tennis courts, Endee Field, financed mainly through the New Departure Mutual Aid Association, became the site of ND's Inter-Departmental League and a hot spot for softball, a game that was growing wildly in popularity for its more inclusive treatment of women and older men compared to baseball.

That is not to say, however, that women were not creating their own baseball history at Muzzy Field. While the heyday of the New Departure baseball teams of the 1920s also included women's baseball teams, the 1930s gave rise nationally to many talented female baseball players and traveling teams.

One of them, the All-Star Ranger Girls of Chicago, was started by women's baseball impresario Maud Nelson in 1927. Their appearance at Muzzy Field on July 6, 1934, stirred up no shortage of fascination and interest in the local newspaper.

"Girls, real girls, attired in the regulation makeup of full-fledged baseball players, and possessing all the characteristics of big league aspirants, make up this outfit from the middle west," the Bristol Press crowed rather incredulously, adding that the club presented "a natty appearance" with hair tucked under caps as they toured from Maine to California.

In 1934, the Ranger Girls signified the end of a fifty-year era that began in 1875 when the first team of women playing baseball for money emerged in Springfield, Illinois. Fifteen years later, a far more serious and talented group of women surpassed the mere novelty that defined early women's baseball. Dubbed Bloomer Girls for the knickers that they wore on the field, the barnstorming teams that traveled the country, often with sexually integrated lineups, became major attractions for many men's towns, semipro and minor league teams, including those in Bristol (Gregorich 1993).

Nelson, a team owner and manager who was vitally important in creating the earliest momentum and backing for these traveling teams, dressed her teams in traditional baseball garb by the 1920s and scouted the nation in search of talent.

The popular run lasted until the mid-1930s, and 1934 was the final year of the Ranger Girls, who arrived in Bristol with a stocked lineup. Softball, not baseball, was becoming an immensely popular sport among women and men because it was less expensive and less difficult to play, according to Barbara Gregorich, a women's baseball historian.

"No national organization sponsored baseball for women, whereas groups such as the YWCA, Catholic Youth Organization, National Recreation Association, Amateur Softball Association, and National Softball Association all supported softball for women," Gregorich wrote. "Three generations of ballplayers who had played the real thing watched in dismay as corporations and communities everywhere pushed women into softball," which often relied on just one outstanding player, the pitcher.

But the Ranger Girls were going out in style. Nelson, who often hired a band to lead the team and townsfolk to the ballpark, also attracted attention to her club with their off-the-field uniforms.

"They were the most showily dressed of Nelson's players, sporting cowboy hats, silky jackets, and flared skirts modeled after the Hollywood cowboy look," Gregorich noted.

For one member of the All-Star Ranger Girls, a reputation preceded her.

Margaret Gisolo, twenty years old, grew up in the coal mining town of Blanford, Indiana, playing baseball with her brother, Toney, a semipro and minor league player. When American Legion Junior Baseball started in 1928, the then-fourteen-year-old Gisolo joined the team as a second baseman and made an immediate impact upon her teammates and opponents.

In the Vermilion County championship, Gisolo opened the three-game series with a game-winning single in the twelfth inning for an 8–7 victory over rival

Clinton, which protested Gisolo's presence by citing the Legion rule that states "any boy" is eligible to play.

As officials considered the merits of the complaint, Blanford won the series before Indiana American Legion state official Robert Bushee announced that Blanford's upstart girl was suspended for six days. In the interim, Bushee convened with state director Dan Sowers who met with Major League Baseball commissioner Kenesaw Mountain Landis, whose leagues contributed fifty thousand dollars to the national program in 1928.

The three men decided that Gisolo's Legion career could continue on account of no specific rule provision that banned girls.

With the blessing of Landis, Gisolo continued her impressive summer on a team that she characterized as close-knit and highly cooperative. In a one-game play-off against the Terre Haute Blue Devils on July 6, Gisolo collected a two-run hit in a 6–5 victory and around the same time received an autographed baseball from Landis that read, "To Margaret Gisolo, With my very good wishes," according to Gregorich.

Blanford won two more games to capture the state championship before losing in the Indiana-Illinois play-off game in Comiskey Park in Chicago. Gisolo acquitted herself well in seven tournament games with a .429 batting average (9-for-21), ten putouts, and twenty-eight assists with no errors.

After Blanford was eliminated, the American Legion adopted a new rule that excluded girls from their program, a rule that remained in place until the 1970s, Gregorich noted.

Gisolo was not out of baseball for long, joining the Ranger Girls in 1930 and playing until 1934 before embarking on a decorated career in education, attending college at the University of California and New York University and earning lieutenant commander rank in the navy.

At Muzzy Field against the Polish American Club, Gisolo played first base and batted cleanup.

Eighteen-year-old Rose Gacioch of Wheeling, West Virginia, was a rookie pitcher/outfielder for the Ranger Girls in 1934 having earned a spot on the team after Jack Felton, president of the corrugating plant where Gacioch worked, watched her play some baseball for the factory team. Felton happened to know Maud Nelson and apprised her of this talented player in West Virginia, and Nelson signed her after a workout.

Gacioch lost both of her parents by the time she was fifteen and was living with her aunt and uncle when she joined the traveling team. At five foot six and

134 pounds, Gacioch was a self-taught pitcher who learned to throw a sharp curveball by hooking the ball between two trees in her backyard, Gregorich noted.

While Gisolo and Gacioch were the queens of the diamond, the Ranger Girls
lineup at Muzzy Field included other talented women and men. In fact, "of all
the Ranger teams, the one of 1934 may have been the best," Gregorich opined.

"On the East Coast, so many teams wanted to play against the All-Star Rang-
ers that year that Margaret Gisolo remembers a few days on which the team
played *three* different ball games," Gregorich revealed.

Team captain Elizabeth "Fargo" Pull of North Dakota started in left field;
Beatrice "Peanuts" Schmidt was a heavy-hitting second baseman from Kenosha,
Wisconsin; and Cecil "Montana" Griedl was the center fielder.

Lee Chandler, a pitcher and shortstop, batted third, which followed Nelson's
practice of placing a male player every three batters to even out the lineup, Gregorich stated. Other unknown players in the lineup were Kerns, who played left
field and second base; Ronalto, the catcher; and Flarito, the third baseman and
shortstop.

The Ranger Girls were a popular bunch and "generally amassed tributes, particularly for the playing of Schmidt, Gisolo and Gacioch."

Against the Polish American club, they took a quick two-run lead before the
home team tied it on a home run in the third; then leading 3–2 in the sixth, the
Ranger Girls allowed a single, double, and wild throw that provided the Polish
Americans' winning margin, 4–3.

An anemic box score reveals that Schmidt finished 0-for-3, Chandler 1-for-4,
Gisolo 1-for-4 with a run scored, Pull 1-for-3, Griedl 0-for-3, and Gacioch 1-for-
3.

After the Ranger Girls dissolved at the end of the season, most of the personnel retired from the game, including Nelson, as they were advancing in age. But
the young Gacioch had yet to reach the prime of her career. For ten years, she
played softball, a game she learned from former Boston Red Sox pitcher "Sad
Sam" Jones, and earned as much as fifty dollars for two days' play on the weekend, Gregorich noted.

When she was twenty-eight, she benefited from the formation of the All-
American Girls Baseball League and spent the next eleven years of her life becoming one of the most decorated players in that league while earning the moniker
"Rockford Rosie." She joined the league during World War II after hearing about
it while working in a Wheeling factory.

Her career began with the South Bend Blue Sox, but when she landed on the
Rockford Peaches team, her career blossomed as the club won four AAGBL

championships. She had been moved to the outfield in 1945 and set an all-time league record with thirty-one assists while also hitting nine triples and driving in forty-four runs. She had thirty outfield assists the next season and thirty-one again in 1947.

At thirty-three years old in 1948, Gacioch returned to the mound and posted a 14–5 mark with a 2.21 ERA as the Peaches won their first of three consecutive championships. She went 9–2 the next year and capped her finest individual season in 1951 with a 20–7 record and 1.68 ERA, the league's only twenty-game winner.

Gregorich's research indicates that the 1934 Ranger Girls team that appeared at Muzzy Field not only comprised important players of the Bloomer Girl era but also were a vital link to the significant baseball history created in the AAGBL.

As the baseball season continued, local teams provided all of the excitement at Muzzy Field, but women were earning their time on center stage, albeit in softball. Prior to a WEAC game in early September, the West End All-Stars battled the Northside Girls in a one-sided 14–3 victory for the West Enders. A week later on September 16, that same West End club conquered the Celtic Athletic Club women, 16–1.

Often these games served as precursors to the baseball games. The September 16 event preceded a WEAC-Celtic winner-take-all game for the city championship that attracted five hundred fans. WEAC won despite a base hit and run scored by Fay Vincent, first baseman that day for the Celtics.

Gradually, the football season overtook the sporting interests of the city, and the WEAC eleven were more powerful than usual, winning their first three games by a combined 97–6 score. Fans of the time apparently wanted to see closer games rather than cheering on a blowout victory for the home team because the gate began to suffer from the low caliber of opponents.

The road games, however, were nothing short of scintillating, and WEAC's performances at Thomaston (0–0) and at powerhouse Danbury (a 7–6 loss) near the end of October cemented the Bristol team as one of the most competitive in the state.

Sugar Hugret had rejoined the team that fall and emerged as a major factor in the return game against Thomaston on November 11 at Muzzy Field. The game was so important, in fact, that club president Rebelle Carpenter lobbied New Departure executives to give running back George Alexander the day off so he could play in the game. Apparently, he was persuasive.

In front of thirty-two hundred fans, Hugret threw a second-quarter touchdown pass to Phil Alexander while George burst across the goal line in the fourth as WEAC prevailed, 13–0.

They followed up the next week with a 20–7 home victory over the New Haven Boys Club as George Alexander scored two touchdowns in front of nearly fifteen hundred fans, and then disposed of the New Britain Blues, 9–7. On Thanksgiving morning, the Wallingford Walcos were due in town but ultimately backed out for unreported reasons. Their replacements, the All-Hartfords, were a tattered bunch who displayed "a putrid attraction" in which "intoxicated players combined with a frail line made the contest miserable," the local newspaper reported.

Much keener competition awaited three days later with another trip to Danbury and another close loss (7–0) that boiled down to a controversial touchdown pass that caused much irritation among Bristol faithful.

The 1934 season was to extend into the second weekend of December, but wind blew down Muzzy Field's center-field fence, canceling the game the day before it was scheduled and ending the season in anticlimactic fashion. WEAC finished 7–2–1 in one of their most successful campaigns to date.

◆　　　◆　　　◆

News from Muzzy Field in 1935 focused on the deteriorating fence. In late April a nearby rubbish fire spread erratically and soon ate away at seventy-five feet of the wooden fence, which had been used to keep out nonpaying customers or "chiselers." The fire was large enough that the local fire department was called to extinguish it at three fifteen in the afternoon, leaving the fence in poor shape and prompting local columnist Charles McCarthy to call for more wood to burn down the fence completely.

By mid-May, the fence still was wanting for repair and smudging the city's image.

"Without any question or a doubt the situation at Muzzy Field is certainly an eye-sore to the city of Bristol," McCarthy opined.

A game in early July was emblematic of the problem that took so long for the city to fix. When one thousand fans descended on Muzzy Field to watch a baseball game between the Italian and Polish clubs, only twenty-four dollars was raised; most of the spectators never paid to watch the game due to the dilapidated state of the surrounding fence.

Three weeks later, the city council and board of finance approved a chain link fence to be erected with white pine trees, measuring eight to twelve feet in height, to be planted just inside. Those trees remain today.

An exterior fence of corrugated metal coated with green vitrified clay, locked into concrete posts, would stretch down the baselines behind the grandstand. The total cost of the project was $5,825.

During the course of this discussion, an interesting point was made by corporation counsel Francis V. Tracy. He noted that the original deed to Muzzy Field stated that the park was to remain public and no person could be denied free admission if he insisted on not paying at the gate. Technically, attendance was based on an honor system, but overall, the citizens of Bristol, persuaded in all probability by city leaders and civic-minded folks, seemed not to press the legality of the deed and seek a free pass, despite a report in mid-August that people just sat beyond the nine-foot-tall chain link fence and observed the action.

The local baseball scene was only mildly interesting and often sparsely populated, though it included a unique game of baseball with players riding donkeys, a popular novelty of the time. That exhibition drew a reported 732 fans.

Citing the poor playing conditions at Muzzy Field and the high cost of operation, WEAC did not field a baseball team for the first time in many years. Arguably, interest was too weak to support a team from the city's oldest athletic club anyway.

Football remained the popular attraction, and WEAC fielded another strong club. With many of the same players and Hugret serving as coach, WEAC won their first four games by shutout while outscoring their opposition 91–0. The dominant start to the season set up another highly anticipated meeting with Danbury in what was quickly becoming one of the premier rivalries in the state.

Again, the game was hosted by Danbury, and again, WEAC lost a tight 7–6 battle.

They recovered the following week on November 11 with a 21–6 win over the New London Diesels in front of twelve hundred paid fans at Muzzy Field who watched Hugret catch two touchdown passes, one for sixty-five yards.

For the rest of the month, poor weather hampered the team, and on two occasions heavy rain and then six inches of snow postponed an appearance by the West Point Colored Cavalry, who made a sharp impression by showing up to Muzzy Field in their military uniforms.

There was discussion of a rematch with Danbury on the Sunday after Thanksgiving, but the teams' management squabbled over the split of gate receipts as

Danbury reportedly requested WEAC take 40 percent win, lose, or draw. WEAC officials would have none of it, and the teams failed to strike a deal.

On December 1, the weather was agreeable enough that the West Point Colored Cavalry could display their wares. Conquerors of Danbury the year prior, West Point fashioned an 8–0 record on the strength of their offensive backfield: elusive Hewitt Teabout, who averaged ten yards a carry, Okie Boone, a bruising two-hundred-pound fullback, and another talented runner, Frank Caesar. With their passing attack, however, WEAC rendered West Point powerless and emerged with a surprisingly easy 47–0 win in the final game of the season.

◆　　◆　　◆

The financial problems that prevented WEAC from fielding a baseball team in 1935 befell the Polish American club in 1936. People simply did not care for semipro baseball as they once had in Bristol.

Most attention on the amateur game was paid to the Bronx where Fordham University enjoyed an auspicious start to their season due in part to the talented local duo of Andy Palau and Albie Gurske. Palau was batting .398 for Fordham by early June and earned a tryout with the Detroit Tigers, though he reportedly said he would not sign until he graduated. Gurske, meanwhile, overcame his wildness and fanned fourteen New York University batters in late May for his first varsity win.

Still, several memorable and historic baseball moments took place on the Muzzy Field diamond. First was the appearance of a semipro team from Hoboken, New Jersey.

Providing the opposition in WEAC's home opener on May 24, Hoboken's lineup featured Buck Wingo, a one-armed right fielder. Field manager George Scott's charges lost the game, 8–3, but it was Wingo's performance, nearly ten years before one-armed outfielder Pete Gray made headlines with the St. Louis Browns, that was most noteworthy.

In front of a sparse crowd of 350 paid fans, Wingo went 1-for-3 with an RBI and stopped cold a WEAC rally with a "spectacular shoe-string catch" in the fourth inning, which earned him a "tremendous ovation" from the appreciative Bristol fans.

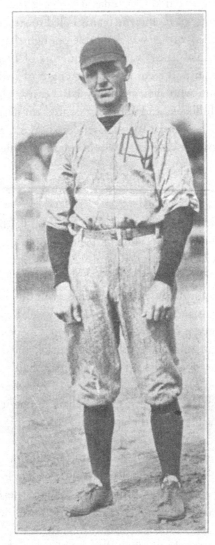

Catcher Waters.

Clyde Waters, who played minor league baseball in New Haven before
1919, was considered one of the finest semipro catchers in the region
when he joined New Departure. (Courtesy: Bristol Public Library)

On June 4, WEAC made history as participants in the first night game in
Muzzy Field history. The Connecticut Nighthawks of Winsted, the only semipro

team in the state to use lights, took a page from the House of David and carried around their own portable lighting system to attract paying customers not only for the novelty of night baseball but also for the intrigue of rarely seen technology. Playing games against the Eastern League teams in Hartford and New Haven, the Nighthawks' motorcade included a mammoth truck that hauled their 100,000-watt generator, a 250-horsepower gas engine cooled by a special radiator, and several sets of lights mounted on 50-foot poles to be placed around the field.

Though attendance at Muzzy Field's first night game, which started at 8:45 PM, was unreported, the spectacle provided much excitement in the local paper. Apparently, the WEAC players took some time to adjust to the nocturnal side of the game as none of them had ever before played at night. They surrendered ten runs in the first inning to the Nighthawks and committed five errors. But the team eventually found their stride and nearly completed an amazing comeback until George Scott, who hit a home run in the game, and his scrappy players used up their outs before falling, 11–8.

Local fans received another treat at the end of June.

Many of the big-name players from the New Departure clubs in the 1920s lived in the area and agreed to get together for a game against the Yesteryear Stars, whose lineup was filled with former major leaguers.

The local side was dotted with the ballplayers whose names elicit so many memories of fantastic baseball moments at Muzzy Field: Clyde Waters, Eddie Goodridge, Gus Forslund, Smoke Halbach, Eddie Zielke, Les Lanning, George Scott, and Swat McCabe, who was coaching the Celtics Athletic Club baseball team that summer.

The Yesteryear Stars featured team captain John Michael Henry, who at seventy-seven was reportedly the oldest active ballplayer in the world. Henry spent parts of four seasons in the National League and American Association from 1884 to 1890. He logged sixty games with the Cleveland Blues, Baltimore Orioles, Washington Nationals, and New York Giants.

Art Nichols, who played six seasons with the Chicago Orphans and St. Louis Cardinals, was a sixty-five-year-old center fielder on the team.

But it was Meriden resident and World Series champion Big Ed Walsh who garnered the most attention. At fifty-five years of age, Walsh was ten years away from his induction into the Baseball Hall of Fame in Cooperstown after winning 195 games and striking out 1,736 batters in a 14-year career, mainly with the Chicago White Sox, as arguably the greatest spitball pitcher of all time.

In the White Sox's 1906 championship season that culminated with a cross-town World Series against the Cubs, Walsh compiled a 17–11 mark and 1.88 ERA. He tossed a 2-hit gem in Game 3 of the World Series, striking out 12 against a team that had compiled an astounding 116–36 record and scored 705 runs during the regular season. He came back two days later and pitched six innings for the victory as the White Sox outlasted the Cubs on their way to winning the Series, 4–2.

Walsh posted even more impressive individual statistics in ensuing seasons. He went 40–15 with 269 strikeouts, 42 complete games in 49 starts, and 11 shutouts in 1908, and he posted a career-low 1.27 ERA in 1910, the last of 5 consecutive seasons in which he posted an ERA under 2.00. He won twenty-seven games in both 1911 and 1912 before a dead arm eventually ended his major league playing career. From 1913 to 1917, he pitched in just thirty-three games, logging 2,965 innings in his career.

Walsh's 1.82 career ERA is considered the lowest of all time, though the number was not considered an official statistic until 1913.

Eight hundred fans showed up to watch Walsh battle Lanning at Muzzy Field on June 28, a day when Walsh was honored with a silver cup presented by the hosts for his service to the game.

Both teams made decent showings. The New Departure Oldies collected thirteen hits off of Walsh, who also struck out four and walked four more. Lanning, who got a hit off of Walsh, struck out five, walked five, and surrendered seven hits, one of them to Walsh. Henry started in left field and finished 0-for-2 and Nichols went 0-for-1.

New Departure, on the strength of their brightest former stars, outlasted the opposition, 9–3.

Prior to that contest, WEAC notched a win over Sanitary Laundry of Southington, 3–2, as the Fordham boys, Gurske and Palau, formed the WEAC battery with Gurske striking out six; both went 0-for-2 at the plate. In his next start, Gurske tossed a complete-game four-hitter, allowing one run as he was putting together another solid summer season.

To gauge how popular softball was becoming, the New Departure women's softball team scored a 15–0 decision over the Ingraham Clock women's softball team on July 14 in front of seven hundred fans, just one hundred fewer than what showed up to watch former major leaguers, albeit aged, two weeks prior.

But baseball regained center stage in September when a three-game series for the city championship was played between WEAC and the Celtics. A fiercer baseball rivalry within Bristol had not existed. Though Gurske and Palau were due back to Fordham for classes and football practice, they received special releases from head coach Jim Crowley to participate in the series, including missing an exhibition against the New York Giants to play Game 2 on September 6.

Swat McCabe's Celtics had drawn first blood, 4–1, in the first game, turning the second contest into a must-win contest for WEAC. Gurske responded with a complete-game effort including ten strikeouts, no walks, and one run allowed on four hits. Both he and Palau collected a hit while Louis Laponte drove home the winning run with a triple to the edge of the cinder track in left-center field for a 4–1 win.

In the throes of such an exciting series, it is not inconceivable to consider that many of the fans and players spent that late summer evening after the game listening to the soulful sounds of famed jazz pianist Fats Waller emanate from the Lake Compounce band shell.

Bristol once again embraced the game of baseball in a way that it had not in many years. "Not since the halcyon days of Joe Carroll's original New Departures has Bristol fandom taken its baseball serious," the city's newspaper crowed. More than thirteen hundred fans jammed Muzzy Field on Sunday afternoon for Game 3, many hopeful that Gurske could replicate his performance on the mound and secure the city championship for WEAC.

Though reportedly banged up in football practice that week, Gurske did not disappoint. In another complete-game outing, the bespectacled right-hander scattered eights hits, struck out eight, and walked one as WEAC prevailed, 8–2. Laponte, who had two hits, notched a pivotal two-run triple in the game and completed the 1936 season on his fourth consecutive city championship team after winning with the Celtics in 1935.

Palau struggled in the series, hitting just .153 with three runs scored. Gurske was 5-for-12 with two runs and two RBI, and Laponte went 4-for-13 with four RBI.

Soon after a grand close to a baseball season that peaked at the end, news circulated that the Mount Vernon (NY) Pros of the American Professional Football Association were scheduled for WEAC's football season opener, a portent of the home club's bolstered schedule.

They abandoned the idea of playing only Connecticut-based teams. Instead, club officials chose to follow the New Departure baseball model of the 1920s and bring in heavyweight opponents believing fans would respond in kind. It was a profitable gamble.

Mount Vernon featured Cliff Montgomery, the star quarterback and MVP of Columbia University's 1934 Rose Bowl champions that defeated Stanford, 7–0.

Montgomery spent time with the Brooklyn Dodgers football team after college but soon signed with Mount Vernon when that team offered more money. The Pros' lineup included other players from Eastern colleges such as Princeton, Colgate, Fordham, and New York University.

WEAC cast their regular lineup of performers, intent on maintaining the momentum of consecutive impressive seasons. Quarterback Arthur "Charlie" O'Keefe and his brother, Ed, a halfback, teamed with fullback Twirler Phelps, halfback Ed Saba, and star left end/head coach Sugar Hugret to form one of the strongest teams in the state.

Under Hugret's direction, WEAC attacked with a precision passing game, especially against Mount Vernon, and drove down the field seemingly at will. Saba threw a touchdown pass to Hugret; Charlie O'Keefe scored two touchdowns and converted point-after kicks; and Phelps added another touchdown in a 27–7 thrashing in front of 1,620 fans.

Roused by the hometown club's performance, Bristolites also kept close watch on the Fordham Rams led by Palau, now a senior quarterback. Gurske was a junior and second-string halfback.

The Rams stood among the top teams in the country in 1935 before a loss to Purdue and ties against powerful Pittsburgh and high-flying St. Mary's (CA) dropped them to eleventh in the national rankings following their 6–1–2 campaign.

The crowning achievement had been the traditional Thanksgiving Day battle against NYU. The Violet fielded a strong team in 1935, but Fordham shut them down, 21–0, in front of seventy-five thousand fans at Yankee Stadium. Palau emerged into the national spotlight with a touchdown catch, two interceptions, impressive punt returns, and strategic punting; for his efforts, he earned the coveted Madow Trophy as the game's MVP.

Not surprisingly, Fordham boosters and national pundits expected the Rams to challenge for national supremacy, and the cries of "From Rose Hill to the Rose Bowl" rang out across the Bronx campus in the autumn of 1936.

Meanwhile, WEAC was scheduled to play their second game of the season against the Newark Bears of the minor-league American Association, a team that reportedly had defeated the Philadelphia Eagles the previous week, 24–0.

But when WEAC jumped out to a 27–0 lead in the first quarter in front of nearly eighteen hundred fans, something seemed amiss. As it turned out, promoter Nat C. Strong, who had been on the business end of negotiating the Muzzy Field appearances of famous baseball teams in the 1920s, sent the wrong team to Bristol. As WEAC piled up the points on the imposters, to the final tune of 52–0, the club and their fans grew irritable.

Team officials reacted quickly, issuing passes for the following week's game against the Providence Steam Roller and demanding that Providence post a bond to insure their legitimacy.

Providence had been a member of the National Football League from 1925 to 1931 and remains the last team not currently in the NFL to have won the league championship, which they accomplished in 1928. Financial difficulties precipitated by the Great Depression forced the team, which had been established in 1916, to drop out of the NFL and cease operations. One of the team's original founders, Pearce Johnson, revived the name and operated the team as a semipro outfit.

This was the team that appeared at Muzzy Field, and Johnson was the man who posted the bond. Providence came to town on October 4 with Alex Pike, former Ohio State quarterback in 1934, leading the offense.

Assured of the Steam Roller's credentials, Bristol fans arrived thirteen hundred strong and witnessed a well-played tussle that featured a blocked punt by Hugret, two interceptions by the WEAC defense, and a stout response to the Providence offense on a goal-to-go situation in the fourth quarter. Hugret's block also set up a Saba touchdown, the only one of the day in a noteworthy 7–0 triumph.

Meanwhile, the day before, Fordham opened their season with a 66–7 pasting of Franklin & Marshall as Gurske scored three touchdowns.

WEAC's grueling schedule continued the next two weekends at Muzzy Field with matchups against the Stapleton Pros of Staten Island and the Orange (NJ) Pros, both members of the APFA. Stapleton got the best of WEAC in front of 2,413 fans when former Cornell star Wally Switzer scored a touchdown on fourth down in the 7–0 win; Orange had an easier time, winning 20–7 and handing WEAC their worst lost since 1932.

The hometown club brought in the Norristown (PA) Pros of the Keystone State Professional League on October 25 and hammered out a 26–0 win. Former Fordham backfield star Jack Gallivan scored two touchdowns.

Three days later, the *Bristol Press* announced that Fordham would appear in a benefit game at Muzzy Field the Sunday after Thanksgiving to raise money for a local toy drive. The only thing that would change those plans was if Fordham was chosen to play in the Rose Bowl in Pasadena.

Vince Lombardi was one of the cogs in the Seven Blocks of Granite at Fordham when he appeared at Muzzy Field in November 1936 for a benefit game between his Fordham teammates and the West End Athletic Club. (Courtesy: Fordham University Sports Information)

WEAC spent the month of November tuning up for Fordham and inflating their winning percentage. Following an impressive 48–0 victory over the all-black New York Blackhawks on the first of the month, the club followed with a rematch against the Stapleton Pros. In a physical battle on rain-soaked Muzzy Field, the Bristol team outlasted Stapleton, 7–0, on the strength of a seventy-yard touchdown drive capped off by Charlie O'Keefe in front of another strong crowd of sixteen hundred fans.

The victory avenged one of WEAC's two losses, and the club crafted a five-game winning streak through the month with victories by a combined 48–6 over town teams from Middletown and Wallingford. The latter provided the opposition on Thanksgiving Day, three days before the arrival of Fordham.

◆    ◆    ◆

Following Gurske's impressive opening-game performance, the Rams enjoyed a fine 1936 campaign. Crowley, one of Notre Dame's famed Four Horsemen, molded Fordham into a national power during his nine-year tenure that began in 1933, "Handy Andy" Palau's freshman year.

That class was a talented one composed of young men from New England factory towns and one undersized guard who later become a football legend on the sidelines: Vince Lombardi.

His teammates called him "Butch," biographer David Maraniss revealed.

The *Bristol Press* acknowledged the Brooklyn native toward the bottom of its pregame story. Lombardi often was an overlooked member of the team.

"No. 40 Vincent Lombardi, the right guard, is Fordham's work horse–steady and deadly effective on close-up plays," the paper reported, listing Lombardi at five foot eleven and 188 pounds.

Palau was one of his closest friends, often bringing him to his parents' home in Bristol across the street from Muzzy Field where Palau's mother gave him food. As the two friends grew into adulthood, Palau said in a 2004 interview that Lombardi visited frequently, enjoying his time with Palau and his parents, Helen and Gustav.

Lombardi was coming off a disappointing junior season in which he injured his shoulder early in the season against Vanderbilt and lost his starting job to Ed Franco. But the 1936 campaign featured sixteen top returning letterman and immense expectations, despite a difficult schedule that included Southern Methodist, St. Mary's (CA), Pittsburgh, Purdue, Georgia, and New York University.

Franco and Al Babartsky had been moved from guard positions to left and right tackle in 1936 to make room for Lombardi at right guard and Nat Pierce at left guard. The center, future Pro Football Hall of Fame inductee Franklin "Alex" Wojciechowicz, anchored the line with Leo Paquin and Johnny "Tarzan" Druze at the left and right end positions.

They formed a formidable line and on defense shut down the high-flying St. Mary's offense in October 1936, prompting Crowley to gush to the *New York American* that he had witnessed "the greatest defensive team" he's ever seen.

Based on that performance, Fordham publicist Tim Cohane borrowed a nickname he remembered from a 1930 Associated Press photo caption and inserted it into the game program the following week against vaunted Pittsburgh. Thus, the timeless moniker "The Seven Blocks of Granite," though not born that day, certainly was applied for posterity to the Fordham line and their stonewalling capabilities.

The Rams lived up to the hype, fighting Pitt to a scoreless tie in front of fifty-seven thousand at the Polo Grounds.

"Their attitude was typified by a custom the guards and tackles had of staring straight into the opponents' eyes during that long moment of tension after the opening kickoff when the linemen crouched, ready to spring into action when the ball was snapped for the game's first play," Robert W. Wells wrote in his biography of Lombardi. "There was no talk. There was just the open-eyed and menacing stare before the two lines crashed together, the opponents' flesh and sinew meeting the Rams' granite barrier. The Fordham stare was a psychological weapon that the players were convinced gave them an edge."

The offense was not shabby, either, with captain and fullback Frank Mautte working in the backfield with Palau, who told Maraniss that Lombardi's motivational exhortations in the huddle often forced Palau to tell him to quiet down so he could call a play. Fordham's attack centered, not surprisingly, on a shift-heavy scheme taken from Crowley's alma mater.

"As the quarterback in Crowley's Notre Dame box formation, Palau lined up a few yards behind center, then shifted to the left or right before the snap, often ending up behind the right guard," Maraniss wrote. "On many plays, he and Lombardi had the same blocking assignment, pulling out to double-team an opposing guard or tackle. Vin hit from inside, Andy the outside. Palau was 165 pounds, 20 less than Lombardi. Palau said Lombardi was a brilliant blocker, a determined perfectionist."

After the tie against Pitt, Fordham entertained Purdue at the Polo Grounds and disposed of the Boilermakers, 15–0; thinking a Rose Bowl berth in easy reach, the Rams got too cocky against Georgia the next week and played to a 7–7 outcome. Despite a 5–0–2 record, Fordham still had a shot at Pasadena if they could beat out New York University in the mud and sleet in Yankee Stadium on Thanksgiving Day.

But as the Rams ruined a good NYU season in 1935, so too did the Violet derail Fordham's planned trip west in 1936. Palau, knocked out of the game with an ankle injury, was not on the field at the end of the surprising 7–6 loss.

As it turned out, Palau was not the only Ram not playing at full strength that day. For several weeks during the season, some players were joining semipro teams in New Jersey on Sundays to earn extra money under fictitious names.

Dick Healy, an end for Fordham, told Maraniss that "several of the guys were hurt in the semipro game the Sunday before the NYU game. Ed Franco was hurt in that game. But they covered it up."

Palau corroborated the story to Maraniss, but exonerated his close friend.

He said, "Sure, it's true. Ahhh, jeez! It's true. Three linemen and one back. Can't say who. Not Vinnie. That's probably why we lost. Yeah. Ah, Jesus. Some of the players were banged up. And they were pooped and it's a shame. A shame! I was sure pissed off when I found out about it. A chance to go to the Rose Bowl and they screwed it up. Ahhhhhh!"

Though the Rose Bowl turned down the Rams, the Orange Bowl in Miami extended an offer, "but it would've been humiliating to settle for second best and Fordham turned them down," Wells wrote.

So instead of heading to Pasadena, Fordham readied for a trip north to Bristol for, ironically, a Sunday game against a semipro team. Actually, the first scheduled stop was New Bedford, Massachusetts, that Saturday, but when the team arrived in town, Paquin noticed that the game's advertisements touted them as the Fordham Rams instead of calling them the Fordham Collegians as they did in Bristol.

Paquin pulled the squad from the field in New Bedford where thousands of fans had come to see them play.

"We had no license to use the school's name and we didn't feel as though we should risk the chance and get tossed out of school," Paquin told the *Bristol Press*. "If they had advertised us as they did here in Bristol, everything would have been satisfactory."

Fordham's game against WEAC was the first college-semipro game ever played in Bristol, and the Rams arrived in town with three of the Seven Blocks of Granite: Paquin, Pierce, and Lombardi.

**THE SEVEN BLOCKS OF GRANITE**
**FORDHAM UNIVERSITY 1936-37**

Fordham's famed Seven Blocks of Granite included, front row, left to right, John Druze, Al Babartsky, Vince Lombardi, Alex Wojciechowicz, Nat Pierce, Ed Franco, and Leo Paquin blocking for quarterback Andy Palau. The three running backs behind Palau are unidentified. Joining Palau for the benefit game at Muzzy Field in November 1936 were Paquin, Pierce, and Lombardi. (Courtesy: Fordham University Sports Information)

Celtic club members opened their homes to the Collegians, and undoubtedly many, if not all, of them composed the record-setting crowd of forty-three hundred fans at Muzzy Field for the two o'clock kickoff.

Also suiting up for Fordham were left tackle James Lawlor, center William Cronin, right tackle William Ney, right end Healy, Palau at quarterback, left halfback Warren Mulrey, a right halfback named McDermott (who was either William or Frank), and fullback Joseph Dulkie.

The presence of WEAC left-end/head coach Sugar Hugret renewed the Fordham-NYU rivalry for one more week, and another familiar face was on the field that day. Clyde Waters officiated the Fordham-WEAC game the day after he worked the Army-Navy game in Philadelphia in front of one hundred thousand people.

For Waters, it was quite a weekend officiating Army-Navy in the years preceding World War II followed by Lombardi's appearance at Muzzy Field.

Fordham took little time to show their mettle and prove that they were not simply going through the motions. In the first drive after the kickoff, Dulkie sprinted thirty-seven yards to the WEAC twenty-eight-yard line before McDermott hit Palau with a twenty-seven-yard pass. Dulkie then bulled his way in from a yard out, Palau added the extra point, and Fordham led, 7–0, an advantage that held through halftime.

WEAC struck back in the third quarter with their efficient passing game when Charlie O'Keefe hit Jimmy O'Brien on a thirty-five-yard scoring play. A missed extra point, however, kept WEAC at bay, 7–6. Fordham then salted away the contest when Pierce intercepted a pass near midfield. McDermott then rushed down to the seven-yard line, and on fourth and goal, Dulkie pushed across another touchdown before Palau missed the extra point.

The precision blocking of Lombardi and two of the Granite Blocks proved too much for the host club, and the thousands of fans rejoiced the return of Palau. Little did they know that the smallish yet bulldog-tough right guard was to become a football immortal.

That night, a banquet was held at Cadillac Grille on North Main Street with Bristol mayor Joseph Harding, and the Fordham players received watches from representatives of the Ingraham Company. The season was complete.

Palau and Lombardi became inseparable in the ensuing years. When Palau's baseball career fizzled in the New York Yankees farm system, he took a job in 1939 replacing former teammate Pierce as football coach at St. Cecilia, a small Catholic high school in New Jersey.

The first coach he hired on the staff was Lombardi, who earned seventeen hundred dollars a year—not much, but it was more attractive to Lombardi than working on the waterfront for his father, working for a finance company's collection agency, or joining the priesthood, which were all considerations at the time. Lombardi turned to coaching and shared a boardinghouse room and king-size bed for $1.50 a week.

One of Bristol's most dazzling athletes, Andy Palau became quarterback of the Fordham Rams in the 1930s and close friends with Vince Lombardi, his lineman. After college, Palau gave Lombardi his first coaching job at St. Cecilia's High School in New Jersey at a salary of seventeen hundred dollars per year. (Courtesy: Fordham University Sports Information)

They developed a rivalry in chess and gathered empty beer cans after dinner and tried to outsmart each other with formations. Palau also taught Lombardi the basics of basketball so that Lombardi could take over the coaching duties of St. Cecilia's team (Maraniss 1999).

During Christmas break and off-season vacations, Lombardi was a frequent visitor to Bristol and the Palau family, Palau said. He was then a young man just starting his journey and was always receptive to a plate of Helen's pierogi.

"He liked my father's wine, too," Palau added.

By 1942, the two had parted ways. Palau, the college star, soon ceded the limelight to Lombardi, the onetime backup who achieved unrivaled greatness.

◆     ◆     ◆

Momentum generated by the sport of football carried over into the spring of 1937 when word circulated in late May that WEAC was negotiating a deal to bring the Brooklyn Dodgers of the National Football League to town that autumn. Aside from the crash of the Hindenburg and the lecture presented by writer and poet Carl Sandburg in the Bristol High School auditorium, the potential agreement with the Dodgers was some of the biggest news around town that month.

By this part of the decade, club members discussed football more enthusiastically than baseball, although WEAC did sponsor a baseball team and hosted a significant visitor in July at Muzzy Field.

In mid-July, the Hawaiian Good Will Baseball Club was scheduled to arrive in Bristol with one of baseball's most famous pitchers in tow—Virne Beatrice "Jackie" Mitchell.

Six years prior, Chattanooga Lookouts owner Joe Engel signed the local girl, then seventeen years old, to pitch in an exhibition against the mighty New York Yankees who were traveling north at the end of their spring session. The five-foot-seven, 130-pound left-hander inked the minor league contract with her father, Dr. Joe Mitchell, acting as her agent.

Six years before pitching at Muzzy Field, Jackie Mitchell of Chattanooga earned national fame by striking out Babe Ruth and Lou Gehrig in an exhibition game. Mitchell, who was seventeen at the time, is shown here on that cold and wet day, April 2, 1931. (Courtesy: Getty Images)

As much as the transaction was designed to attract fans to the ballpark in those lean times, Mitchell was no stiff on the mound. When she was about eight years old, her neighbor, future Hall of Fame pitcher Dazzy Vance, taught her how to pitch, and as she grew older, Mitchell developed a sharp breaking ball. In the weeks prior to her appearance against the Yankees, Mitchell attended a baseball school hosted in Atlanta by former major leaguer Norman "Kid" Elberfeld.

Her appearance on a cold and wet April 2 reportedly attracted four thousand fans to the ballpark in Chattanooga, and Mitchell warmed up in front of the right field bleachers while Clyde Barfoot started the game for Chattanooga, according to William E. Brandt's game story in the *New York Times*.

After the first two batters reached base, Mitchell was called into the game to face Babe Ruth, Lou Gehrig, and Tony Lazzeri.

"Without so much as powdering her nose or seeing if her lipstick was on straight, Jackie strode to the mound ..." the *Washington Post* reported the next day.

Her showdown with Ruth whipped the crowd into a frenzy.

"The Babe performed his role very ably," Brandt wrote, hinting that Ruth may not have been trying his hardest, though maybe the reporter simply was in shock of the outcome. "He swung hard at two pitches, then demanded that [the umpire] inspect the ball, just as batters do when utterly baffled by a pitcher's delivery.

"Then the 17-year-old lefthander shot a third strike over the plate. The Babe didn't swing, but when [the umpire] called him out he flung his bat away in high disdain and trudged to the bench, registering disgust with his shoulders and chin."

As the crowd roared, Mitchell prepared to face Gehrig. He went down on three pitches in stunning fashion, and the fans gave her a standing ovation that lasted at least ten minutes, Mitchell recalled to Gregorich.

After a foul ball on the first pitch to Lazzeri, Mitchell walked the third consecutive future Hall of Famer she faced and was subsequently pulled from the game as Barfoot reentered.

News of Mitchell's feat traveled quickly via the large gathering of reporters, wire services, and the film crew from Universal Newsreel. Mitchell became an overnight sensation, but baseball commissioner Kennesaw Mountain Landis quickly stepped in and voided Mitchell's minor league contract on the basis that baseball was "too strenuous" for a woman.

Not all of the press reports were favorable, though.

Ring Lardner, writing in the *Chicago Daily Tribune* on April 6, quoted then-Pittsburgh Pirate George Grantham in his colloquial column, "... a woman's place is in the home and a left hander's place is in the asylum and when the two of them is rolled into one, a regular ball player's place is in the bottom of the ocean."

The *Washington Post* weighed in piggishly on April 5, "Engel seems to have gotten all of the publicity possible out of signing this young lady, and the chances are that she will not be heard of again in baseball, as one of the Chattanooga sports writers said in his column recently: 'Jackie is a better cook than she is a pitcher, and I've never tasted any of her cooking.'"

Landis's ruling did not make Mitchell less attractive to traveling teams, and the press could not have been more off base. Though Mitchell was prohibited from competing in major league-sanctioned competition, she played with Engel's

Junior Lookouts against semipro and town teams across the country. Eventually, she joined House of David, earning one thousand dollars a month and playing with them from 1933 to 1937.

"The story of a young woman overcoming barriers excited people trapped in the midst of the Great Depression," Gregorich wrote.

Still, Mitchell was placed in demeaning situations, such as competing in donkey baseball, and often was treated as a novelty act. Mitchell eventually tired of the traveling baseball life and returned to work with her father in Chattanooga.

Her appearance at Muzzy Field in July 1937 quite possibly was one of the final games of her career, though there was no hint of the end in contemporary newspaper reports.

"My greatest ambition is to pitch in a World Series game," Mitchell was quoted as saying in the *Bristol Press* three days before the game. "That would satisfy me completely as far as baseball is concerned. After that I would be glad to quit the game and settle down as a housewife."

Mitchell and her drop balls garnered much attention in Bristol, and the girl who had always taken to baseball in the fresh air instead of music, dance, or drama, stood on the mound at Muzzy Field as a young woman whose legacy would long outlast her short career on the field.

The local newspaper reported on the efficacy of her pitches and marveled at her ability to juxtapose the grace of a lady. "She dresses more like a debutante than an athlete and always is accompanied on her trips by her mother or a woman chaperone," the *Bristol Press* noted, adding that Mitchell also "displays all the polished charm of a typical southern belle."

Six hundred fans showed up on Monday, July 19, to watch WEAC and the Hawaiian Good Will Baseball Club. Buck Lai, forty-two years old and speedy, captained the visitors, but Mitchell was the star.

Her appearance was fleeting, though. Similar to her historic duel with the Yankees, Mitchell pitched only one inning, and an incomplete box score reveals that she allowed no runs and no hits. Mitchell never recorded an official at-bat, but she nonetheless left her mark on the Muzzy Field diamond, rendering WEAC's 7–6 victory otherwise irrelevant.

The rest of the baseball season passed rather quietly, though Palau signed with the Yankees and was farmed out and Gurske returned to pitch a few games for WEAC.

August brought the announced hiring of Henry L. Brophy, newspaperman and promoter extraordinaire, as the new manager of WEAC football. He would play an integral role in bringing historically important football teams and players to Muzzy Field from 1937 to 1943.

One of the first had been booked before Brophy's arrival.

The football Brooklyn Dodgers had compiled a 29–50–4 record since their inaugural NFL season of 1930 and turned to new coach George "Potsy" Clark to rejuvenate the franchise in 1937. Clark had recently left the Detroit Lions organization after winning forty-eight games in six seasons, including the 1935 NFL Championship.

Unfortunately for Clark, the Dodgers had little firepower until Clarence "Ace" Parker, the talented Duke University All-American, joined the team in November. Through the first seven games of the season, the Dodgers averaged just a shade more than four points per game.

It was in these early stages of what became a 3–7–1 campaign that the Dodgers arrived at Muzzy Field, two days removed from a season-opening, 13–7 victory at Philadelphia.

Dodgers' ownership in 1937 included George "Shipwreck" Kelly, the ex-Kentucky Wildcats star who came from old money, and Dan Topping, whose foray into professional football predated by eleven years his part-ownership of the New York Yankees baseball empire. A 1971 *Bristol Press* account of Muzzy Field's history indicates that Kelly made an appearance in Bristol on game day, September 12, but there is no proof of that in contemporary game reports.

There were two notable members of the Dodgers on the field that day. Ralph Kercheval, who was in his fourth NFL season, was considered "easily the greatest kicker of all times," according to local reporters in 1937, and his legacy has endured such that he remains in the elite group of kicking greats. Reports of the time claimed he averaged fifty yards a punt for his career to date, was an accurate placekicker from fifty yards out, and booted a ninety-one-yard punt in the air. If true, his punt would rank among the longest in NFL history.

Another member of the Brooklyn club was six-foot-three, 231-pound tackle Bill Lee from the University of Alabama, captain of the famed 1934 Crimson Tide team that featured Paul "Bear" Bryant and Don Hutson. The 1937 season was Lee's final one with Brooklyn before he moved to the Green Bay Packers. "He is regarded as one of the great tackles of this era," wrote Stan Grosshandler of the Professional Football Researchers Association.

One notable WEAC player, right end George E. Mulligan, had spent the previous season with the Philadelphia Eagles, the summation of his NFL career.

Kercheval, who also lined up as quarterback and halfback, played an integral role for the Dodgers in front of four thousand excited fans at Muzzy Field. Aside from his kicking duties, the University of Kentucky alumnus caught a touchdown pass and threw one against WEAC as the Dodgers displayed their esteemed passing attack. With contributions from Lee, the Dodger defense smothered WEAC, never allowing the hosts inside the Brooklyn thirty-yard line.

The result was a 19–0 Brooklyn victory in a game refereed by Clyde Waters and umpired by Eddie Goodridge.

But the real news happened after the game.

At 1:20 AM on September 13, Muzzy Field groundskeeper Tony Rafaniello noticed flames around his beloved ballpark's wooden grandstand, which had been partially renovated with new planks three years prior, and immediately called the fire department.

Four companies responded to the scene, and "the place was a seething mass of flames when the firemen arrived," the *Bristol Press* reported. The intense conflagration was visible fifteen miles away and attracted a crowd of several thousand near the site. The town watched as its West End gem was devoured by flames that spat sparks wildly.

In the end, damage was estimated between $5,000 and $7,500, part of which was recovered from the grandstand's insurance policy. Investigators determined that the cause of the fire was an errant cigarette flicked away by a spectator of the previous afternoon's Dodgers-WEAC game.

The fire did not slow down the WEAC football season at Muzzy Field. Temporary bleachers for twelve hundred spectators were trucked in and the schedule never missed a beat. Next up was the Brooklyn Eagles football club, defending champions of the American Football Association, the league that included the Newark Bears and served as a minor-league feeder to the NFL. The Eagles also were the same team that in 1939 featured Vince Lombardi, who had yet to break into the coaching ranks.

Two days before the football game, WEAC officials announced that "Handy Andy" Palau was coming back to town to coach the club's football team. He had spent the summer trying to work his way up the Yankees farm system and would spend part of his off-season back on familiar turf in Bristol, though the Yankees forbade him from playing football. He kick-started the team by speeding up the offense with passes, laterals, and reverses, a nod to his experience in the shifty Fordham attack.

But against the Brooklyn Eagles, the offense got nothing going. The defense, however, shut down the Eagles, who featured former Lehigh halfback Harold Ock—who played one game with the Brooklyn Dodgers baseball team in

1935—and former University of Denver standout quarterback Joseph "Cowboy" Fena.

In the end, the teams battled to a scoreless tie.

WEAC welcomed the Stapleton Pros the following weekend, and the visitors' roster included Reds Weiner, a member of the 1934 Philadelphia Eagles. Weiner did not stick around long, though. He and WEAC guard Dan Harrigan got into a fistfight and both were kicked out of the game. Meanwhile, Chick Kaufman, a former Princeton player, suited up for WEAC and recorded a forty-five-yard interception return for a touchdown. Points came often for WEAC to the delight of two thousand fans who cheered the 26–6 victory.

Brophy's wheeling and dealing brought in two opponents from the American Football League, which was one of the more legitimate professional leagues competing against the NFL in the 1930s and 1940s.

The first were the Boston Shamrocks, defending champions of the AFL by virtue of their 8–3 record and the highest scoring team that year.

Scheduled for an October 3 game against WEAC, the Shamrocks arrived at Muzzy Field with a roster of college stars and several other players who had logged NFL experience. Ernest "Rick" Concannon, a former teammate of Sugar Hugret at NYU, played in twenty-five games over three seasons as a guard for the Boston Redskins while left halfback Swede Ellstrom of the University of Oklahoma played fifteen games in the NFL with the Redskins, Eagles, Pittsburgh Pirates, and Chicago Cardinals from 1934 to 1936. Left end Herm Davis of Birmingham-Southern played two games with the 1936 Cardinals, and quarterback Joe Zapustas saw action at end in two games with the 1933 New York Giants. Guard Jim Zyntell of Holy Cross also played with the 1933 Giants and later the Eagles, eventually competing in twenty-six NFL games in three seasons.

The Shamrocks were a stiff challenge, and the locals appreciated the opposition's talent. With another crowd of two thousand in the stands, WEAC found it difficult to slow the Shamrock passing attack after stymieing their running game, and the Shamrocks emerged victorious, 18–7, with Charlie O'Keefe accounting for WEAC's lone touchdown.

Boston ended their AFL season with a disappointing 2–5 mark.

WEAC took off the next week from the field but not on the business end of things. Negotiations were under way with the Los Angeles Bulldogs, the first West Coast professional football team in a coast-to-coast league that did not play all of their games on the road, according to Bob Braunwart's research for the Professional Football Researchers Association.

Crowds gather for another event. (Courtesy: Bristol Public Library)

The Bulldogs were formed in 1936 and played as independents. In 1937, they joined the AFL and ran roughshod through the league with an 8–0 record and an aggregate scoring differential of 219–69.

Bing Crosby and his fellow Hollywood star Joe E. Brown held 48 percent ownership of the Bulldog franchise, with the American Legion Council of Los Angeles owning the remaining 52 percent.

Under the direction of Elmer "Gloomy Gus" Henderson, the Bulldogs were arguably the strongest non-NFL club ever to appear at Muzzy Field. Henderson, who guided the Southern Cal Trojans to national prominence from 1919 to 1924, had former St. Mary's (CA) All-American halfback Al Nichelini on his roster. Nichelini, who had played the previous two seasons with the Chicago Cardinals, stood six foot and 207 pounds and was a feature of the Gaels' high-scoring attack in college.

The Los Angeles club quartered at Burritt Hotel in New Britain and practiced at Muzzy Field on Friday and Saturday. Their starting lineup on Sunday also included left end Malcolm Frankian of St. Mary's, who played the 1934 and 1935 seasons with the New York Giants football team; left tackle Steve Sinko of Duquense, who played the 1934–36 seasons with the Redskins; and left guard Peter Mehringer, an All-American at Kansas in football and wrestling who enjoyed a distinguished career. Mehringer, who learned how to wrestle through a mail-order correspondence course, was the 1932 Olympic heavyweight wrestling gold medalist, played in the first college all-star football game and spent time with the Cardinals prior to the Bulldogs. He also acted alongside Ronald Reagan in the movie *Knute Rockne, All American* and doubled for Bob Hope in *Road to Zanzibar* in his film career as an extra and stuntman. In 1983, Mehringer was honored as a Distinguished Member of the National Wrestling Hall of Fame.

Starting at center for the L.A. Bulldogs was Bernie Hughes, who played for the Boston Braves and Cardinals in the early- to mid-1930s. A player named Clemons was a right guard next to right tackle Harry Fields and a player named Moore, the right end. Robert "Poi" Miller joined Nichelini in the backfield when he was not kicking in his trademark barefoot style that he learned in Honolulu while stationed in the army.

Notable substitutes in the game were Bill Howard from USC; Gordon Gore, who spent the 1939 season with the Detroit Lions; and Bert Pearson, a lineman who played eight years with the Chicago Bears.

Los Angeles attacked efficiently with Miller and Nichelini "zig-zagging downfield" for touchdowns, the newspaper stated. The Bulldogs scored one touchdown per quarter, outpacing WEAC, 28–7, in front of 2,214 fans.

WEAC's first road game arrived the following week, a 7–7 decision against archrival Danbury, before the club recovered back at home with an easy 13–0 win over the New England Pros, whose roster included former Eastern collegiate players.

On November 7, the rematch with Danbury at Muzzy Field was scheduled, and 5,977 fans jammed into the West End ballpark for the highly anticipated meeting. WEAC struck in the first quarter after Wally Switzer, who had signed with WEAC in early October, returned a punt forty-eight yards to the Danbury two-yard line, setting up a touchdown plunge by Charlie O'Keefe for a 7–0 lead following George Mulligan's kick.

That score held through halftime. In the third quarter, Danbury's Fritz Petella churned across midfield on a fifteen-yard run, and before he was dragged down lateraled to Deke Pillsbury at the WEAC forty-five-yard line leading to a remarkable touchdown. Art O'Keefe blocked the extra point attempt to keep WEAC ahead.

In the fourth quarter, Danbury player-coach Jack Thompson shanked a punt into WEAC territory, but it hit an unaware WEAC player and Danbury recovered on the twenty-yard line in an incredible turn of fortunes in the game. Three running plays later, Danbury kicker Warren "Red" Negri booted a thirty-nine-yard field goal for the decisive points.

Danbury dominated the statistics, amassing 266 total yards (214 on the ground) compared to WEAC's 78 total yards. Danbury also gained ten first downs to WEAC's two. Following the unimaginable loss by WEAC, there was talk of a Danbury jinx. The Muzzy Field gatekeepers thought otherwise as their coffers swelled with the 5-cent head tax imposed on each ticket sold, allowing the city to make $298.85.

WEAC disposed of the Naugatuck Gems on November 14 to improve to 3–4–2, but fans clamored for another contest with Danbury. The Bristol club hit the road and were welcomed by a large crowd that saw them shatter any perceived jinx and register an impressive 19–0 whitewash of the powerful Danbury club, reportedly their worst loss ever to a Connecticut team.

WEAC immediately proclaimed themselves state champions after four straight years of finishing behind Danbury.

It was a fitting end to a good football season at Muzzy Field. Another Fordham game had been discussed but the university's athletic director, Jack Coffey, a former pro baseball player and longtime Fordham baseball coach, banned all postseason games and forbade players from performing with an outside team after the regular season.

Bristol football fans were forced to satiate themselves through the winter months with the memories of an impressive three-game series with Danbury and the most colorful home football schedule to date.

◆     ◆     ◆

Though the imported bleachers were a suitable stopgap in the autumn, Muzzy Field would not regain its identity without a grandstand, and even then, it was apparent by 1938 that it was the end of the wooden era.

WEAC football manager Rebelle Carpenter threatened to cancel the football season in early May, and by early August the newspaper reported that the city was seeking Public Works Administration funds to build a brick and steel grandstand. Mayor Joseph W. Harding and city engineer Carleton W. Buell estimated the cost at forty thousand dollars.

During a meeting in May, a special Muzzy Field committee estimated a steel and brick grandstand at twenty-six thousand dollars and submitted sketches of an all-steel stand from the Pittsburgh-Des Moines Steel Company, which came in at approximately twenty-nine thousand dollars.

The committee further suggested that the new grandstand be named for *Bristol Press* city editor Thomas A. Tracy, who died the night the grandstand burned down. The Parks Commission later approved the measure.

Few noteworthy baseball moments occurred at the field, save for Smoky Joe Wood Jr., a Yale freshman, earning a complete-game victory and driving in a run for his New Haven semipro team versus WEAC in mid-June. All other baseball news revolved around the minor league exploits of Andy Palau and Albie Gurske, both of whom bounced around the Piedmont League, Florida State League, Northern New York League, and South Atlantic League during the summer.

Softball continued to gain a foothold in the local sporting landscape, attracting participants far and wide.

"Having always considered the game a 'girls' sport, we were somewhat surprised to see some of our A No. 1 baseball players cavorting around the miniature diamond," columnist Charles McCarthy wrote in late August. "We failed to get a kick out of the proceedings ... Certainly softball has taken big strides around these parts this summer, but we would not like to see that game displace baseball entirely which some seem to think will happen."

Football reigned supreme in Bristol as the WEAC management attracted high-profile teams and fed the city's football appetite, though for some unexplained reasons, the fans did not take fully to the out-of-towners. The club also attempted to bring back Palau, this time as a quarterback because the Yankees had released him in June. But Palau, who worked on his master's degree at the University of Vermont while playing baseball in Burlington, had larger plans for the football season. He signed with the Union City (NJ) Rams of the American Professional Football League, a farm club of the Brooklyn Dodgers, in September.

WEAC did, however, add Jack Batten, captain of the 1936 Cornell football team and talented baseball player at six foot one and 189 pounds. At the time, he was working as manager of the Hartford Club before taking a position as a hotel manager in Bermuda. He died suddenly in 1940 of a kidney ailment at age twenty-five. The team also added 1937 Colgate backfield star Albie Burke, former Boston Shamrock back Bill Pendergrast, and former NFL and Shamrock guard Rick Concannon. Burke was the focus of preseason bidding wars between Danbury and WEAC, and shortly after WEAC announced they had secured Burke, they went out and signed 223-pound tackle Walter "Uzzy" Uzdavinis, a former Fordham player who spent the 1937 season with the NFL's Cleveland Rams. Though impressive in name, Uzdavinis apparently did not pan out on the field because he was fired immediately after the first game.

The strengthened WEAC eleven again hosted the Brooklyn Dodgers to open the season, and the Dodgers also were an improved team that would finish 4–4–3.

Brooklyn's major attraction was quarterback Ace Parker, a decorated three-sport athlete at Duke University where he earned All-American football honors in 1936 when he was a kick return and punting specialist. Connie Mack signed him to a baseball contract with his Philadelphia A's, and he played ninety-four games at shortstop in the 1937 and 1938 seasons while obtaining permission from the A's to try pro football in 1937.

Though his pro baseball career ended after he twice suffered broken ankles, Parker, a five-foot-ten, 178-pound dynamo, continued to be a threat in the NFL and won the league's most valuable player award in 1940. In 1955, Parker was inducted into the College Football Hall of Fame in South Bend, Indiana, and seventeen years later the Pro Football Hall of Fame in Canton also welcomed him into its hallowed halls.

At Muzzy Field in 1938, he embarked on his first full professional football season, and by kickoff of the September 11 game, Parker had gone through only three days of football practice.

Along with Brooklyn's usual array of former college standouts, Beattie Feathers joined Parker in the backfield. Feathers was an All-American halfback at the University of Tennessee where he scored thirty-two touchdowns in thirty games from 1931 to 1933. During his stay in Knoxville, the Volunteers posted a 25–3–2 record, and Feathers's 1,888 career-rushing yards stood as a school record for 37 years. His illustrious college career led to his 1955 induction into the College Football Hall of Fame.

As a professional, Feathers became the first player to rush for 1,000 yards when he accumulated 1,004 on 101 carries (a record 9.9 yards-per-carry average) and scored 8 rushing touchdowns in his 1934 rookie year with the Chicago Bears, smashing the previous rushing record by 267 yards. He also caught a touchdown and passed for a score during the season.

Playing in a backfield with Bronko Nagurski and Red Grange, Feathers and the Bears compiled a 13–0 mark as Western Conference champions before losing the NFL Championship to the New York Giants, a game Feathers missed with injuries. Feathers never again enjoyed such a magnificent individual season as he rushed for 980 yards combined in his final 6 years in the NFL.

The Dodgers roster at Muzzy Field also featured Ralph Kercheval, who entered the game as a substitute with Parker and Feathers. The starting lineup included Bill Waller, left end; Felix Dixon, left tackle; Gene Moore, center;

Andrew Barberi, left guard; George Stapleton, right guard; James Whatley, right tackle; Harold Hill, right end; Boyd Brumbaugh, quarterback; William Reissig, left halfback; Ronald Henderson, right halfback; and Jack Stringham, fullback. Brooklyn also used numerous substitutes throughout the game.

The two thousand fans in attendance that day were treated to an appearance by famed actress Arline Judge, who was the wife of team owner Dan Topping. Their party arrived by plane, landing at Bristol's airport across town, and once at Muzzy Field, "the distinguished Hollywood lady favorably responded to a suggestion calling for her to execute the first kickoff," a 1971 *Bristol Press* story recalled. "Just as she hoisted her foot in an attempt to kick the ball, off flew her shoe to the delightful reaction of a capacity crowd."

Not much else amused Bristol fans hoping for a home team victory that afternoon.

Parker proved an exceptional athlete, nabbing an interception and returning it seventy yards for a touchdown and recovering a fumble and returning it ten yards for a score. End Jim Austin of St. Mary's (CA) fell on another WEAC fumble for a touchdown.

WEAC's Batten got into the mix by intercepting a Parker pass and returning it for a touchdown, the length of which McCarthy described as 110 yards. Though certainly an exciting play for WEAC, regardless the distance, it was all they could muster as Brooklyn won, 20–7, a week before tying the Washington Redskins in their NFL opener.

The only solace for locals was an opportunity to dance to jazz great Gene Krupa and his swing orchestra at the Lake Compounce Music Shell that evening.

Ten days later, an unprecedented weather disaster hit Long Island and New England when a Category 3 hurricane dubbed the Long Island Express created a seventeen-foot storm surge and fifty-foot waves in Rhode Island and Massachusetts. Six hundred people in New England were killed—one hundred on Long Island—and eighty-nine hundred homes were destroyed leaving sixty-three thousand people homeless. The economic impact was more than six million dollars in 1938 figures.

Several people were killed in Bristol as a result of the hurricane and ensuing floods, and football was the last thing on everyone's mind when the Massachusetts State Police told the Boston Shamrocks not to make the trip to Bristol for their scheduled game on September 25.

Muzzy Field sustained no damage, and WEAC returned the first weekend of October to battle the Providence Steam Roller, which featured five former WEAC players including Ed Saba, Charlie and Art O'Keefe, and Phil and Dave

Couhig. Before the season, Charlie O'Keefe and the Couhigs reportedly told Manager Brophy that they would not play unless Saba and Art O'Keefe were given their old positions on the team. Rather than acquiesce, Brophy cut all five players, "but not without reluctances," the *Bristol Press* reported.

They were not unemployed for long, signing deals to compete with the Steam Roller, and Saba especially got the last laugh.

Tied at fourteen in the fourth quarter, Providence was on the WEAC one-yard line ready to take control of the game when the Steam Roller fumbled and WEAC's George Mulligan recovered. Backed up against their goal line, WEAC elected to pass their way out of the hole, but Saba nabbed a Burke aerial at the twenty-yard line and raced to the end zone for the decisive score in Providence's 20–14 win.

Also around that time, work on the new Muzzy Field grandstand started on the strength of city and federal funds.

The Waltham Pros of Massachusetts arrived the following Sunday, October 9, with coach Bill Hardy, a former Harvard captain. Reports on the team indicated a strong opponent, but WEAC rolled to an easy 32–0 win in front of 750 fans in the temporary bleachers. WEAC held Waltham to one first down, an indication that the visitors did not exactly show up as advertised.

It was after the Waltham game that the newspaper reported that local fans were requesting WEAC play only in-state teams instead of the colorful, yet often unknown, out-of-state visitors that usually defeated the home club. WEAC's management responded in kind with a scheduled game against the Naugatuck Gems on October 16 with former New York Giant Stu Clancy serving as coach.

WEAC struck quickly with a first-quarter touchdown pass from recently signed Wally Switzer to Burke before Switzer added a touchdown run and Batten scored later in the game. The 20–0 victory came before a healthy crowd of two thousand fans, and WEAC evened their record at 2–2.

Despite the Naugatuck turnout, attendance had been far from superb at Muzzy Field, and that could have been owed to the warm weather conditions and devastating hurricane as much as the lack of a proper grandstand. Still, when Danbury came to town, people paid attention.

A lengthy buildup to the Danbury game preceded the kickoff, and gates at Muzzy Field opened at noon, more than two hours before the start, to accommodate the rush of fans who were buying tickets. No reserved seats had gone on sale for the game, and five thousand fans arrived by the time the game started. If the public wanted natural rivalries such as Danbury, they certainly responded at the ticket office.

The game lived up to expectations.

Through the first three quarters, the teams battled to a scoreless tie and the anticipation grew in the bleachers. Those bleachers began to sway in the second half because of all the weight sitting on a soft area of turf, and one of Muzzy Field's most anxious moments was about to occur.

Sometime in the fourth quarter, play-by-play announcer Harry Ginsburg warned the fans to evacuate the overloaded, teetering bleachers, but not everyone was quick to react. After his announcement (newspaper reports said the time elapsed was at least thirty minutes), eight sections of bleachers collapsed suddenly, sending seven hundred people to the ground in a frightening fury. Fortunately, what could have been the ballpark's most disastrous afternoon was averted when only fourteen people reported injuries ranging from sprains to bruises, though one man went to the hospital for X-rays on his ankle.

"It was like an avalanche," Waterbury reporter Ken Alyta told the Bristol paper.

Once players ascertained that family members were fine, the game resumed, and Danbury was able to scratch out a field goal by Warren "Red" Negri for a 3–0 lead.

Burke fielded the ensuing kickoff and weaved through the Danbury coverage. He reached midfield and had one man to beat, Negri, but the kicker wrestled him down at the Danbury forty-five.

With inspiring field position, WEAC began moving the ball. Two passes to Burke positioned WEAC at the opposition's fifteen-yard line. Two running plays advanced the ball to the nine for a third-down play. Pendergrast dropped back to pass and had Hugret in his sights, but the ball slipped through Hugret's fingers. WEAC decided to go for the tie with George Mulligan lining up the kick, but he pushed it wide by a slight margin and WEAC endured another close loss to their rivals.

There was more bad news in the business office.

While the collapsing bleachers probably ratcheted the urgency for a rebuilt Muzzy Field grandstand, the overall reports from the gates also hastened activity. By the end of October, WEAC football was staring at a six hundred dollar deficit.

With two of their final four games on the road and no big-ticket opponents coming to Bristol, WEAC had virtually no chance of breaking even. The game on October 30 did, however, feature the Colonial Brown Bombers and left halfback David Myers, another former teammate of Hugret at NYU.

By the time the ex-Violets got together in 1938, Myers had become one of the pioneer black players in the NFL, competing in thirteen games with the 1930

Staten Island and 1931 Brooklyn teams as one of the first fifteen black players in professional football altogether.

Myers could not do much for the Brown Bombers though, and WEAC won, 20–0, to move their record to 3–3.

Another difficult loss at Danbury (6–0) was followed by a blowout win (40–13) in Waterbury in a charity game to provide Thanksgiving and Christmas baskets to needy families. In the last game of the season on Thanksgiving Day, WEAC signed local high school captain Richard "Stonewall" Jackson, and the youngster scored a touchdown against an overmatched Middletown team sponsored by the Sons of Italy club. The 25–0 triumph gave WEAC a winning record to close the year.

◆      ◆      ◆

At the dawn of 1939, the new Muzzy Field grandstand was close to completion with a target date of February 12. Work had commenced the previous September and moved ahead quickly as a Public Works Administration project and in the end cost $34,720. The city picked up 55 percent ($19,096) of the costs with the remainder paid from a government grant. Former New Departure President DeWitt Page also contributed a five thousand dollar gift.

Local contractors P. Allaire & Sons won the contract with a bid of $30,078.

In mid-January, Euclid J. Allaire, treasurer of the company, announced that seats would arrive in February, and the new grandstand would seat about thirteen hundred spectators. One of the special features of the structure was its locker rooms located under the grandstand and connected to the dugouts, both of which were located on the third base side and separated by a brick wall and wire barrier. Previously, players had to walk out of the dugout and around the old wooden grandstand to the players' dressing quarters. Another highlight of the new structure was a press box for newspapermen halfway down the third base line at the top of the stands that included seating for eleven and additional standing room. Glass windows at the front of the press box could be opened on the hottest days, as could the glass windows that were placed in the brick wall of the stands near the ceiling of the locker rooms.

On April 27, the *Bristol Press* proudly announced the completion of the Thomas A. Tracy memorial grandstand, and upon inspecting the completed project, legendary Bristol athletic coach Thomas M. Monahan remarked, "There may be bigger grandstands in New England but I doubt if there are any better."

Inside the main gate, four entrances filtered fans into rows of wooden bleachers with back supports under the overhang, and several rows of box seats stretched out closer to the field. Two public drinking fountains were installed on both ends of the grandstand.

"The new stand has the same general shape and outline of the old, is constructed on the same site and has only slightly larger seating capacity, between 1,200 and 1,300," the *Bristol Press* stated.

For the first time, the grandstand was enclosed completely, whereas the wooden structure was open behind the last row of seats.

Many elements of the Tracy grandstand, including the dugouts and locker rooms, were borrowed from major league stadia architecture. The locker rooms included "needle showers and toilet facilities" and could be accessed through doors in the back of the grandstands.

There also were men's and women's restrooms located under the stands, and all such rooms were heated by a gas radiator. A concession stand, storage room, and office for the groundskeeper also were built into the ground level of the grandstand.

The details of the grandstand remain largely the same today as they were in 1939 save for the relocation of the concession stand, restrooms, and groundskeeper's office. As for the playing field itself, the new structure adjusted it slightly when home plate was moved ten feet farther out in the infield. Still, the ballpark presented a yawning divide between home plate and a home run.

"Muzzy Field's present modernistic grandstand of steel and concrete and its beautifully kept baseball diamond, its eye-filling wire enclosure ornated with hundreds of fir trees, are a far cry from the wooden-fenced, dusty ballyard, where athletes of two decades ago romped," columnist Lou Bachman observed a couple of years later.

Secured to the grandstand's wall was a plaque honoring Thomas A. Tracy, which remains today.

Despite all of the excitement surrounding the impressive new facilities, baseball continued falling out of favor among Bristol's sporting crowd. The high school game that was supposed to serve as the dedication ceremony was rained out on April 26, and the official dedication did not take place until August.

In early May, WEAC officials announced that they would not sponsor their traditional semipro team, and the manager, Harry Dzilenski, resigned the same night the club cancelled the season.

The high school team was the only squad making use of Muzzy Field on a regular basis.

"Back a few years ago, I remember when there weren't enough fields in town to take care of the baseball players around the city," former high school captain Louie Goulette lamented in a story published by the *Bristol Press* that June. "Now, we've got one of the best ballparks at Muzzy Field, and there's no baseball to be had."

Softball had taken root in the city, and locally sponsored teams popped up as baseball teams had in the 1920s. The Coty Roofers, Blue Lantern Inn, Federal Hill Aces, New Departure, Italian-Americans, Sessions Clock, Polish Americans, Yarde's Grille, Eagle Lock, and Bristol Phantoms all participated in local leagues.

Many of the purists cringed at the echoes of loneliness inside Muzzy Field in the summertime.

"The ballpark is like a race track without any horses," Bill Shipman, a tailor on Main Street, told columnist McCarthy.

By July, softball teams were using the field for their games but also had to share with the Junior City League, which sponsored a baseball team for teenaged boys. Two of these junior teams got together on August 20 for the Thomas A. Tracy grandstand dedication. Tracy's widow, Lucia, attended with about four hundred others who took in the scheduled doubleheader.

With little baseball on the calendar, many fans looked forward to the football season and WEAC, which announced that they would focus on competition within the newly formed Connecticut State League.

Head coach Sugar Hugret said in early August that he was tired of coaching big names who came to Bristol on the weekend and cared little about their performance. His players' erratic schedules prohibited him from holding practices during the week, and he was more interested in coaching local talent. Hugret also tightened the reins by changing pay day. No longer did players earn paychecks after games on Sunday. Instead, money was doled out on Monday, and anyone missing Friday or Monday practices would be fired, Hugret said.

The general de-emphasis in the WEAC football program led to ticket prices slashed from seventy-five to fifty-five cents for general admission. WEAC's league schedule included Stratford, Wallingford, Fairfield, and New London with each team playing two games home and away.

The club's team included a furniture salesman, two teachers, a policeman, a gas station owner, and a truck driver, all decked out on gameday in WEAC's green and white duds. One player, John Frank, reportedly left the team in October to study law at Georgetown University.

WEAC won two of their first three before the announcement that Muzzy Field's first night football game was taking place on Thursday, October 12. A lighting company from Long Island provided the mobile illumination and Wallingford the competition for the event.

Fay Vincent also returned to Bristol to work as head linesman. He and the 1,263 paid customers saw a well-fought game, won by Wallingford when they scored the game's lone touchdown on a blocked kick in the first quarter.

After winning their next game at Muzzy Field against the New London Diesels, WEAC dropped a 13–0 decision at Danbury at the end of October in front of two thousand. It was the smallest crowd in the intense series until the next weekend when 1,750 customers paid to watch WEAC drop a 7–0 contest at home against the Danbury club. George Mulligan, the former Philadelphia Eagle and WEAC member, had joined Danbury in the off-season along with former Cleveland Rams and Washington Redskins fullback Dick Tuckey.

After two road wins, WEAC ended up the season at home on December 10 with a 20–0 win over Stratford in front of fifteen hundred. The victory sealed the club's championship in the inaugural CSL and came against a team that was coached by Ivan Fuqua, who won gold in the 1932 Olympics as the first leg of the American 4x400m relay team.

But with a combination of bad weather that postponed or canceled several football games and some resulting small crowds, the first year of the remodeled ballpark was an uninspiring one. WEAC reportedly lost two thousand dollars on the venture and decided to go back to paying players a split of any proceeds at season's end instead of remunerating them after every game.

# 1940–1950: Confluence of the Spectacular

The next decade at Muzzy Field opened with another lethargic season, from an historical standpoint. Plans for a City Baseball League were scrapped in May after WEAC backed out and refused to pay the twenty-five dollar entry fee after club members' opposed fielding a team. The decision followed the Celtics' abandonment of the league, as well.

McCarthy, ever the baseball supporter, observed that the clubs had no problem supporting softball when members voted on those issues.

"It's a shame to see softball given preference over baseball—especially by West End Athletic Club—often labeled as one of the leading athletic plants in the state," he wrote on May 23, 1940.

There were three senior league teams playing throughout the city, including Muzzy Field, but it was little more than local amateurs playing in front of two hundred fans, at best.

Hartford Senators manager Jack Onslow, who appeared at Muzzy Field with the 1926 Pirates, was one of the lamenters of the current situation. "You've got one of the nicest parks in the country right here," he told the *Bristol Press* in August. "Why, look at that infield. You could play pool out there."

WEAC stuck with their football downsizing, too, and many familiar names bolted for better football opportunities, meaning more money. Defectors included Sugar Hugret, who played in Holyoke, Massachusetts, on Sundays and in a Waterbury league during weeknights—both teams sponsored by his former player, George Mulligan.

WEAC did play two tie games in September and October that attracted around a thousand fans, but otherwise, Muzzy Field was a quiet and relatively empty place during the 1940 outdoor sports seasons.

Not much changed in 1941, either. At that time, the most popular attractions were at Lake Compounce where Benny Goodman, Tommy Dorsey, and Glenn Miller were featured entertainers.

Several local businessmen made an effort to revive baseball with the formation of the Bristol Baseball Club in May, but there were only token vestiges of years past, most important their coach, George Scott. Albie Gurske returned to pitch a game in June after he had given up organized baseball, but even he left Bristol for more money with a town team in Massachusetts.

The most popular game of the summer came against the Florida Hoboes on June 22 in front of twelve hundred, and that contest—a 9–4 Bristol win—was notable simply for the stage names of the visitors: Peter the Tramp, Coal Car, Hoggy Railroad, Fat Stuff Baker, Oil Can, Gatorbait, High Hip, Lazy, Rollem Red, and Rags.

Some other local teams, the Bristol Merchants and Jack's Radio Nine, also fielded teams and included in their lineups some players who were able to clear the right field wall at Muzzy Field with home runs.

WEAC football never got off the ground in 1941, and only the Bristol Hoboes played occasionally during the autumn to little fanfare.

When Americans' lives changed on December 7, 1941, in the Pacific Ocean, activities at Muzzy Field slowed remarkably. Boxing had a run in the spring and summer and some town teams played baseball, but the weight of the country's involvement in World War II smothered most everything on the playing field. WEAC, however, did field a football team, and the war effort attracted many out-of-state athletes from the Deep South and Midwest who worked in the local manufacturing plants.

While 1942 was quiet, the realities of war and the eventual refocusing on entertainment outlets combined with savvy business dealings to provide Muzzy Field several magnificent moments in the next three years.

◆   ◆   ◆

Travel restrictions imposed during World War II in 1943 prohibited Major League Baseball teams from their annual trips to Florida for spring training and instead relegated teams to more northern, regional locales. The St. Louis Cardinals hosted the southernmost spring training in the river town of Cairo, Illinois.

The chilly and damp April days in Connecticut traditionally passed with sports news of local basketball contests and wire reports from sunny Florida retreats, but in the war years, there was a more tangible energy courtesy the Boston Braves organization, whose spring training site became the Choate School in nearby Wallingford.

On March 24, Braves officials announced the team would play an intrasquad scrimmage in early April, a game sponsored by the Bristol Community Chest's United War Fund charity program for the entertainment of war workers in the city.

Bristol mayor Daniel Davis was excited about the news, calling the team's appearance at renovated Muzzy Field "a wonderful thing for the city." From the United War Fund's perspective, the scheduled game fit perfectly into its mission "to provide wholesome entertainment for local war workers, who because of rationing and lack of time will be unable to make pleasure trips to the larger cities."

Prior to the game on April 5, team president Bob Quinn toured Muzzy Field and gauged the facilities. Quinn was no greenhorn in baseball at that time. At age seventy-three, Quinn was in the final years of his reign as president and part owner of the Braves. Previously, he had served as general manager of the St. Louis Browns (1917–22), owner and president of the Boston Red Sox (1923–33) in the post-Harry Frazee years, and general manager of the Brooklyn Dodgers (1934–35) before joining the Braves.

After his retirement from the Braves in 1945, he was president of the Baseball Hall of Fame in Cooperstown from 1948 to 1951.

He had seen plenty of major league and minor league ballparks around the country, so when he endorsed Muzzy Field's fine layout during a forty-five-minute inspection, it meant something.

"Just wait until [manager] Casey Stengel has a look at that outfield," he said to columnist Lou Bachman. "What a spot for him to make our pitchers run and take off some excess poundage."

The newspaper report said Quinn admired many aspects of the ballpark from its well-manicured mound to its spacious dressing rooms, dugouts, and modern grandstand. He especially took notice of the plaque honoring Tracy.

"I'd be prouder of a thing like that than all the expensive monuments in the world," he said.

When told that Muzzy Field did not host an organized ball club, Quinn said it was a pity for "so fine a park." He urged the Community Chest committee to change that after the war and told them, "Don't try to make any money out of it. Content yourselves with knowledge that you'd be educating a lot of young boys in the fine points of a fine game ..."

He then offered a timeless bit of advice. "Take care of the fans and they'll take care of baseball."

Alfred H. Breckbill, chairman of the United War Fund's recreation committee, reported strong ticket sales a few days before the game. More than 800 of the 1,100 reserved grandstand seats had been sold for $1.25 each through Lou Harrison's Smoke Shop on Main Street, and another 3,000 general admission seats for 85 cents (adults) and 30 cents (children) went on sale the day of the game. Men and women in the armed services were admitted free as guests of Harry Simon, proprietor of the Terryville Furniture Store.

City residents offered to do anything to accommodate the Braves. Eleven members of the Bristol Lions Club, including Mayor Davis, volunteered to drive down to Wallingford and pick up Braves personnel. In turn, the Braves were taking a minority percentage of receipts from the game so that the war fund could profit, and Stengel secured three baseballs autographed by the team that were given away in a game-day raffle.

The Braves' traveling contingent included the elder Quinn; his son, John, who was president of the Hartford farm club; former Boston Red Sox outfielder Duffy Lewis (member of Boston's famed "Million Dollar Outfield"), who was the Braves' road secretary; and Charlie Blossfield, business manager of the Hartford farm club. When the team arrived at Muzzy Field an hour before first pitch, the New Departure band greeted them, and once again, baseball mattered in Bristol.

A lot of the pregame buzz centered on newly acquired pitcher Vernon "Lefty" Gomez whom the Braves purchased from the Yankees on January 25. Gomez was scheduled to start at Muzzy Field, which was quite a treat for fans who had followed his 14-year major league career in which he won 189 games and 5 World Series championships, and was undefeated in 7 World Series starts.

Unfortunately, the offbeat left-hander, known as "El Goofy," was scratched from the game "due to an injured thumb which he had cut a few hours before in Wallingford while closing a zipper on his traveling bag," according to *Bristol Press* reports. Gomez did, however, work out with the Braves during pregame drills at Muzzy Field and later took a bow from the dugout.

His time with the Braves was short. The team released him in May, and he signed with the Washington Senators soon after. He pitched in one game for Washington before the team released him in July, thus ending Gomez's Major League Baseball career that culminated in 1972 with his induction into the National Baseball Hall of Fame.

Stengel divided his squad into two teams: the Regulars and the Yannigans, a term used to describe the marginalized players who were in camp but rarely stuck with the club. The future Hall of Fame manager did not see much of his Braves that year, though. Two days before the season opener, he suffered a broken leg when a Boston cab driver hit him with his car, sending Stengel into traction for two months. George Kelly and Bob Coleman then took over managing duties of a ball club with a thin depth chart.

Though the Braves were stuck in a seven-year cycle in which they never won more than sixty-eight games, the high-water mark came in 1943 when they finished sixth in the National League, ahead of Philadelphia and New York.

But Bristol fans did not care about Boston's recent record. They arrived as a group of 3,031 to watch a major league team in action, albeit one whose roster was filled with many players who were forced out of the majors once the regulars came back after World War II.

The Yannigans' batting lineup included Charles Aickley at shortstop, Nick Rhabe in right field, Connie Creeden in left field, Tony Cuccinello at third base, Kerby Farrell at first base, Phil Masi at second base, Butch Nieman in center field, Bob Ayotte behind the plate, and pitchers Al Javery, Nate Andrews, and Reardon.

Among position players, only Masi and Nieman were Braves regulars that season, and Masi made two All-Star appearances during a fourteen-year major league career, mainly as a fine defensive catcher with uncommon speed at the position. Cuccinello, at thirty-five, was a seasoned veteran coming off the bench for Boston. He played in only thirteen games in 1943 before Boston released him in July and the White Sox signed him as a free agent. As a thirty-seven-year-old third baseman two years later, Cuccinello earned the second of his two All-Star nominations in his career and retired after that season.

Among the Yannigans' pitchers, Javery and Andrews were two of Boston's most effective in the 1943 season. Javery earned the first of two consecutive All-Star game appearances with a 17–16 mark, the lone Boston hurler to finish over .500 and the only time he did so in his seven-year career. Andrews won fourteen games in 1943, though he led the National League with twenty losses, and he earned an All-Star nomination the following year.

The Boston Regulars featured a batting lineup of Whitey Wietelmann at shortstop, Eddie Joost at second base, Tommy Holmes in center field, Johnny McCarthy at first base, Chet Ross in left field, Joe Burns at third base, a player named Neill (possibly Tommy, who debuted in the major leagues with the

Braves in 1946) in right field, Clyde Kluttz at catcher, and pitchers Manny Salvo, Lou Tost, and Red Barrett.

Four starters for the 1943 Braves were part of this lineup, the most notable being Joost and Holmes. One year after committing a league-high forty-five errors in 1942, Joost went on to bat .185 in 1943, the lowest batting average ever for a player with four hundred or more at-bats. He resurrected his career with the Philadelphia A's later in the decade and earned an All-Star nomination in 1949. Holmes turned in a solid but unspectacular season immediately following his appearance at Muzzy Field. But it was his 1945 performance that remains historically significant when he won the National League MVP award after fashioning a thirty-seven-game hitting streak, which stood as a twentieth-century National League record until Pete Rose broke it in 1978. Holmes batted .302 with 88 home runs and 581 RBI in his 11-year major league career.

Salvo and Barrett were starting pitchers who won a combined seventeen games in 1943.

The exhibition game at Muzzy Field was loosely played, and the teams combined for eighteen runs, twenty-two hits, and six errors—one by Joost—on a cold afternoon. Creeden and Holmes blasted home runs out of the park to the right side. Creeden's blast over the right-center field wall 375 feet away reportedly was on par with Babe Ruth's and Johnny Moore's of two decades earlier.

Cuccinello and Masi were the Yannigans' hitting stars with three apiece and five combined RBI as their side won, 10–8. Joost, Holmes, Burns, and Kluttz all garnered two hits while Ross smacked three for the Regulars.

In all, it was a fine manner in which to begin the outdoor sporting year in Bristol.

William P. "Hank" O'Donnell of the *Waterbury Republican* left the field impressed, as did several of the Boston writers who accompanied the Braves.

"Northern training camps may have their drawbacks but the Boston Braves discovered ... in Bristol that this section is a fertile field for exhibition games," O'Donnell penned. "The field was in splendid shape, the fans were enthusiastic and the Bristol city officials cooperative ..."

At the gates, the strong fan support allowed the city to pay off the remaining balance of the fence repair work from 1935.

The success of the Braves' appearance convinced the Bristol Community Chest and United War Fund committee that such exhibitions were sensible and profitable ventures both for charity and the city. In late May, they announced a partnership with an agency that provided toilet kits to soldiers overseas, and the

"Kits for Servicemen" exhibition baseball game involved the Philadelphia Phillies against a semipro team from Meriden.

Brophy helped negotiate Philadelphia's appearance, which occurred during several off days between road games against St. Louis and New York, after meeting with team officials in Philadelphia in May.

As bad a shape as the Braves were in that season, the Phillies were worse off. In six of the seven preceding years, the hapless Philadelphia franchise had finished in last place in the National League. By February 1943, team owner Gerry Nugent was so deep in debt on rent and bank loans and so highly resented by other National League clubs that the league bought out his shares for fifty thousand dollars and obtained ownership of the club (Westcott and Bilovsky 2004).

In searching for a suitable buyer, in stepped William Drought Cox, a thirty-three-year-old entrepreneur who was educated at Yale, where he was a track and baseball athlete. He spent the 1930s as a successful dealer of American art, and he also established a lumber business in Oregon that supplied all of the pilings used to reinforce the Panama Canal during World War II. For eighty thousand dollars, the keen businessman bought the Phillies and set about reinventing the franchise.

His first order of business was hiring manager Stanley Raymond "Bucky" Harris, who entered the managerial ranks as a twenty-seven-year-old player/manager of the 1924 Washington Senators and led them to a World Series title. Harris would guide a Philadelphia team that had only fourteen players in spring training, due to Nugent's selling them off in a failed attempt to keep up with his bills.

As a lumber broker, Cox worked long hours and carried his habits over to his baseball team ownership, and he expected his manager to be accessible at all times. But Cox was a different breed. After his postgame meeting with the press, he usually was not available until two hours before the next game (Holtzman 2004).

Almost immediately, friction emerged between owner and manager, and the season began with tension and power struggles, even though Harris's team was more successful on the field and at the gate than many Phillie clubs from previous decades. In one instance, Cox brought in a trainer and director of physical fitness, Harold Bruce, without Harris's input. It has been reported that Bruce was Cox's high school track coach. Cox, certainly an involved owner, was said to have invaded the dressing room at will and called in players to give them inspirational pep talks while berating umpires from his box seat, according to reports that year in the *Washington Post*.

He also alienated his thirty-member board of investors with ill-advised personnel moves (Holtzman 2004).

Meanwhile, news in Bristol reported on Philadelphia's upcoming appearance and the 1,200 reserved seat tickets selling for $1.25 apiece. There was more excitement when the locals learned that Albie Gurske would pitch for Meriden against the Phillies, who were due to arrive in Bristol by train from New York at 4:02 on Friday afternoon, June 11. Cox reportedly said he was joining the team on the trip.

In the days leading up to the Phillies game, plans were made to include performances by the Bradley Air Field Band from Hartford and to schedule an Army Air Corps Aviation Cadet recruiting drive concurrent with a swearing-in ceremony at Muzzy Field of eleven such cadets.

Big Ed Walsh also would throw out the first pitch of the game.

On June 10, baseball commissioner Kennesaw Mountain Landis handed down a disappointing decision when he ruled Gurske ineligible to compete in the game. Apparently, when Gurske retired from baseball two years prior, he had failed to report to Augusta, Georgia, of the South Atlantic League after leaving a team in Binghamton, New York, thereby rendering his retirement unofficial even though he had spent the last two years working in a New Britain war plant. Baseball's laws prohibited any major league team from playing against any other team that had a player on its roster who was on the ineligible list of any major or minor league clubs, as Gurske was with Augusta for failing to report.

Negotiations failed with Landis's office in Chicago to reinstate Gurske for the Phillies game.

Instead, Meriden used Mickey DeLuccia, a southpaw who had played with Buffalo of the International League during his organized baseball career. He dueled against Walter "Boom Boom" Beck, a journeyman right-hander who spent twelve years in the major leagues, losing twice as many as he won, and appeared in four regular season games for the 1943 Phillies.

Baseball historian William Brashler wrote that Beck supposedly earned his nickname with the 1934 Brooklyn Dodgers. Upset over manager Casey Stengel's decision to remove him from a game with the Dodgers leading, Beck furiously threw the ball into right field in Philadelphia's Baker Bowl where it caromed off the wall and hit the center-field wall. "The 'boom-boom' of the rebound roused center fielder Hack Wilson, who was relaxing during the pitching change and thought the game had resumed," Brashler noted. "Wilson pursued the ball and fired a strike back to the infield."

Philadelphia's batting lineup also included Danny Murtaugh at second base, Ron "The Round Man" Northey in right field, Buster Adams in center field, Jimmy Wasdell at first base, Babe Dahlgren at third base, Paul Busby in left field, Charlie Brewster at shortstop, and Tom Padden as catcher.

Murtaugh, Northey, and Dahlgren were the most notable position players for the Phillies at Muzzy Field. Murtaugh was a solid player but later made a name with World Series championships in 1960 and 1971 as manager of the Pittsburgh Pirates.

Northey was a hefty left-handed hitter with a remarkably strong throwing arm and a penchant for clutch home runs, evinced by his three pinch-hit grand slams and eight career grand slams. According to historian Jim Langford, "Dodger outfield Carl Furillo claims that he and Northey were the only two players to hit the famous sign on Ebbets Field's right-field wall and win a free suit from Abe Stark."

Dahlgren was the New York Yankee who on May 2, 1939, played first base for an ailing Lou Gehrig, thus ending the Iron Horse's streak of consecutive games played at 2,130. Coming into the game at Muzzy Field, Dahlgren was leading the National League with a .367 average on his way to his lone All-Star game appearance at thirty-one years old, though his average dipped to .287 by the end of the season.

Philadelphia players rode the train from New York and ate only sandwiches before their arrival in Bristol. A large dinner party was scheduled after the game at Fuller's Restaurant in Bristol. If the players were in a foul mood because of their scant meal, they certainly did not enjoy the sight of DeLuccia.

More than fifteen hundred fans jammed Muzzy Field for the game, and Meriden struck in the first inning following a Brewster throwing error and two singles. Then Jake Banks smashed a Beck offering off the right-field wall to score two more, but Northey's exceptional defensive ability revealed itself when he gunned down Banks at second base to end the threat.

Quickly, the Phillies trailed, 3–0.

DeLuccia found trouble in the third inning with an infield hit by Busby and a single by Brewster. After DeLuccia forced Busby at third, Brewster stole third base to set up the "most electrifying play of the day," according to *Bristol Press* reports.

Beck crushed a pitch to left-center field where an outfielder named Dombroski "raced some 100 feet and with his back to the plate speared the drive with his outstretched hand," which allowed Brewster to tag up.

With a 3–1 lead, DeLuccia locked down and "slow balled the Phillies into submission" the rest of the evening. Philadelphia threatened in the ninth with a

Northey single before fly outs from Adams and Wasdell. Dahlgren then hit a slow roller to short, and the fielder sailed the ball over the first baseman's head instead of forcing Northey at second. DeLuccia then walked Stewart to load the bases, but he managed to coax Brewster into a fly out to end the game with the potential winning run stranded.

DeLuccia scattered five hits, struck out five, and walked three.

For Meriden, it was a remarkable win and an equally deflating loss for the Phillies. Murtaugh finished with two hits, a double, and four assists. Northey, Busby, and Brewster earned the remaining Philadelphia hits, and DeLuccia held the National League's hottest batter at the time to an 0-for-3 performance with two walks.

Reports stated that Harris and his players were impressed with Bristol's ballpark and surprised to learn that Johnny Moore, himself an ex-Phillie, had launched his major league career from that same field.

After the game, Harris told James P. Jennings, president of the Community Chest, that the Phillies will "always be glad to play a game in Bristol again."

The bonhomie did not exist between Harris and Cox, though.

Their strained relationship came to a head at the end of July when the Phillies were on an extended road trip to the Midwest. The impatient Cox decided to fire Harris and announced it during a press conference in Philadelphia with the team in St. Louis. Harris and the team learned of the news through the press.

Though the Phillies threatened to strike over the mistreatment of their manager, Harris convinced them to take the field against the Cardinals, and they won the game that night.

Infuriated by Cox's treatment of him, Harris returned to Philadelphia and met with the media, not mincing words on his ill feelings toward the young owner. As an historical coup de grâce, Harris added, "He's a fine guy to fire me when he gambles on games his club plays."

A news report later revealed that Harris inadvertently learned of Cox's actions early in the season while speaking to a stenographer in Cox's lumber business office in New York. In the middle of dictating to the stenographer, Dorothy Massey, Harris said she looked at her watch and excused herself to make a phone call on Cox's behalf that she said she made every day.

Massey told Harris, "It's the morning line—you know, the odds on the ball games."

An amazed Harris asked, "Do you mean that Mr. Cox is betting on ball games?"

"Oh, yes," Massey answered. "I thought you knew."

With that explosive bit of information, an investigation into the life of Cox revealed that he did bet on his team, though he said the allegations were ridiculous and then later claimed to be ignorant of Major League Rule 21 (d) forbidding such action. Commissioner Landis had told Cox earlier in the year to get out of horse racing because of its betting.

Eventually, on November 23, Landis permanently barred Cox from baseball for placing "approximately 15 to 20 bets of $25 to $100 per game on Philadelphia to win," according to Landis's ruling.

"Your betting of baseball games of the Philadelphia National League Club ... require[s] me ... to declare you to be permanently ineligible to hold any office or employment with the Philadelphia National League Club or any other club or league party to the Major League Agreement or Major-Minor League Agreement," Landis stated.

Cox did not appeal and stated on a WOR (Newark, NJ) radio address the following night, "I have endeavored in every way to lead an exemplary life and conduct myself with the proper viewpoint to this great sport. Good luck and goodby[e] to everyone in baseball."

In a December 7, 1943, column, famed sportswriter Red Smith addressed the matter and included a sentence that began, "Inasmuch as there never was anything like it in baseball before and, praise be, probably never will again ..."

Cox went on to hold ownership of the Brooklyn Dodgers football team when that club moved into the All-America Football Conference.

For decades, as Red Smith had hoped, Cox was the last man to be banned from baseball for betting, until the drama of Pete Rose unfolded.

Following the Phillies game at Muzzy Field, the baseball season proceeded in a low-profile manner defined by local amateur teams. One of those teams was a union club, New Departure CIO, which competed in a small state league. Their most notable games came against the old New Departure players who defined baseball at Muzzy Field in the 1920s.

With many of the old-timers still living in the area, it was easy to cobble together a competitive team, as the CIO club found out in their two contests against them.

The old-timers' lineup included Clyde Waters, Les Lanning, Eddie Zielke, Jimmy Malcolm, George Scott, Smoke Halbach, Eddie Goodridge, Gus Forslund, and Swat McCabe. They failed to start quickly in the first game on July 15, though.

CIO jumped out to a 10–3 lead before they chipped away slowly and eventually tied the game at ten in the seventh inning. CIO then pushed across the winning run in the bottom of the seventh and held on, 11–10, as three hundred fans looked on.

The second game was scheduled for August 29 to benefit the Kits for Servicemen agency, and the old-timers got the last word with a 12–8 victory. McCabe went 3-for-3 and officially ended his career by walking off the field after his third hit late in the game. As usual, he went out on his own terms.

A couple of weeks before that game, Scott announced that WEAC would sponsor a football team in the fall, but the club dropped those plans a week later when only eight players attended a tryout. Many of the eligible and interested players had been called to the war front.

Therefore, the autumn season was quiet, except when Muzzy Field hosted Army Day in late October and displayed to the public Axis weapons taken in the war, such as a Mark IV tank and Nazi equipment captured by United Nations forces in Africa.

Quiet, that is, until Brophy, the promoter, happened to pick up a pro football magazine in a West Hartford newsstand at the beginning of November. He outlined the anatomy of a monumental deal in a 1971 *Bristol Press* story that he authored.

Brophy noticed that the Green Bay Packers schedule included a road game at Brooklyn on November 21 and then a week off before playing in Philadelphia on December 5. This quirk resulted from the direct effect of World War II on the rosters of both the Philadelphia Eagles and Pittsburgh Steelers. Thin ranks on both sides prompted the teams to merge as one franchise, the Phil-Pitt Steagles, during the war years, and one of the unexpected advantages befell Brophy and other football aficionados in Bristol.

Brophy immediately placed a call to Dennis Shea, business manager of the Brooklyn Dodgers, with whom Brophy had a relationship based on Brooklyn serving as WEAC's home opener in previous years. When Brophy informed Shea of his idea, the Dodger representative dispatched a note of recommendation to Packers coach and administrator Earl L. "Curly" Lambeau.

Shea figured the Packers' monetary demands would be about five thousand dollars, but he also thought it was doubtful that Green Bay did not have something already lined up for the bye week. Regardless, Brophy also sent a letter to Lambeau detailing the advantages of playing an exhibition game at Muzzy Field. A few days later, Lambeau sent a telegram to Brophy reading, "Considering Bristol, must have more details."

Brophy jumped on the telephone to the Green Bay front office and learned that the Packers were negotiating another appearance somewhere on the East

Coast the weekend of November 28. Due to the wartime travel restrictions, the Packers planned to stay at the Rye, New York, Country Club between their trips to Brooklyn and Philadelphia.

Opportunity in hand, Brophy negotiated with Lambeau over the phone long enough to rack up a twenty-seven-dollar bill on the call. Lambeau wanted five thousand dollars guaranteed for the Packers' appearance at Muzzy Field, but Brophy eventually negotiated him down to three thousand dollars, and a game between the Packers and the powerful semipro outfit New London Diesels was cemented.

The NFL in 1943 suffered through the same personnel depletion as other major sports, and the war era marked a dilution of league talent. At the start of the season, 376 players who had roster spots in the previous three years were in the military service, according to pro football historian Stan Grosshandler. The Cleveland Rams disbanded in 1943 because their owners were called to service, and their players were lent to other teams. Creation of the Steagles franchise gave the league its fewest members since 1932. Rosters were cut back to twenty-eight, helmets became mandatory, and a ten-game schedule—one fewer than the previous year—was implemented, Grosshandler noted.

Still, the name value of the Green Bay Packers, one of the strongest teams in the Western Division, and the inclusion on their roster of one of the finest players in the history of the sport guaranteed a successful game in Bristol.

Additionally, the Packers lent twenty-five players to the war effort in 1942 and 1943, while teams like the Detroit Lions (45) and New York Giants (44) had many more servicemen on their rosters, historian Bob Barnett wrote in 1983.

"One of the reasons more of our players weren't drafted was that we were a bunch of broken-down stumblebums," Charles "Buckets" Goldenberg told Barnett. "A bunch of us tried to get in but were rejected."

But enough of the Packers went off to war that end Don Hutson postponed his retirement plans in 1943 and returned to the team in August, "not because he wanted to play especially, but because the manpower shortage had left Curly on the spot," an Associated Press story reported at the time.

"I feel I owe the professional game something," Hutson is quoted as saying in the November 20 *Bristol Press* article.

Because of that decision, Muzzy Field can boast one of the finest receivers in the history of football among its many celebrated visiting athletes. Some college football historians believe Hutson would have been the run-away winner of the Heisman Trophy had the trophy existed during his All-America season at the University of Alabama in 1934.

As dominant as the speedy six-foot-one, 183-pound end was in college, he became a legend when the Packers signed him after the Crimson Tide won the 1935 Rose Bowl. Hutson's legacy partly is owed to then-NFL president Joe Carr. Hutson signed contracts with both the Packers, who embraced the forward pass, and Brooklyn Dodgers, a more run-oriented team. "Carr ruled that the contract with the earliest postmark would be honored," according to the Pro Football Hall of Fame, and the Packers postmarked theirs seventeen minutes before Brooklyn.

Hutson immediately made an impact on a league that was just learning how to use the lethal forward pass, and in fact, "the Alabama Antelope," who ran the 100-yard dash in 9.5 seconds, revolutionized the passing game. He is credited with creating Z-routes, buttonhooks, hook-and-gos, and numerous other pass patterns, maneuvers, and fakes. Legendary Chicago Bears coach George Halas actually created special defenses designed to slow down Hutson. He rendered NFL defensive backs helpless in his eleven-year career and held eighteen NFL records when he retired, many of which still stand. He led the NFL in receiving in eight of his eleven years and in scoring five consecutive years. In 1941 and 1942, he was named league MVP.

Hutson finished his career with 488 catches, 7,991 yards, and 99 touchdowns and scored 811 points, 193 as a placekicker. His closest receiving competitors had 190 catches and 37 touchdowns. He also rushed for 284 yards and 3 scores, and for good measure in the days of single platoon football, Hutson intercepted 30 passes in his final 6 years and scored once. He even completed one pass in 1943 for a touchdown.

He was possibly the most influential and dominant player in professional football history.

Hutson also was a civic leader and local businessman in Green Bay. Prior to his arrival in Bristol, a newspaper report described how he had difficulties finding reliable workers to staff his Green Bay bowling alleys during the war and how he was chairman of the Brown County Red Cross drive in Wisconsin while also serving on a committee to study the possibility of creating a community airport.

When news broke about Green Bay's exhibition game, orders flew out of Bristol's park commission's office to ready Muzzy Field for a large crowd.

Prior to the start of the 1943 season, All-Pro quarterback Cecil Isbell had spent five seasons throwing dozens of touchdown passes Hutson's way, but he surprised the Packers when he announced his retirement and took a coaching job at Purdue University.

In stepped rookie Irv Comp, who split time with Tony Canadeo that year. Comp was the only passing back used at Muzzy Field. At six foot one and 205 pounds, Comp was a passing, running, and kicking threat at the University of Wisconsin where his coach Harry Stuhldreher called him the "greatest prospect I have ever seen." He then transferred to St. Benedictine's College before joining the Packers as a third-round draft pick in 1943. Defective eyesight kept him out of the army, and Comp spent his off-seasons working in a Milwaukee defense plant during the war.

Many of the Packers who made the trip to Bristol were veteran NFL players whom the military rejected for various health reasons. In the ten days leading up to the game, the *Bristol Press* published profiles of some of Green Bay's players to feed the public's excitement.

One particular favorite was Harry Jacunski, an end from nearby New Britain. Jacunski played collegiate football at Fordham, where he served as co-captain, and was Hutson's backup for the Packers. The 1943 season was his finest as he caught 24 passes for 528 yards and 3 touchdowns.

Another ex-Fordham player was tackle Paul Berezney, teammate of Jacunski, who was playing his second NFL season with the Packers while on hiatus from Marquette Medical School. Chet Adams was his fellow tackle. A four-year star with the Cleveland Rams, Adams joined the Packers when the Rams liquidated and Lambeau reportedly drew his name out of a hat. It was a fine choice, because the six-foot-three, 225-pound lineman enjoyed a ten-year professional football career.

Lineman Buford "Baby" Ray was a hulking six foot six, 250 pounds, and too big for military service. Considered one of the most talented linemen in the NFL, Ray spent all eleven of his NFL years with the Packers, and the former Vanderbilt standout played in 116 games. In the off-season, Ray lived in Antioch, Tennessee, and operated a liquor store in Nashville.

Goldenberg, a thirty-two-year-old guard, was the glue of the Packers' line. With eleven years' NFL experience by 1943, the five-foot-ten 225-pounder whose main attributes were his "experience and fight" played two more seasons before he retired a lifelong Packer. Early in his career, Goldenberg also played as a fullback, halfback, and quarterback. He reportedly had experience as a professional wrestler, too, and owned a restaurant in Milwaukee.

Right halfback Andy Uram was in the final year of a six-year NFL career. The former University of Minnesota star was a versatile back who finished with 1,073 rushing yards at 4.5 yards per carry, 4 touchdowns, and 1,083 receiving yards at 18.7 yards per catch with 10 touchdowns in his career. He often was Green Bay's second option to Hutson in their passing game.

With the war effort in full swing, New London was not lacking in football talent. Several former college players from around the country landed in town either with navy submarine contractor Electric Boat or the Coast Guard. The Diesels roster included one notable in particular, tackle Norman Olsen of Alabama who went on to play with the Cleveland Rams in 1944–45. Other players came from North Carolina, Wisconsin, Kentucky, Minnesota, and St. Mary's.

In honor of Jacunski, the seventy-piece marching band from New Britain High School played in front of a large delegation from that city along with a reported eighty-five hundred fans, the largest crowd in Muzzy Field history, including nine hundred servicemen. Reserved seats for $1.85 were available only to New Departure war workers, and general admission tickets went for $1.10 for adults and 55 cents for children. Proceeds from game program sales went to buy cigarettes for New Departure employees in the service.

On the morning of the game, the Packer team ate a large breakfast at Nick's on North Main Street and then convened at Muzzy Field to face the Diesels.

Green Bay's starting linemen included left end Tony Falkenstein; left tackle Joel Mason, who also was a professional basketball player; left guard Milburn "Tiny" Croft, who stood six foot four and weighed 287 pounds; center Sherwood Fries; right guard Forrest McPherson; right tackle Glen Sorenson; and right end Ade Schwammel. The backfield included Comp, Joe Laws, Dick Evans, and Larry Craig, who was deferred from the war because he was a farmer, a valuable occupation at the time.

Substitutes were Hutson, Ray, Bob Flowers, Goldenberg, Adams, Jacunski, Uram, Charlie Brock, Berezney, and Ben Starrett. They marched on to Muzzy Field clad in their trademark navy blue jerseys with gold shoulders and numbers, tan pants, and navy socks.

Immediately, Green Bay showed their wares as one of the most formidable professional franchises in any sport. Comp scored in the first quarter on an eleven-yard sweep set up by his two passes to Mason. With a modest 7–0 lead, the Packers exploded for thirty-four points in the second quarter on a thirty-five-yard Comp-to-Jacunski pass that delighted the crowd, which was followed by Hutson's conversion kick. Then Craig scored on a ten-yard run set up by a twenty-five-yard pass to Hutson and a ten-yard Brock run. Hutson converted that kick, too, but either was hit in the face during the attempt or otherwise struck because he left the game at that point with a badly cut nose. Lankas, Evans, and Mason all followed with touchdowns, and Uram also began passing all over the field in the quarter.

Don Hutson, far left, Curly Lambeau, and Irv Comp were responsible for a revolutionary passing attack in the National Football League and also contributed to the most magnificent football moment in Muzzy Field's history. They are shown here at training camp in Bear Mountain, New York, nearly one year after their historic appearance in Bristol in 1943. (Courtesy: Associated Press)

After halftime, Comp connected with Laws for two touchdowns and then found Evans for another touchdown in the fourth quarter covering thirty-one yards.

In the end, the Packers overwhelmed the Diesels in all phases, including 62–14 on the scoreboard, and connected on every conversion except one, during which Ray slipped and missed the kick. Comp completed twenty-seven of his thirty-four passes, and under the direction of future Hall of Fame coach Curly Lambeau, the Packers displayed the passing attack that had separated them from other teams in the NFL.

"There may be better teams than the Green Bay Packers," K.H. "Pop" Simmons wrote, "but it wouldn't do to start that kind of talk in Bristol today."

The locals were thoroughly impressed with the display, and a happenstance moment in a West Hartford newsstand led to what "all agreed ... was the finest sports exhibition ever seen at Muzzy Field," the *Bristol Press* proclaimed.

The cap was on the 1943 sports season at Muzzy Field, and five Packers (Hutson, Adams, Brock, Ray, and Comp) were named All-Pro or honorable mention All-Pro.

Green Bay went on to win their final game against the Philadelphia-Pittsburgh aggregation to finish their season 7–2–1.

◆     ◆     ◆

On the heels of a successful venture into Bristol during spring training, the Boston Braves scheduled another exhibition game in early April 1944 as a side trip from their training grounds in Wallingford. Bob Coleman had replaced Casey Stengel as manager, and Benny Bengough and Tom Sheehan joined him as coaches. Sheehan pitched in 146 games in his 6-year career that began with the 1915 Philadelphia A's, and Bengough played 10 years with the New York Yankees and St. Louis Browns starting in 1923.

Many of the Braves players were the same, and Bristol fans responded one thousand strong on a chilly second day of April.

Butch Nieman provided the offensive firepower with a solo home run in the sixth inning over the 360-foot mark in right-center field and into the pine trees and added a run scored when Connie Ryan grounded into a double play. That was all the Regulars needed as they defeated the Yannigans, 2–0, behind a combined five-hitter by Ben Cardoni and Vince Shupe. Carl Lindquist pitched for the Yannigans with Hal Schacker, who combined to scatter seven hits.

The team, however, suffered through another painful season, compiling a 65–89 record for sixth place, forty games behind the World Champion St. Louis Cardinals.

Bob and John Quinn took in the action at Muzzy Field and shortly after the exhibition's conclusion, John announced that his Hartford farm club would use Muzzy Field and Bristol as their spring training base. Some of the Boston Braves players became intimately familiar with the ballpark through their workouts with Hartford.

Managed by former Brooklyn Dodgers first baseman Del Bissonette, the Hartford Laurels arrived in Bristol on April 10 and quartered in the federal housing project on Peck Lane while taking their meals at the New Departure cafeteria.

They were guests of the New Departure Recreation Council and one of the few minor league teams in America that played through World War II.

During the team's three-week stay, they worked out each day from ten thirty in the morning to two thirty in the afternoon, practicing during the noon hour for the public's enjoyment and then taking lunch at the park. Thirty-five players composed the club during spring training, and the facilities were top-notch in Bissonette's eyes.

"This is a grand spot, one of the best baseball parks I've ever seen in a city of Bristol's size," he told the newspaper after he arrived a few days before his team reported.

Players who competed in the Braves scrimmage and came back with the Laurels were Shupe, Schacker, and Steve Shemo. Other notable Hartford players were Charles Aickley, Stan Wentzel, James Francoline, Mike Sabena, Merle Settlemire, Walter Sorgi, Francis Messenger, and John Dione.

Though talent was thin during the war, Bissonette compiled a group that became one of the finest clubs that ever played in the Eastern League. They hosted intrasquad games and scrimmages against other Eastern League teams at Muzzy Field, including the Albany Lawmakers managed by former Gas House Gang member and All-Star Ripper Collins on April 23. Their games routinely attracted three hundred to five hundred fans that spring.

In their last game in Bristol, the Laurels dropped a 5–4 decision to Albie Gurske and his Meriden club, which benefited from a two-run double from Gus Dugas, who spent four years playing for the Pittsburgh Pirates, Philadelphia Phillies, and Washington Senators in the early 1930s.

But it was after spring training that Hartford flourished. Behind the strength of southpaw pitcher and Duke University product Pete Naktenis, the Laurels tore through the Eastern League with a 99–38 record and finished eight and a half games ahead of second-place Albany.

Shupe batted a team-best .339 with a league-leading 187 hits and drove in 109 runs. Shemo hit .316, Wentzel .323 with a league-high nine home runs, and Roland Gladu batted .372 with 102 RBI.

In Naktenis, Schacker, and Warren Mueller, the Laurels boasted three eighteen-game winners, and Naktenis led the league in winning percentage (just three losses) and sported the Eastern League's lowest ERA at 1.93.

Paired against third-place Utica (69–69) in the league play-offs, Hartford promptly dropped the first two games, 1–0 and 5–4, in eleven innings. They scratched back to tie the series but dropped the deciding game, 9–8, after Naktenis uncharacteristically threw two wild pitches late in the game and the defense foundered with six errors. One of the finest season-long performances of any minor league team went for naught with sloppy play and Utica's good pitching.

Baseball season at Muzzy Field did not end with Hartford's spring training departure. The aggregate sponsored by New Departure CIO started their second season on May 8, three days before the city lost a fine sportsman and official in Clyde Waters, who died of a heart attack at fifty-five.

As an amateur team, the ND CIO club was among the finest on the East Coast and qualified for the All-American Amateur Baseball Association tournament in Baltimore in September following a strong regular-season showing. They finished third out of fourteen teams and competed against clubs from New York, Maryland, and Washington, D.C.

While the Braves made a repeat visit to Muzzy Field, so too did the Philadelphia Phillies on June 9. Following the fiasco of the Bill Cox regime, the Carpenter family of Wilmington, Delaware, purchased the club, and Robert R.M. Carpenter Jr. served as team president. In that capacity, Carpenter attempted to generate more interest in the maligned franchise by initiating a contest to rename the team, the winner to receive a one hundred dollar bond.

More than five thousand entries came in, and the nickname Blue Jays was chosen. So apathetic was the attitude toward Philadelphia's National League entry that the only reaction to the renaming came from Johns Hopkins University students. The prestigious Baltimore school had been called the Blue Jays for nearly seven decades when Carpenter made his choice; in response, the Johns Hopkins student council passed a resolution, which it sent to Carpenter, calling Philadelphia's adoption of the nickname, "a reprehensible act which brought disgrace and dishonor to the good name of Johns Hopkins University" (Westcott and Bilovsky 2004).

With seventeen last-place finishes in twenty-eight years beginning in 1919, few held Philadelphia's National League baseball team in high regard, JHU students especially.

Though the 1944 season failed to change Philadelphia's fortunes as they finished last at 61–92, a major league ball club always got Bristol residents interested in their arrival. The Blue Jays again were pitted against the semipro outfit out of Meriden, but this time, Albie Gurske had been designated a free agent and was eligible to compete. Meriden's lineup included several other players with minor league experience, including Dugas.

Philadelphia's lineup, under new manager Freddie Fitzsimmons, winner of 217 games in a 19-year major league pitching career, included several new faces from the previous year.

The chief attraction was Tony Lupien, a former Boston Red Sox player who Philadelphia claimed off waivers in April 1944. Lupien was a Connecticut native who starred at Harvard and played six seasons with the Red Sox, Blue Jays, and Chicago White Sox. In 1942, he beat out Jimmie Foxx for the first base job in Boston, which led to Foxx's release. One of Lupien's finest years was 1944 in which he hit .283 with five home runs, fifty-two RBI, and eighteen stolen bases.

Also making their first trips to Muzzy Field were Fitzsimmons, Ray Hamrick, Benny Culp, Ted Cieslak, Moon Mullen, Andy Karl, Andy Seminick, Charlie Letchas, and Glen Stewart. Buster Adams, Jimmy Wasdell, and Ron Northey were back in Bristol for a second time.

With Gurske on the mound, many locals probably hoped for and expected a similar outcome to 1943 when Meriden surprised the major league visitors. But the Blue Jays had none of it and came out hitting Mickey DeLuccia and Gurske hard in front of nine hundred paid fans and nearly as many local schoolboys who were admitted free as guests of New Departure on a Friday afternoon.

Adams smacked a line drive back at DeLuccia in the fourth inning and knocked him out of the game. But even before he left, he was unable to master the opposition with his changeup, surrendering nine hits and five runs in his stint. Gurske came in and gave up a home run to Lupien over the right-field fence. Philadelphia cruised to a 12–1 victory and took advantage of six Meriden errors, whose lone standout was Dugas. The first baseman collected two hits including a solo home run off of Fitzsimmons, who started on the mound for Philadelphia and pitched three innings.

Karl relieved and scattered three hits the rest of the way. Offensively, the Blue Jays received support from Hamrick (3-for-6, two runs, double, two triples, and four assists) and Lupien, who drove in two runs and scored three. Northey, Wasdell, and Adams combined for four hits, four runs scored, and two RBI. Fitzsimmons also drove in a run.

It was a rare high point for the 1944 Blue Jays.

The other notable baseball moment that summer came in late June when the New York Black Yankees arrived for a night game played under a portable lighting system. The visitors were in the midst of horrible 4–24 season in the Negro National League and competed against the ND CIO team.

The New Yorkers proved superior to the amateurs, though, and routed them, 19–8, as ND CIO committed six errors and surrendered seventeen hits.

Their lineup included leadoff batter and second baseman Marvin Barker, one of the most versatile players in the Negro National League and a fourteen-year veteran of the Black Yankees. He collected three hits, including a double, and scored three runs against ND CIO. Unfortunately, an incomplete box score in the local newspaper leaves several game details lost to history.

First baseman Zack Clayton was a light-hitting but solid ballplayer who spent two years with the Black Yankees in 1943–44; he was more famous for his time spent with the Harlem Globetrotters basketball team but carved out a respectable twelve-year baseball career. He also collected three hits and scored three times at Muzzy Field.

Shortstop Carlos Rivero was a light-hitting, yet versatile, infielder in his Negro League-playing days, the last of which were spent with the Black Yankees in 1944. He hit .227 in his final season and had two hits and scored twice in the game.

Center fielder Harry Williams was a veteran of the Negro League circuit by 1944 and is considered "an underrated player" with a good bat who "could play any infield position," James A. Riley wrote. He spent five seasons playing for the Black Yankees and ten playing for various other teams before returning to the Black Yankees as manager in 1950. He was a big stick in the New York lineup at Muzzy Field, smashing a home run and a double and scoring three runs.

The Black Yankees' reported third baseman, Al Starks, does not appear in Riley's *Biographical Encyclopedia of the Negro Baseball Leagues*, but could actually be James Starks, who spent seven of his years in the Negro Leagues with the Black Yankees, including the 1944 season. If so, Starks was a six-foot-two, 225-pound hitter with good power who was adequate otherwise, Riley stated. He hit .300 for the Black Yankees in 1941 but was relegated to reserve status for the remainder of his Black Yankee career because of sub-.200 batting averages. The Starks who played at Muzzy smashed a home run, collected three hits, and scored four runs.

Hapgood, the New York right fielder, is unknown to Riley and no information other than his surname is published in the local newspaper. He also hit a home run and scored twice against ND CIO.

Catcher William Kelly, a Black Yankee rookie in 1944, was one of the few visitors who failed to get a hit. A reliable backstop, he earned a spot in the starting lineup during the war years and later become one of several catchers brought in by the Homestead Grays in 1947 to replace the legendary Josh Gibson following his death.

John McFarland, a pitcher who spent four seasons with the Black Yankees in the mid-1940s, played right field for New York and went 0-for-5 with a run scored.

Percy Forrest was the starting pitcher for New York and also collected a hit. He spent more than ten seasons in the black big leagues, three with the Black

Yankees. Incomplete game information does not reveal how many innings Forrest pitched, but he was followed by hurlers named "Ziegler" and "Russel," according to the *Bristol Press*. Neither appears in Riley's exhaustive documentation.

By the time the ND team straightened out and finished strong in the Baltimore tournament, WEAC football was under way at Muzzy Field. The athletic club's participation in football had been sporadic in the years immediately before and during World War II, and the autumn of 1944 offered little in the way of historically significant football moments. With a focus on competing against local teams, WEAC struggled to attract enough fans at Muzzy Field to remain solvent and shifted their home base to Torrington in early November. Sugar Hugret, who was coach of the WEAC team, took to playing for the more competitive New London Diesels by the end of the season.

◆          ◆          ◆

Despite New Departure's baseball success, the team lost several thousand dollars in 1944, and the company did not field a team the next year. Springtime bloomed while Muzzy Field sat idle and quiet, save for some schoolboy games, and threatened to remain that way through the summer. Focused on the war or distracted by other entertainment options, people simply did not show up at the gates.

"... With the field that we have, it is little short of criminal that baseball cannot be a regular Sunday and holiday occurrence at Muzzy Field throughout the summer," Simmons penned in April.

By July, however, two local teams had formed in the Bristol Townies and Bristol Tramps, and the Tramps called Muzzy Field home while the Townies played at Page Park. Organized by local softball and basketball maven Julie Larese, the Tramps boasted Gurske and Dugas in their lineup, but neither team received the kind of attention that local baseball clubs had generated in previous decades.

When the WEAC football team attracted twenty-nine players to their tryout in late August, very few box scores were appearing in the newspaper.

About a month later, though, Brophy the promoter announced that the New Departure Recreation Council was sponsoring an appearance by the vaunted New York Yankees in an exhibition game against the Savitt Gems of Hartford on Tuesday, September 25.

A week before the game, tickets went on sale at local smoke shops, pharmacies, and haberdasheries at $1.65 reserved and $1.25 general admission for adults

(75 cents for children), and 5,000 extra bleacher seats were made available. While the Yankees suffered like other Major League Baseball clubs during the lean war years, they were America's premiere sports franchise, and local officials expected a large crowd.

New York arrived in Bristol due south from Boston on an off day following a three-game series against the Red Sox. They finished up against the Philadelphia A's and Red Sox at Yankee Stadium on their way to an 81–71 record and a fourth-place finish.

Nearly thirty players accompanied ten New York baseball writers on the train to Berlin where a motorcade met them while a police escort awaited them at the Bristol town line. Extra buses ran from the New Departure plant on North Main Street and the downtown area to Muzzy Field, and a twenty-two-piece New Departure band greeted the mighty Yankees.

Famed WTIC radio announcer Bob Steele conducted his "Strictly Sports" show live at the ballpark where twenty policemen were dispatched to handle the crowd and traffic.

The mass of people, however, was not enough to impress local reporters, who chided the public for a "disappointing" turnout. Sportswriters gathered at the Chippanee Country Club before the game, a report stated, and almost as many people were there as were at the ball game, "which characterizes this little sporting town about as well as anything could."

The Yankee lineup did not necessarily shine with historical brilliance, but they were well regarded for their time. Their top hitters were second baseman George "Snuffy" Stirnweiss and first baseman Nick Etten. Stirnweiss, a former star halfback at the University of North Carolina, won the batting title on the last day of the 1945 season and finished with a .309 average, leading the league in hits (195), doubles (32), and runs (107) for the second consecutive year. He also earned the first of two consecutive All-Star game appearances.

Etten was New York's main power threat in 1945 with 18 home runs and 111 RBI, second and first in the league, while hitting .285 and earning the only All-Star nomination of his career.

The Yankee lineup at Muzzy Field featured Stirnweiss at second base; Bud Metheny in right field; Tuck Stainback in center field; Charlie "King Kong" Keller, an eventual five-time All-Star in his thirteen-year career, in left field; Etten at first base; Oscar Grimes, an All-Star in 1945, at third base; Mike Milosevich at shortstop; and Herb Crompton at catcher. The pitchers were Hartford native Monk Dubiel, a ten-game winner for the Yankees in 1945, and Al Gettel, a nine-game winner.

And of course, there was esteemed manager Joe McCarthy, who had won the last of his seven World Series championships with the Yankees in 1943 and entered the Hall of Fame in 1957; by the time he retired in 1950, McCarthy had managed 3,487 games in 24 years and recorded a .615 winning percentage.

Though the Savitt Gems managed four runs on ten hits, they were no match for the Yankees, who scored six runs in the fifth inning and collected fifteen total hits in the game for a 9–4 triumph.

Metheny drove in three runs and scored twice with two home runs, and Stirnweiss added two runs scored with six assists in the field. Stainback, Keller, Milosevich, and Dubiel all collected two hits and drove in a combined two runs while Grimes and Crompton drove in three with two hits combined. Etten finished 1-for-5, and Gettel smacked a double and scored a run.

Dubiel earned the win with five innings pitched, though he gave up all four Gems' runs on nine hits. Gettel finished the game with one hit allowed in four innings while striking out three.

Nothing else topped the Yankee appearance for the rest of the year, including WEAC's football triumph over five-time state champion and traditional power New London.

WEAC had signed quarterback Wes Holden, a former local high school standout who starred at Columbia University, but even he could not attract paying fans. The apathy forced WEAC officials to react.

"Convinced that sports is a losing proposition in Bristol and the only way to lure fans into Muzzy Field is to probably book some attraction and charge one crackerjack box top for admission, Manager Frank Longo will take his fine club on the road," the newspaper reported, noting that the team lost one thousand dollars on three home games.

WEAC folded the season in October.

◆　　◆　　◆

The following year passed rather quietly at Muzzy Field. Boxing returned in early June, and softball games attracted as many as fifteen hundred while the New Departure Interdepartmental Softball League debuted at Muzzy Field on June 10.

In July, Roy Dissinger, a Connecticut native and longtime scout with the St. Louis Cardinals and Boston Red Sox, conducted a tryout camp at Muzzy Field on behalf of the Triple-A New Orleans Pelicans, of which Dissinger served as general manager, chief scout, and director of its farm system. He rated the field highly and suggested Bristol field a minor league-caliber team.

One major obstacle to such a proposition was the lack of a lighting system, but that was addressed in mid-August when a city board was created to study the feasibility of installing such a system at a cost of twenty thousand dollars. A permanently lighted Muzzy Field would be a reality within a year.

Certainly the potential still existed to draw big crowds. The North Atlantic Regional softball tournament hosted at Muzzy Field the last weekend of August attracted more than forty-six hundred fans. Unfortunately for the WEAC football program, no more than a few hundred showed up throughout the fall, and the club became largely irrelevant, despite the presence of local football star Richard "Stonewall" Jackson.

◆　　　◆　　　◆

The push toward a baseball renaissance in Bristol began during the winter months of 1947 and culminated in the creation of the Bristol Sports Promotions, Inc., a group of local-minded sportsmen who desired a return to the days when their ballpark on the West End buzzed with excitement in the spring and summer.

Unsatisfied with fielding an amateur team with a few big-name opponents sprinkled on the schedule, the group sponsored the semiprofessional Bristol Bees baseball team and immediately hired Edward Jeremiah Donahue as their manager, assisted by local legend George Scott.

Donahue was no stranger to high-level competitive athletics, having served as football, basketball, baseball, and track coach at Clemson University from 1917 to 1920. He coached all four sports during the 1918–19 school year before getting into baseball.

The local benefactors wanted Bristol to boast a high-caliber team with a high-end facility to attract large crowds at the gate. With entertainment options more readily available than when Bristol last fielded such a competitive team in the 1920s, the group needed to invest in a quality team and the town needed to invest in a lighting system; the local newspaper continually mentioned the large crowds that were attracted to the semipro night games of the West Haven Sailors and the Meriden Insilcos (sponsored by the International Silver Company) under the lights at their fields.

Bristol Sports Promotions wanted its team to ascend to similar levels, and it believed the novelty of night baseball was the answer. Night games became an attractive feature of Bees baseball in the summer. They also needed talent on the field, and Donahue began accumulating such in April with the signings of Eddie Wilson, a former Brooklyn Dodgers catcher for the 1936 and 1937 seasons, and Jim Sheehan, who played one game with the 1936 New York Giants.

Jack Westley, a standout hitter the previous season for St. Petersburg of the Florida State League, was the team's main offensive threat. He was joined by second baseman Ray "Scooter" Scussel, a former Yale football player who also signed with the Los Angeles Dons of the All-America Football Conference. Steve Shoplick, Ray Curry, Charlie Horvath, Johnny Utke, Jake Banks, Johnny Chomick, and Bill Miller, brother of All-Star Eddie Miller, rounded out the position players. Even George Scott, then fifty-two years old, got into a game in August and collected an RBI double with a run scored.

Donahue managed to sign an able pitching staff of George Klimak, Bristol native Dick Redman, Bill Connolly, and Dick Manville. Connolly and Manville were Ivy Leaguers who had been ruled ineligible from their college teams (Harvard and Yale) after playing in minor league circuits.

Though there was no formal agreement, the Bees served as a repository of young talent for the Boston Braves while playing as an independent team.

Manville spent only two months on the Bees team before the Braves signed him in mid-June and optioned him to the Milwaukee Brewers of the American Association. He broke into the major leagues in 1950 and pitched in twelve games in his short career with the Braves and Chicago Cubs.

Bristol's new team was a highly capable bunch. They started quickly and played strong, winning baseball through the summer months on their way to a 34–24 mark.

The Bees' inaugural game took place on Thursday, May 8, a cold day that restricted the turnout to about six hundred fans to watch the visiting Ottawa Nationals. Ottawa was an interesting opponent. Owned by National Hockey League cofounder, Stanley Cup-winning coach, and future Hall of Famer Tom Gorman, the team's manager was former St. Louis Cardinal pitcher Paul "Daffy" Dean. Ottawa was training in Saratoga Springs, New York, in preparation for their season in the Class C Border League in which they would be pennant winners and champions.

But the Bees got off to a better start and won 8–5 as Westley hit a home run—estimated at 350 feet—over the right-field wall and finished with 3 hits, 5 RBI, and 11 putouts at first base. Some of the runs came against Dean, who inserted himself near the end of the game as the third of four pitchers used.

That weekend, the Bees battled another Border League entry, the Ogdensburg Maples, managed by Steve Yerkes, a seven-year major league infielder who won a World Series ring with the 1912 Boston Red Sox. They split at Muzzy Field, losing the first game but recovering in front of more than 1,150 fans as Manville shut down the Maples on the mound and delivered 4 hits with 7 RBI. Manville won one more game with the Bees before signing with the Braves.

The Bees continued their winning ways through early June and ran their record to 9–1 after a victory over American Bosch of Springfield, Massachusetts. The visitors arrived with Angelo Bertelli, teammate of Scussel's on the Los Angeles Dons football team. Bertelli was a highly decorated football player at Notre Dame where he won the 1943 Heisman Trophy despite playing only six games before the Marine Corps activated him. He was the catalyst for Notre Dame's famed T-formation and passed for 2,582 yards and 29 touchdowns in 26 games in his Irish career, earning a College Football Hall of Fame induction in 1972.

At Muzzy Field, Bertelli played error-free in center field and finished with a single in four at-bats with no putouts or assists.

Meanwhile, BSP was working in the background to bring additional attractions to Muzzy Field. In mid-June, it announced that the New York Yankees of the All-America Football Conference would play an intrasquad game in August, a short trip from their preseason training headquarters at Cheshire (CT) Academy. Donahue was to coach a football version of the Bees, which would serve as training grounds for future Yankee players.

As a baseball manager, Donahue continued to strengthen the Bees, signing pitcher Tom Casey of New York University, one of the best college teams east of the Mississippi River that season. Yale, featuring first baseman and future president George H.W. Bush, edged NYU for the Eastern championship and played California in the first College World Series.

On July 2, Casey made his Bees debut against the Kokomo (IN) Clowns in front of 1,240 fans under portable lights at Muzzy Field.

With his fastball, sinker, and curve, Casey did not disappoint in striking out eighteen and tossing a two-hitter in a 1–0 victory; the only Clown hits came from players named Elmer and Ha-Ha. Billy Moore, the brother of former New Departure standout Johnny Moore, added an RBI single in the ninth inning for the winning run as the Bees ran their record to 14–5.

The team and their ownership saw what a field with permanent lights might mean at the gates when the Bees traveled to West Haven on July 4 to play a night game, which they lost, 3–2, in front of four thousand fans at Exhibition Park. News reports from late spring indicated that Muzzy Field would have its lights by

June, but that month had passed without any stanchions erected on Bristol's West End.

Bristol suffered a rare setback on July 13 when the New York Cops defeated them, 6–1, in front of nearly nine hundred fans in a Sunday night game. One of the main contributors to the visitors' victory was Eddie Turchin, a thirty-year-old second baseman who had played eleven games for the Cleveland Indians in 1943. Batting in the fifth spot, Turchin collected two hits and scored twice off of Klivak and Redman.

That same day, Donahue signed Roy Teasley, captain-elect of the NYU baseball team whose 9–0 record was the only one better than Casey's.

Better news followed when it was announced that steel light stanchions were on order and would arrive by July 19.

By then, the Bees had defeated the Puerto Rican All-Stars and had attracted nearly twelve hundred fans in two home games, which they split. Teasley pitched a six-hitter with nine strikeouts against the All-Stars, whose lineup included Fontanez in right field, Ville Fame at third base, Cabrera in center field, Lanauze at first base, Montalvo at catcher, Hernandez in left field, Santiago at shortstop, Pedrozo at second base, and Pulliza and Fernandez on the hill. No other details were found about these players.

On July 27, the Bees improved to 21–10 with a 9–1 home victory over the Meriden Insilcos, which featured seventeen-year-old Jimmy Piersall, a Waterbury native and one of the finest players ever to come out of the state of Connecticut. In 1950, he began a seventeen-year major league career with the Boston Red Sox and eventually played with five other teams on his way to hitting .272 while playing strong defense in the outfield, ending with ninety-five assists and thirty-nine errors in his career.

Piersall and his Meriden teammates accomplished little against Casey and the Bees, however, as Casey scattered four hits—one of them a single from Piersall—and struck out nine batters. Piersall scored the lone run on a Jack Westley throwing error.

The Bees closed out July winning two of three.

August's first day brought the Staten Island Dodgers, a Brooklyn farm club that the Bees had defeated handily back in June. But one major change in Staten Island's lineup stood out and news of it spread quickly and enthusiastically throughout the city.

Jimmie Foxx, who was inducted into the Hall of Fame in 1951, signed on with the Dodgers and made his first appearance at Muzzy Field. The coming of Foxx—a three-time MVP, two-time World Series champion, and one of the game's finest hitters with a .325 average, 534 home runs, and 1,921 RBI in twenty seasons with the Red Sox, Athletics, Cubs, and Phillies—was a gate attraction that swelled attendance to nearly 2,000 at Muzzy Field.

As successful as Foxx had been on the diamond, his personal life was chaotic.

A contentious divorce from his first wife, Helen, cost him financially, and he had lost money on a Florida golf course investment that closed during World War II, according to biographer John Bennett. Prior to the divorce, Foxx was estranged from his sons for long periods of time and began drinking heavily. But by the time he arrived in Bristol, he was happily remarried with another son, Bennett wrote.

Foxx, then thirty-nine years old, batted cleanup and started at first base for the Dodgers. The team, which included no other former or future major league players, faced Klivak, who performed admirably.

Foxx collected two singles in four at-bats, but Klivak got the better of him in the seventh with a strikeout. Still, the Dodgers had enough to defeat the Bees, 4–3. Foxx would soon return to Bristol.

Meanwhile, stanchions were going up at Muzzy Field for the first night game played under permanent lights on August 5 against the West Haven Sailors. The newspaper reported that ten light towers now encompassed Muzzy Field, each of them standing eighty feet tall. Soon after the Bees secured Teasley by contract, the Sailors swooped in and signed him away with a more lucrative offer, which certainly added some spice to an historic game played between two of the better independent semipro teams in the state.

More than three thousand fans crammed into Muzzy Field for the game, which West Haven won, 7–5. Curry had a two-run triple for the Bees, but their pitching staff was hit harder than they hit Bob Barthelson, who had spent part of the 1944 season with the New York Giants mound corps. The Sailors also featured third baseman Vince Ventura, a former Washington Senator who went 0-for-4 at Muzzy, and second baseman Arnie Sergicomi, who reportedly had been a Nazi prisoner during the war. Sergicomi collected a hit in three official plate appearances.

The Dodgers' appearance was so popular that the Bees brought them back on August 8 and drew another thirteen hundred fans for Foxx's second game at Muzzy Field. This time, the Bees gained the upper hand as Ray Curry had three hits and scored the winning run on Redman's single in the sixth for a 4–2 victory. Foxx, who played first and third base, was 1-for-2 with a run and hit into a double play.

In their final years of fielding ball clubs, the House of David played two games in Bristol and split against the Bees. Bristol won the second game, 7–5, with Westley's two-run home run, and he became the first man to hit three home runs out of Muzzy Field in one season. A team from Freeport, Long Island, knocked off the Bees the next day, dropping them to 26–15.

Football then took center stage as the New York Yankees arrived from Cheshire. Clad in their silver and blue uniforms and coming off a 10–3–1 season in 1946, the Yankees were considered the class franchise of the All-America Football Conference along with the Cleveland Browns.

Millionaire businessmen formed the AAFC in 1944 as a competitor to the NFL on the belief that an influx of professional football talent would be available immediately after World War II. In their first season, 1946, the Yankees won the four-team East but lost, 14–9, to the Browns in the championship game.

The Yankees again were favorites in 1947 under the direction of Ray Flaherty, a future Pro Football Hall of Fame inductee who had played end with Red Grange's Yankees in 1927–28. He then joined Steve Owen and the New York Giants, becoming a playing coach in 1933. Three years later, Flaherty became a head coach at age thirty-two with the Boston Redskins and coached them to league championships in 1937 and 1942. Flaherty is credited with two innovations in professional football—the behind-the-line screen pass and a two-platoon offense, one that emphasized the ground game and the other the passing game. In ten years as a head coach, Flaherty compiled an 80–37–5 mark.

His intrasquad scrimmage at Muzzy Field included one team running the T-formation and the other running the single wing, which was New York's offense of choice in the regular season.

The "T" team included Bob Flowers and Lou Sossamon as centers; Roman Bentz, John Perko, Jack Quinn, Chuck Riffle, and Don Cumley as guards; Chuck Elliott, Nate Johnson, Frank "Bruiser" Kinard, and John Sanchez as tackles; Bruce Alford, Mel Conger, and Roy Kurasch as ends; and Harry Burrus, Lloyd Cheatham, Jack Fellows, Dewey Proctor, John Sylvester, Fred Cardinal, Frank Dornfeld, John Moddy, and Bob Sweiger as the backfield.

Despite Johnson earning AAFC All-League honors in 1947, Kinard was the star of this group. In three seasons at the University of Mississippi, Kinard was named All-America his junior and senior seasons after he was on the field for 708 of 720 minutes the Rebels played his sophomore season. He is considered one of the finest players in Southern college football history (Barnhart 2000).

A third-round pick of the Brooklyn Dodgers in 1938, Kinard was an under-sized tackle (weighing 216 pounds at his heaviest) but fast and aggressive and a

60-minute player. In his nine-year NFL and AAFC career, Kinard missed only one game, and "even then, it was doctor's orders, not a lack of willingness to play that kept Bruiser on the sideline," his Pro Football Hall of Fame biography stated.

Kinard, a sure tackler and smothering blocker at six foot one, earned All-NFL recognition from his rookie season in 1938 through 1944, after which he entered the military for one year. In 1946, he joined the Yankees and earned All-AAFC honors, becoming the first pro football player named All-League in both leagues. His appearance at Muzzy Field marked the beginning of his final season in professional football, and he was inducted into the Pro Football Hall of Fame in 1971.

New York's single-wing team included Jack Baldwin and Ralph Stewart as centers; Mike Karmazin, Joe Yachanich, Ed Grain, Oliver Poole, and Ed Sharkey as guards; Derrell Palmer, Vic Schleich, Ted Ossowski, and Jack Durishan as tackles; Preston Flanagan, Van Davis, Archie Harris, and Roy Ruckusky as ends; and Ed Prokop, Bob Kennedy, Orban "Spec" Sanders, Frank "Fireball Frankie" Sinkwich, Lowell Wagner, Jack Kelley, Harvey Johnson, Del Owens, and Bob Krejsa as the loaded backfield.

The single-wing notables were Sanders, Sinkwich, and Prokop, a former All-American at Georgia Tech.

Sanders led the AAFC in 1946—his rookie year out of the University of Texas—with 709 yards rushing, 6 touchdowns, and more than 5 yards per carry. With high expectations on a talented team, Sanders far surpassed his own benchmark in a season that hinted at no sophomore slump. At twenty-nine years old in his second year, the six-foot-two, 196-pound back became the only runner in AAFC's short history to run for more than 1,000 yards when he finished with 1,432 yards and 18 touchdowns in 14 games while also passing for 1,442 yards and 14 touchdowns.

Stan Grosshandler quoted Yankee fullback Buddy Young in his brief history of the AAFC. "I would consider Spec Sanders one of the five or six truly great players I have seen," Young said. "He was in a class by himself. You could say he was a late maturation factor [after spending time in the military]. He really came of age when he got to the Yankees."

Young was playing in the prestigious college all-star game in Chicago at the time the Yankees came to Bristol, which would explain his absence from the roster despite playing a significant role on the team that year.

Before Sanders's breakout season, Sinkwich was the more decorated player. A consensus All-American in 1941 and 1942 at the University of Georgia, he became the first player from a Southern school to win the Heisman Trophy in

1942. The five-foot-ten, 185-pound Sinkwich ended his Georgia career as one of the finest offensive players in college football history after compiling 2,271 yards rushing and 2,331 yards passing and scoring 60 touchdowns in 3 seasons.

The Detroit Lions then made him the top draft pick in 1943, and Sinkwich responded in kind with All-Pro honors in his rookie season. The next year, he passed for 1,060 yards, rushed for 563, and accounted for 18 touchdowns while intercepting 3 passes; in turn, he was named NFL Most Valuable Player. His NFL career seemed destined for things as great as or better than college, until he joined the air force in 1944. During a football game with his team in Colorado Springs, Sinkwich suffered a major knee injury that required two surgeries, and he never recovered completely.

At twenty-five, his career was essentially over, though he played two more seasons in the AAFC. "I was foolish to try to come back and play in the AAFC," Grosshandler quoted Sinkwich as saying. "I couldn't do a thing. I've always thought what might have been had I been able to play with a set of good knees."

Sinkwich, however, acquitted himself well at Muzzy Field as a starting left halfback for the single-wingers, completing seven of eleven passes.

The football exhibition, of which announcements had been made over the public address system at Yankee Stadium during baseball games, drew an admirable crowd of thirty-five hundred on a midsummer Friday afternoon. Bristol Sports Promotions hired Fay Vincent to handle the officiating duties, and he presided over a well-played game.

The "T" team, captained by Kinard, struck first when Proctor capped off a sixty-nine-yard drive with a short touchdown run and a successful conversion kick by Karmazin. The team added another touchdown in the second quarter when Prokop passed to Sanders only to have Dornfeld snatch it away and take it in for a touchdown, followed by a Karmazin kick, for a 14–0 halftime lead.

Sanders finally got his team on the board in the fourth quarter with a fourteen-yard scamper to cap a seventy-four-yard drive followed by Harvey Johnson's kick. Sinkwich's passes and Sanders's running highlighted the drive, but only Sanders's performance was an indication of the season to come. Sinkwich played sparingly while Sanders thrived at the midpoint of his short professional football career.

For Bristolites, their attention returned to the Bees and the baseball diamond.

But the Bees were not playing great baseball at the end of the summer and closed out the last two months with a 9–10 mark. There were, however, noteworthy games played during that time.

On August 18, nearly two thousand fans showed up for a game against Hartford's minor league team—then called the Chiefs—which the Bees lost, 4–1. Hartford's roster included Piersall (0-for-4) and third baseman Nick Picciuto, who was 2-for-5 with a run and an RBI. The twenty-five-year-old had played 36 games in a reserve role for the dreadful 1945 Philadelphia Phillies, who lost 108 games.

A home-and-home doubleheader with West Haven on August 24 caused a big stir, but the Bees lost both games as Vince Ventura, the former Washington Senator, collected two hits and scored a run at Muzzy in front of fifteen hundred fans.

During Labor Day weekend, the New York Black Yankees made their first appearance since 1944 and drew a good crowd. New York's lineup featured a player named Fitzgerald in center field, who was replaced early in the game by Marvin Barker, making his second appearance at Muzzy Field.

Second baseman Dick Seay batted second, and though a light-hitting player, he was known for his bunting and hit-and-run skills. Seay enjoyed a twenty-two-year career in the Negro Leagues and is considered the best defensive second baseman in black baseball in the 1930s. He played for three consecutive Negro National League champions in the mid-1930s and provided "defensive contributions to his team's success [that] were immeasurable" (Riley 1994).

"The amiable and popular player was always in demand by ball clubs in the Negro Leagues and in Latin America, especially Puerto Rico, where he is still a national hero," Riley added.

Seay's appearance was one of his last in Negro League baseball, as he retired after the 1947 season.

John Smith, the right fielder, also was on the back end of his career after spending three prosperous years with the Chicago American Giants before joining the Black Yankees in 1946.

Hard-hitting rookie first baseman George Crowe batted cleanup at Muzzy Field and started his career with the Black Yankees, hitting .305, before eventually breaking into the major leagues with the Boston Braves in 1952. He also enjoyed successful seasons in Cincinnati and St. Louis and compiled a .270 lifetime major league average in nine seasons with eighty-one home runs. After retiring from baseball in 1961, his life took an interesting turn. "He became a recluse, living in the rural Adirondacks without modern conveniences," according to Riley.

Shortstop Clyde "The Dude" Parris was a week shy of his twenty-first birthday when he arrived in Bristol, near the end of a season in which he hit

.246—thirty points higher than the previous year. Parris stayed with the Black Yankees until the Negro National League folded after the 1948 campaign, and he then spent nearly a decade in the minor leagues before finishing his career in Mexico. A native of Panama, Parris returned home nearly every winter to play baseball.

Johnny Hayes batted sixth for the Black Yankees as their catcher, near the end of his seventeen-year Negro League career. Regarded as a left-handed slap hitter with little power, Hayes earned an All-Star game nomination in 1947 while hitting .257; his braininess in calling a game made him one of the better catchers in baseball.

Hayes and Crowe both played for Hartford in the Eastern League after their time with the Black Yankees.

Joe Spencer manned third base at Muzzy Field, three years after he was a part-time starter with the Homestead Grays on their World Series championship team. Spencer was never much of a hitter in his playing days as his .179 average in limited play with the 1947 Black Yankees attests.

Hugh "Honey" Lott roamed the outer garden in left field and spent just a handful of seasons in the Negro National League before it folded. He then enjoyed a five-year career in the organized minor leagues, playing in five circuits around the country.

John "Neck" Stanley began his lengthy Negro League career in 1927, and the five-foot-eleven, 215-pound left-hander made a name for himself in games against white all-star teams with his repertoire of ten pitches, some of which were illegal. Stanley's spitball was his hallmark, but he also wielded "an excellent slider, a good screwball, drop and change and had an average curve, fastball, sinker and knuckler, and he was also highly proficient with a 'cut ball,'" Riley wrote.

"The hefty southpaw mixed a wide assortment of off-speed breaking pitches to keep batters off stride, and excelled at holding runners on first base," Riley continued, "but acknowledged that an emery board and good control were key ingredients to his mound success."

Stanley pitched for Satchel Paige's All-Star team that barnstormed against Bob Feller's All-Stars in 1946, but he was dropped for his use of illegal pitches following a protest from Feller's team members. The white all-stars refused to continue the tour unless Stanley was cut from the team after he shut out their club, 4–0, in front of twenty-seven thousand at Yankee Stadium.

Stanley, who spent eighteen years with the Black Yankees, is credited with five no-hitters and "was a consistent 20-game winner for more than a decade," Riley stated. Two of his wins included 8–0 and 6–0 decisions over Babe Ruth's All-Stars and Dizzy Dean's All-Stars.

At Muzzy Field, he allowed the Bees few scoring opportunities in throwing a complete game in front of almost fifteen hundred fans. Stanley scattered four hits and allowed two runs with four strikeouts and five walks, but it took a pivotal double play in the seventh inning to preserve New York's lead and eventual 4–2 victory.

For the Bees, Lefty Perzan matched Stanley most of the way, but a three-run third inning proved his undoing when he surrendered two singles, a double, and a walk.

The Black Yankees' offensive surge came from Crowe, who smacked an RBI double; Parris, who had three hits and drove in a run; and Smith, who scored twice and drove in one run on two hits. Hayes also drove in a run and Seay came around to score once.

The Bees split the next two games at home before challenging the Eastern League All-Stars at Muzzy Field on September 9. The All-Stars, whose lineup included ex-Phillie Nick Picciuto, tied the game in the eighth on a three-run double and won it in the tenth, 4–3, with a ground ball deep in the hole at short-stop that scored a runner from third.

A similarly impressive crowd of nearly thirteen hundred showed up five days later for a game against the International League All-Stars. On a damp Sunday evening, the Bees got the better of the IL squad, 7–3, as the teams combined for eleven errors with a wet ball on a torn-up infield.

The most effective IL player also was the game's most notable. Joe Buzas played thirty games with the 1945 New York Yankees, but his true legacy in Bristol came almost thirty years later when he became the owner of the Bristol Red Sox of the Class AA Eastern League and called Muzzy Field home for ten years before relocating to New Britain. Buzas, a second baseman, went 3-for-4 with two runs and an RBI against the Bees.

Another IL player with future ties to the city was pitcher/right fielder Al Barillari, a member of the Baltimore Orioles. After driving in a run and taking the loss on the mound for the International League'ers, he returned in 1949 as manager of the Bristol Owls, the city's Class B Colonial League entry.

Two days after that game, the Bees took on the New York Cubans, then of the Negro National League, on a cold Tuesday night that drew only 761 fans. Unfortunately for the fans who stayed away, they missed out on watching the 1947 NNL champions that became the World Series champions by defeating the Negro American League's Cleveland Buckeyes.

Bristol contracted Fred Collins, who pitched one inning against the IL All-Stars, to start against the Cubans, and Collins, a former teammate of Albie Gurske in Binghamton, tossed a gem against New York's starter Barney Morris.

The Cuban lineup included leadoff batter Orestes "Minnie" Minoso, the offensive catalyst of the championship team. A speedy third baseman with a dangerous bat, Minoso did not remain long in the Negro Leagues before he joined the Cleveland Indians in 1949.

Minoso, five foot ten and 175 pounds, soon was traded to the Chicago White Sox and became a fixture in the outfield. In seventeen seasons with four teams, Minoso won three Gold Gloves in left field and was a seven-time all-star. He led the American League in stolen bases his first three full seasons and throughout his career consistently hit around .300. Minoso also had longevity in the game, playing in five decades and appearing as a pinch hitter in the 1980s.

He was an offensive and defensive force in three decades and finished his major league career with a .298 average, 186 home runs, 1,023 RBI, 1,136 runs scored, 205 steals, 336 doubles, and 83 triples, plus a .459 slugging percentage.

After his time in the major leagues, he played nine more seasons in Mexico until he was in his fifties, including seasons of hitting .360 and .348 during that time.

At Muzzy Field, Minoso played third base.

First baseman Homero Ariosa batted second and played sparingly for the Cubans in 1947, his first of three years with the club.

Shortstop Silvio Garcia was an all-star for the Cubans on his way to hitting .324 in 1947. A fine five-tool player at five foot eleven and 190 pounds, Garcia was one of the best hitters never to play in the major leagues, according to Hall of Fame manager Tommy Lasorda, who pitched against Garcia in Cuba. Hall of Fame manager Leo Durocher also raved about Garcia's defensive abilities (Riley 1994).

Garcia started his career as a pitcher but was struck in the arm while sitting in the dugout during a game, and the injury forced him to the infield. Though he played only two seasons for the Cubans, Garcia played nineteen years in the Cuban Winter League where he posted a lifetime average of .282.

Claro Duany, a left-handed power hitter playing right field, batted behind Garcia. He was a regular in New York's outfield, and he earned the nickname "the Puerto Rican Babe Ruth" both for his ability to clout pitches and for his six-foot-two, 215-pound physique, which often increased to greater proportions. He enjoyed a lengthy and prosperous career in the Puerto Rican, Cuban, and Mexican winter leagues, leading the Cuban league with a .340 average in 1944–45. He then played in Canada and for one season in the American minor leagues before retiring from organized baseball in 1952.

Ray Noble began his career with the Cubans as a catcher, but he played left field against the Bees where he could unleash his powerful arm strength. In 1947, he was one of New York's top hitters with a .325 average. After some time spent in the minor leagues, Noble played parts of the 1951–53 seasons with the New York Giants before spending his final eight years at the Triple-A level.

After two sluggish seasons with the Cubans, Cleveland Clark broke out in 1947 and clubbed the pill at a .338 clip as the team's regular center fielder, the same position he held down at Muzzy Field while batting sixth in the lineup. Clark also posted impressive numbers in the Cuban Winter League, such as his .361 average for the 1944–45 champion Almendares club.

Horacio "Rabbit" Martinez played second base in Bristol and was at the end of a career in which he distinguished himself with "his sterling glovework and the skill and ease with which he executed his position ..." Riley commented, while earning consideration as the best shortstop in the league in the 1940s. Though an average hitter most of the time, he shined in his five East-West All-Star game appearances, hitting .545.

Catcher Louis Louden had a powerful arm and pulled most every pitch as a right-handed hitter. He posted a .290 average in 1947 and performed smoothly with some additional help, Riley offered.

"He was a superb receiver whose hustle and pep kept the players on their toes and the fans pleased with his antics," he wrote. "He had a bit of a drinking problem and would sometimes show up so inebriated he couldn't snap his own shin guards, yet still he could catch a flawless game."

Louden made the first of three appearances in the East-West All-Star game around this time, staking his claim as the preeminent catcher of the late 1940s following Josh Gibson's death. Between 1946 and 1949, Louden played with both the Willie Mays All-Star and Jackie Robinson All-Star teams.

Morris was "regarded as the best knuckleballer in the league," Riley noted, and "threw his knuckler as hard as a fastball" with control. The six-foot, 170-pound right-hander began his baseball career in 1932 and along the way earned two East-West All-Star nominations while also throwing an excellent drop ball and a good curve and changeup.

In 1934–35, he played with Neil Churchill's mostly white ball club in Bismarck, North Dakota, and often caught for teammate Satchel Paige, Riley added.

Such an intimidating lineup had no effect on Fred Collins, the Bees pitcher.

He calmly scattered six hits, walked three, and struck out nine, allowing no runs. In the first inning, the Cubans attempted a double steal with Garcia on first and Minoso on third, but Minoso was thrown out at home plate.

Morris was equally stingy, allowing only an unearned run in the first inning after Noble dropped a fly ball with a runner on third base. He allowed little the rest of the way and scattered four hits with three strikeouts and four walks for the game.

Noble redeemed himself with a two-out triple in the sixth inning—the only extra base hit of the game—but Clark struck out to end what proved to be New York's final threat. Garcia picked up two hits while Minoso, Duany, Noble, and Louden collected one apiece.

The Bees scored an impressive 1–0 victory, and knocking off the eventual Negro League champion Cubans was the high point of their season. The team went on to win their final two games, drawing eleven hundred fans in the season finale, to finish their inaugural season at 34–24.

Donahue's debut campaign with the Bristol Bees football team was equally successful, though much less heralded with the team and their opponents lacking star power. The Bees finished 7–2–1 playing teams from nearby towns such as Waterbury, Torrington, and Southington, the latter attracting the largest and most vociferous crowds of the season.

Southington handed the Bees a 6–0 loss on Thanksgiving Day in the last game of the season in front of 1,800 fans, about a month after Bristol won the first game, 9–0, in front of 2,094 at Muzzy.

◆     ◆     ◆

Large-scale player turnover greeted the Bristol Bees baseball program in 1948 as several had signed on with other semipro teams in the area or in the case of pitcher Dick Manville, remained in the minor league system.

As an independent team operating on a small budget, the Bees were destined to see many new faces every year—had they remained solvent. Donahue castigated the city in April for its exorbitant rental fee structure that charged the Bees $175 per game and a 5-cent tax on every fan. With a projected schedule of fifty night games (quite ambitious for the team), Donahue would pay more than eight thousand dollars to the city with an additional three thousand dollars in taxes coming from his projected attendance of sixty thousand.

Though his numbers might have been unrealistically inflated, he made his point when he said the high fees would kill baseball in Bristol. As far as the Bees were concerned, he was right. BSP remained a hometown management team headquartered in the Chamber of Commerce building on Main Street. Without corporate backing such as the old New Departure teams or the Meriden Insilcos, the financial odds were stacked against them.

By the end of August, the Bees had canceled their season due to poor gate receipts, never to take the field again, despite another successful run with a 26–14 record. The inability to make money also caused the Bees football team to fold, and Donahue started coaching a football team in Waterbury that autumn.

Even with the financial bickering and hand-wringing, the 1948 baseball season at Muzzy Field provided several highlights. The Bees' new players—including twenty-three-year-old Yale architecture student and pitcher Walt Gathman—mixed well with the relatively veteran second-year players, and the team started quickly with sixteen wins in their first twenty-three games.

As Buddy Rich, Tommy Dorsey, and Gene Krupa were making headlines for their appearances at Lake Compounce, the first significant event at Muzzy Field did not occur until June 8 when the New York Black Yankees made another trip to Bristol.

Several familiar players appeared in the lineup, including George Crowe, Marvin Barker, Johnny Hayes, and John Smith. The 1948 team also featured Arthur Hefner, the leadoff hitter playing center field who spent just three years in the Negro National League before it folded.

Second baseman Fred Bankhead was one of five Bankhead brothers who played in the Negro Leagues. Fred's lengthy career ended with a one-year stint with the Black Yankees in 1948, and he was known as a slick-fielding and reliable middle infielder with speed, a decent bat, and good bunting skills.

Bud Barbee also was near the end of his professional playing career in the summer of 1948 having played in the Negro Leagues since 1937. The six-foot-three 212-pounder spent most of his career as a Black Yankee and retired after the 1949 season. Primarily a pitcher, Barbee also wielded a powerful bat and played frequently at first base, which was his position in the lineup at Muzzy Field.

Left fielder Ben Little was a part-time starter who enjoyed a short, yet unremarkable, career with the Black Yankees. He was often found in the lower end of the batting order.

It is unclear who Hardy, the shortstop, actually was, based on Riley's work. The lone player with that surname and a history with the Black Yankees was Walter Hardy, a "flashy-fielding, weak-hitting middle infielder," but he was a holdout with New York in 1948. When the team failed to acquiesce to his monetary demands, Hardy joined the New York Cubans, Riley noted. Is it possible that Hardy was signed for a relatively meaningless game against a semipro team in Connecticut?

If so, Bristol fans were treated to the skills of a fine defensive player who was known for "giving the fans a thrill on every play," Riley stated.

The Black Yankees utilized two pitchers in the game: Albert Stephens and Frank Pearson. Stephens's career in the Negro Leagues encapsulated part of the 1948 season with New York, but Pearson enjoyed a more extended stay. The five-foot-six, 145-pound Memphian with a sharp curveball played for four different teams before joining a barnstorming team from Texas in the early 1950s. He also played with an all-white team in Minnesota for one season.

The Bees used right-hander Billy Mackel, a college pitcher soon to graduate from the University of Pennsylvania, and he battled the Black Yankees for nine innings, despite taking a line drive to his pitching arm from Barker and throwing five wild pitches.

New York took control in the fourth inning with four runs, including an inside-the-park home run from Barbee, part of his 3-for-5 afternoon with three RBI and a run scored. Smith also contributed mightily with four hits in five at-bats, and Barker chipped in two hits, two runs, and an RBI while Hayes drove in one. Hefner was the only other Black Yankee to collect a hit.

Stephens struggled with his control, walking five and allowing two runs and two hits before he was pulled after three innings. Pearson went the rest of the way, allowing three runs on five hits with a strikeout and two walks.

Following the loss to the Black Yankees, the Bees played winning baseball through the month of June, knocking off semipro teams from Staten Island, Massachusetts, and the House of David aggregation, and continued as such through mid-July.

The New York Giants announced a weeklong tryout camp at Muzzy Field at that time, conducted by fourteen-year veteran Hans Lobert, a speedy infielder who pilfered 316 bases during the Dead Ball Era.

The Bees had run their record to 16–7 by the time the Black Yankees returned for a Wednesday night game on July 21. Bristol's club was coming off a close win over the Meriden Insilcos that drew only three hundred fans, and local columnists tried to foment support for the team by pointing out that the small group of passionate financial backers should be appreciated for their efforts when a team such as the Insilcos had support from a large, profitable company.

Though probably because of the visitors' talent more than any newspaper column, nearly one thousand fans turned out for the New York game. This time, the Bees got the better of them in a 10–5 victory in which they collected thirteen hits off of John Smith. The only new face in the New York lineup was Rufus "Scoop" Baker at catcher, "an excellent fielder but weak hitter," Riley noted, and pinch hitter Chris Vieira.

Hefner had the best game for the Black Yankees, hitting an inside-the-park home run as one of his three hits. Defensively, New York melted down with six errors.

That weekend, the Jimmie Foxx All-Stars appeared with the future Hall of Famer in a manager's role, and the Bees notched an exciting 4–3 win in eleven innings in front of one thousand fans.

In late July, the New York Cubans appeared with Raul Lopez, a five-foot-eleven, 154-pound southpaw pitcher that the Bees failed to solve. Lopez enjoyed limited success with the Cubans, but mastered the Bees with a complete-game four-hitter and eleven strikeouts in a 6–1 victory.

Along with players such as Cleveland Clark, Ray Noble, and Louis Louden, the Cubans' lineup included shortstop Sammy Gee, a decent hitter with a short Negro League baseball career who also played basketball for the Harlem Globetrotters.

Tommy Sampson might have been the second baseman for New York, though Riley's research shows he played only the 1949 season with the Cubans. If this is the same Sampson, Bristol fans saw a former all-star with the Birmingham Black Barons whose career was altered forever in 1944 as the result of a head-on collision with a drunk driver. Aside from a fine playing career, Sampson also discovered Willie Mays in 1948 and recommended him to the Black Barons, according to Riley.

First baseman Lyman Bostock was another former Black Baron who had been among the Negro Leagues' better players before the war. Solid offensively and defensively, Bostock had earned an East-West All-Star game nomination in the early 1940s and bounced around with other teams before playing just part of the 1948 season with the Cubans.

Miguel Ballestro was at the hot corner for the Cubans in his only season in the Negro Leagues. Ballestro, at five foot eight and 160 pounds, played winter ball in Cuba and throughout organized baseball beginning in the early 1950s but never earned a promotion to the big leagues.

A player named Griggs manned right field for the Cubans.

Noble and Louden inflicted most of the damage for New York with five hits, two runs, and two RBI between them. Bostock drove in one and scored twice while Sampson collected two hits and scored a run. It was a steady game for the Cubans and a fairly easy win against Bristol ace Joe Deutsch.

The remainder of the baseball season passed quietly, and the Bees were unable to overtake the West Haven Sailors for state supremacy. Even worse, their former pitcher, Roy Teasley, was largely responsible for subduing the Bees after he pitched two gems against them in early August.

Bob Maier, who played 132 games with the 1945 Detroit Tigers, arrived in mid-August with the Madison (NJ) Colonels and collected a hit and scored a run in a lopsided Bristol victory.

The Bees ran their record to 26–14 as the crowds dwindled, and the season ended with a late-August loss to a team from Worcester, Massachusetts, in front of 523 fans.

"I can say without fear of contradiction that it has been a financial failure of no mean proportions to those who have honestly and diligently tried to bring baseball back to Bristol," K.H. "Pop" Simmons wrote shortly after the season ended.

With a truncated baseball season and no Bees football team, local fans passed the fall season with an amateur football team, the Bristol Blues, who played an abbreviated schedule against nondescript opponents.

But baseball in Bristol was not to be a lost cause.

◆     ◆     ◆

While Bristol Sports Promotions could not make semipro baseball profitable, two Connecticut natives with deep ties to organized baseball believed Bristol and Muzzy Field were prime locations for a professional minor league baseball team.

John R. O'Connor and Roy Dissinger expressed interest in sponsoring a team in the Class B Colonial League, which had existed since 1945 and included Connecticut entries in Waterbury, Stamford, and Bridgeport. Three New York-based teams were located in Poughkeepsie, Kingston, and Port Chester. Bristol's Chamber of Commerce backed the idea, and Simmons, the columnist, opined that baseball would make money in the city if a set schedule of opponents were in place versus the last-minute scheduling that often accompanied the previous incarnations of baseball teams at Muzzy Field.

Both Dissinger and O'Connor had several years' experience as scouts in the St. Louis Cardinals farm system, while O'Connor also worked for the Boston Braves as a scout and front office executive and assisted Bill Veeck when both were with the Milwaukee Brewers of the American Association. Dissinger's scouting days led to his general manager position with the New Orleans Pelicans, the team under whose auspices he hosted a tryout at Muzzy Field in 1946 when he first mentioned publicly that a minor league team belonged in Bristol.

The Colonial League's original expansion plan called for Bristol to join with a team from Patterson, New Jersey, but when the Patterson entry backed out, Bristol was left as the seventh team in a league that was rife with scheduling difficulties. Its future as a minor league city looked grim.

During some long negotiations and tense moments in the spring of 1949, Bristol finally emerged with Colonial League membership, though it was the result of Port Chester's relocation north to Connecticut. Charter members of the Colonial League, the Port Chester Clippers had won the pennant and the playoffs in 1948, but their proximity to Gotham baseball and the city's endless entertainment options severely limited their profitability.

Team owner and New York stockbroker Lester Osterman Jr. reported that Port Chester averaged slightly more than 450 fans per game to see the best team in the league.

League president John A. Scalzi Jr. of Stamford and the rest of the team owners approved the relocation. This included Waterbury, which waived the territorial rights it held over Bristol to field a minor league team in its backyard.

O'Connor and Dissinger also worked out a rental agreement with the city whereby the team paid fifty dollars per game and a ten-cent head tax. It was quite a discount from the $175 that the defunct Bees paid, and that team still owed more than $603 to the city for unpaid police services in March 1949.

In early April, about a month away from the start of the season, Osterman announced that Al Barillari, who had played at Muzzy Field in 1947, would return as player-manager of the team at thirty years of age. Osterman, who was just thirty-four, served as team president with his business partner, attorney Herbert Huttner, at his side while O'Connor was named business manager. With the Port Chester relocation, Dissinger was no longer involved in the venture, Osterman stated at an introductory meeting. At the same meeting, he solicited the public's input via the newly formed citizens' advisory board.

The team, which was an independent after its 1948 affiliation with the St. Louis Browns, was privately owned and funded by Osterman, O'Connor, and other unnamed associates. A schedule of sixty-three home games was announced.

Though a young executive, Osterman was no stranger to the field. He graduated from the University of Virginia where he was a varsity boxer and baseball player, and he actually suited up in the last game of the 1948 Clipper season and pitched a shutout.

With the Bristol entry a reality, nearly three dozen players began training at Empire Stadium in Port Chester when housing in Delaware could not be secured at their traditional training grounds. A name-the-team contest also began, and the *Bristol Press* received 525 suggestions as of April 9, including 7 entries from Judge William J. Malone, the former town team ballplayer who sent in his entries from his bed at the local hospital.

Eventually, the name Owls was adopted, ostensibly for the night games they were to play at Muzzy Field. The Owls were still adding players to their roster in late April and signed Carlos Bernier, an outfielder from Puerto Rico who became one of the most exciting players to roam Muzzy Field.

Bernier arrived in Bristol as a holdover from the Clippers for whom he played his rookie year of organized baseball in 1948. Though a decent performer, the numbers for the twenty-one-year-old were not outrageous: .248, 3 home runs, 29 RBI, 24 stolen bases and 72 runs in 104 games. His playmaking abilities, however, were evident and burst forth in his first year with the Bristol Owls.

His blazing speed (he reportedly circled the bases in 13.9 seconds in a pregame contest in July) and hitting prowess combined to make him the most dangerous player in the Colonial League and arguably one of the finest players in minor league history. Though he eventually earned a shot in the major leagues in 1953—becoming the first black player for the Pittsburgh Pirates in the process—Bernier played only one season and 105 games before returning to the minors, some argue because of racial bigotry.

But in 1949, local fans were not certain what they would see from Bernier, and he wasted little time showing them, stealing four bases in the first two exhibition games, as reports filtered back to Bristol. He endeared himself less so to Barillari a few days prior. When Bernier's flight to LaGuardia Airport from Puerto Rico landed in late April, he hopped in a cab to Port Chester and charged the $14.20 fare to the team; meanwhile, Barillari was driving a car to the airport to pick him up. The misunderstanding reportedly left O'Connor fuming for thirty minutes.

Spring training in Port Chester involved more than just calisthenics and baseball. One day following a strenuous early morning workout, players assisted workmen in removing bolts from the Empire Park bleachers and breaking them down for shipment to Bristol. As they once did their part in trying to fill the stadium, the players were equally assertive in dismantling it.

After three weeks of training and seven exhibition games, the Owls left Port Chester for good and ventured to their new home in Bristol, replete with an opening-day lineup of career minor leaguers: Roger LaFrance at catcher, Arthur

Kunde at first base, Joe O'Connell at second base, Jackie Moesch at shortstop, Dick Kelley at third base, Lawrence "Rebel" Rowe in left field, Bernier in center field, and player-manager Barillari in right field.

Notable pitchers included right-handed knuckleballer Guy Coleman and left-hander Larry Cauvel. Both were top hurlers for the 1948 Colonial League champions that finished 86–53, Coleman winning seventeen games and Cauvel ten.

The Owls' brass was vindicated for their belief that the city would support a minor league baseball team when 2,681 fans showed up on opening night to get their first glimpse of the talented club they had inherited.

Against the Waterbury Timers, the Owls started with first-inning fireworks when Barillari called for a triple steal and Bernier slid in safely at home for the first run. A couple of home runs highlighted the evening, but those theatrics were upstaged when the home team rallied for three runs in the ninth inning for an exhilarating 7–6 victory.

Thus began Bristol's inaugural Colonial League season and the franchise's defense of the crown.

The Owls ran off with nine wins in their first thirteen games as Bernier collected an incredible eighteen stolen bases. Despite the cold spring weather, fans showed up at Muzzy Field to watch a good team with exciting players while management also brought in attractions such as baseball comedians Max Patkin and later Al Schact and Jackie Price. There were hosiery giveaways for the ladies and typical promotions such as Electrical Appliance Night.

General admission tickets cost ninety cents, students got in for fifty cents, and children under twelve were a quarter. Single-game box seats sold for $1.25 or $60 for the entire season. Ticket packages also were made available at ten dollars for thirteen games. The fans responded and Bristol's Owls infused what Osterman called "the finest minor league park in the country" with the energy of professional baseball.

Osterman proved to be an incredibly supportive owner. In the August 17, 1954, issue of *Sports Illustrated*—the magazine's debut issue—Marjorie Osterman, the owner's wife, recalled her experience in minor league baseball in Bristol in "My Midsummer Nightmare." She recounted how she and her husband's "hopes went soaring" when they saw Muzzy Field for the first time. She also provided a glimpse into their lives during the baseball season:

"In the morning, he (Osterman) drove from Westchester to Wall Street. After a full day at the office, he drove back, collected me and a clean shirt and then drove two hours to Bristol. Once he arrived he never sat still. I traced him by cigaret [sic] butts littering the place where he had been. Usually we didn't get home until 3 or 4 in the morning—and the next day he started all over again."

Early in the season, Stamford and Bridgeport separated themselves as the class of the Colonial League while the Waterbury and New York teams sank toward the bottom. Bristol was somewhere in the middle, within striking distance of first place at certain times and getting dragged down at others. By the end of May, they stood in third place at 14–12.

The Owls then won six of seven against the Kingston Colonials and Waterbury to pull into second place. The lone loss came to the Timers, who were managed by Bert Shepard. During World War II, Shepard's fighter plane was shot down over Germany, and he suffered injuries serious enough that his right leg was amputated. As a POW in a German war camp, Shepard taught himself to walk and then to pitch with a prosthetic leg, according to author Gary Bedingfield.

After returning to America, Shepard caught the eye of Clark Griffith, owner of the Washington Senators, who offered him a job as a pitching coach in 1945. That August, he pitched five innings against the Boston Red Sox, "fulfilling a dream that few could have imagined possible," Bedingfield wrote, and became an inspirational figure.

Shepard also suited up as a player for the Timers during the 1948 season.

Meanwhile, Bristol was signing additional players, especially pitchers. They arrived every couple of weeks—hurlers such as six-foot-four right-hander Tony Sierzega, Jack Early, Bill Zupnik from the University of Maryland, and Rollie Zwick, along with a shortstop, Gary Rutkay.

The Owls quickly became the hot topic in town, especially after a three-game sweep of the front-runner Bridgeport Bees in mid-June that gave them eight straight wins and a 28–16 record, one half game behind Bridgeport.

Bristol fans were not the only ones appreciative of Bristol's arrival to the Colonial League. Bridgeport manager Ollie Byers rated Muzzy Field the best ballpark in New England and told the *Bristol Press*, "No wonder this Bristol club has plenty of pepper at home. Just looking at this place makes a fellow feel like a ballplayer."

But the club could not overtake Byers's team in the standings, dropping two of three to Stamford and then splitting with the Bees. Osterman again sought mound help, and he signed University of Cincinnati product Dick Holmes and Puerto Rico native Ruben Gomez, another pivotal acquisition.

Gomez was a six-foot right-hander who became a celebrated Latin American pitcher prone to wild streaks in both his deliveries and his demeanor. He spent a short time in Bristol, but he and Bernier were the most accomplished former Owls after they left town.

As Bernier was stealing his thirty-seventh base in fifty-two games and Coleman was winning his eighth decision by late June, there were signs of the financial instability that plagued the Colonial League for much of its brief existence. The Waterbury Timers, at 20–31, were placed on the selling block, and stock in the Poughkeepsie club was offered to the public at twenty-five dollars a share.

Meanwhile, the city of Bristol announced that the strong local support of the Owls had allowed it to pay off fourteen thousand dollars on the permanent lighting system with its largest payment coming in early July. The ball club had drawn twenty-seven thousand fans to Muzzy Field by that time.

But fan support could not help the team solve first-place Bridgeport, which won eight of the nine meetings against Bristol. After trading wins with the lower-tier New York teams and splitting with Stamford, the Owls were in third place after the Fourth of July weekend and playing sluggish baseball. Gomez, however, had proven effective in his first start at this time, allowing three runs on eight hits with eight strikeouts and five walks in a win over Poughkeepsie.

After the eighth loss to Bridgeport, a 10–3 setback in front of almost twelve hundred fans at Muzzy Field, Osterman came out on a rampage in the press, lambasting his team that stood in third place at 39–30 and three games out of first place. He sensed divisiveness in the clubhouse and strategically threatened the club before their season unraveled.

"I don't want a third or fourth place club in Bristol and every effort will be made to see that we are on top when the season draws to a close," Osterman told the *Bristol Press*. "They have no hustle," he said of his players. "There are certain personal rivalries which are going to be eliminated ... If there is any continuance of this type of ball against Kingston this Sunday [July 10], the fireworks will be hot and heavy."

Responding suitably, the Owls notched three victories over the weekend: one in Waterbury and the home doubleheader against Kingston, mainly on the strength of good pitching. Sierzega improved to 10–2 with his four-hitter against the Timers, while newly acquired right-hander Al Prior of the New England League tamed Kingston with a six-hitter in a 4–0 victory.

In a week, Osterman had bolstered his lineup by signing pitcher Luis Cabrera and first baseman Saturnino Escalera along with Prior and pitcher Paul Wargo, who had won sixteen games for Barillari in Port Chester the previous year and arrived in Bristol most recently from the Florida State League.

The victories pushed Bristol near the top of the standings and propelled Bernier into the Colonial League record books with the most stolen bases in a season, forty-nine, after barely three months of baseball.

Following Osterman's public upbraiding, the Owls collected seven wins in ten games and slipped into first place on July 22 with a victory at Waterbury combined with Kingston's win over Stamford. Meanwhile, Hamilton "Red" Graham, one of the league's top pitchers for Kingston, was in Osterman's sights for a mid-season acquisition, and Bristol reportedly had the first shot at signing him. But at the last moment, Kingston sold the southpaw to Bridgeport, enraging Osterman and O'Connor and adding another story line to the rivalry with the Bees.

As Bernier continued his marvelous season, he also had his share of transgressions. League President Scalzi fined him twenty-five dollars for using profane language and throwing his bat against the dugout, and later in July, during a pivotal game against Bridgeport, Bernier was fined fifty dollars by Barillari after ignoring a bunt sign and twice attempting steals with poor results in a close game. Bristol lost, 5–2, and dropped to second place. In August, Scalzi suspended Bernier three games after he was kicked out of a game for arguing balls and strikes.

After two wins against Stamford, the Owls swept a pivotal four-game set against Bridgeport with the three games at Muzzy Field attracting more than fifteen hundred fans. Wargo tossed a three-hitter on Saturday night, giving Bristol thirteen wins in sixteen games since his arrival, and Cabrera tossed another three-hitter on Sunday while Gomez hit the game-winning sacrifice fly in the second game. Graham pitched in both games for Bridgeport on Sunday. The next night, Bristol overcame a 5–2 deficit after four innings and pounded Bridgeport's fifteen-game winner, Philip Frick, en route to a 10–6 triumph.

With four straight victories against their nemesis, Bristol's confidence soared going into August, and the team pulled away from the field in the final month of the regular season. Bridgeport ownership reacted quickly and fired manager Ollie Byers after the series that placed the Owls, 59–35, in first by four and a half games. In a matter of a week, Jimmie Foxx was managing the Bees.

Other problems popped up around the league. Cash-strapped Waterbury released Manager Shepard after the board of directors said they could not afford to pay his five thousand dollar salary and Shepard refused a pay cut. This led to Timers players threatening to strike if management failed to rehire Shepard; in the interim, Leo Eastham, one of the league's top talents and stolen base record-holder before Bernier's domination, guided the club until mid-August when Shepard returned.

Meanwhile, the Owls continued to play great baseball and receive meaningful contributions from all parties. Gomez picked up his fifth win against Waterbury on August 4, giving Bristol their eighth straight win and nineteenth in twenty-two games. Escalera had fashioned a twenty-two-game hitting streak, and Cabrera, who was emerging as the team's best pitcher, strung together $34^{1}/_{3}$ consecutive innings of scoreless baseball.

Bernier swiped four bases, giving him seventy-four on the season, when the Owls sold him to the Pirates on a conditional basis, and he joined Indianapolis of the American Association for a brief weeklong stint during which he never had an at-bat.

Before he returned, the Owls welcomed Foxx and the Bees to Muzzy Field and greeted them with a 12–1 pasting as they chased Graham with a five-run first inning. Bridgeport had won a home game against the Owls the week prior, but six losses in their last seven games to Bristol certainly stung the one-time Colonial League front-runners. Cabrera tossed a six-hitter and notched his third win against Bridgeport, having allowed only two runs—one earned—in those contests.

Wargo earned his third win against Bridgeport the following night with a two-hitter.

Stamford was now emerging as the team that the Owls could not knock down consistently. It took the Owls winning three out of four after the Bridgeport series to pull even with Stamford, managed by ex-New York Yankee catcher Joe Glenn, in their twenty-six-game season series. Bristol ended up 12–14 against Stamford and 13–13 against Bridgeport, but those teams' inability to defeat the lower echelon in the final month allowed Bristol's lead to grow as they feasted on Kingston, Waterbury, and Poughkeepsie.

By late August, the Owls were 78–42 with a nine-game advantage, and they soon won the Colonial League championship by six games at 82–47. The regular season evolved successfully on the field and at the gates, where a league-record 59,481 people watched games at Muzzy Field.

The Owls led the league with a .291 team average and forty-seven triples, and Bernier was unquestionably their biggest star. Somewhat of an unknown before the season, Bernier played 120 games and hit .336 with 15 home runs, 56 RBI, 89 stolen bases, 25 doubles, 5 triples, and 136 runs scored.

Without the Owls' affiliation with the St. Louis Browns, Bernier remained in Bristol, save for the short stint with Indianapolis, which excited the locals. Five other players hit better than .300 with Escalera rapping out a .347 average, thirty

RBI, nineteen doubles, fourteen steals, and forty-eight runs scored in fifty-eight games. Barillari chipped in a .271 mark with thirty-five RBI.

Cabrera's 11–1 record, eleven consecutive wins, and a league-best four shut-outs cemented him as staff ace, despite Sierzega's 15-win season and 184 innings pitched and Coleman's 13 wins. Gomez posted a 5–1 mark with eighty-two strikeouts and sixty-six walks in forty-six innings while splitting his time in the outfield.

Wargo, named MVP by the fans, hit .315 in thirty games with seventeen RBI and nineteen runs while going 8–1 on the mound.

Riding high into the Colonial League play-offs, Bristol engaged the Waterbury Timers, who finished in fourth place with a 62–63 record.

Cabrera got the nod and continued his momentum, scattering four hits and allowing one run—an RBI single from player-manager Shepard—in Bristol's 3–1 triumph in the first game of the best-of-seven series. They were tied at one run apiece until Cabrera hit a double to the left side in the eighth inning estimated at 377 feet, advancing to third on a bobble in the outfield. He then scored on Bernier's fielder's choice before the team notched a third run on a throwing error. Bernier added an impressive running catch in the ninth inning with two runners on base.

The Owls displayed offensive fireworks late in the second game when they scored five runs in the tenth for an 11–6 victory, highlighted by Barillari's five RBI and Bernier's three stolen bases. Though the pitching was slightly ragged, Wargo, Gomez, and Zwick outlasted the Timers.

Bristol's defense betrayed Sierzega in the third game, committing five errors as the suddenly snakebitten right-hander lost for the fifth time in six decisions. Shaky pitching defined the next game, too, but Gomez came in late as a reliever and stopped the hitting attack that had knocked around Cabrera and Zwick. It may not have mattered, though, because the Owls had no shortage of runs in the 13–7 victory, giving them a 3–1 series lead.

Primed for a series victory, the Owls came out on Monday, September 13, only to have the Muzzy Field lights fail them in embarrassing fashion before the game started. It was postponed the next day due to rain before the teams tried again on Wednesday. And again, the lights went dim prior to the first pitch, causing a fifty-three-minute delay. Once play resumed for a half-inning, Bernier started things for Bristol with a single, but the field went dark as the ball rolled into the outfield.

After such a memorable regular season, the postseason was becoming an anti-climactic affair. Rain and cool weather already had set in before the lighting system became a serious and unavoidable hazard. The wires that were buried underground apparently were not deep enough because they routinely popped out of the ground in right field where Barillari played.

As a result, night baseball was cancelled for the year and all underground cables were dug up and replaced with a heavier duty carrier.

"The only way is to do the job right and that means an overhauling of the entire wiring system," said parks superintendent E. Gordon Stocks at the time. General Electric later offered to perform all of the upgrades free of charge.

Some speculated that the play-offs would be canceled, and others suggested the format go to a best-of-three. As columnist Pop Simmons wrote, "It is no secret that the clubs have lost money on its playoff games and the players themselves are ready to call off the whole business."

Game five shifted to Waterbury where lights were not an issue, and the Owls finally clinched the series, 2–1, behind Wargo's six-hitter and Joe O'Connell's game-winning single in the third inning that drove home Escalera, who had tripled.

But the victory came under odd circumstances. O'Connell was acting as manager after Barillari unexpectedly quit before the game to chase a tentative offer from a higher-class baseball club. Published information was scant, but the on-field leader's defection seemed to have no effect on the team, and Osterman stated publicly that Barillari would be welcomed back in 1950 if things did not work out for him otherwise. The lineup experienced more changes before the end of the season.

As Bristol outlasted Waterbury, so too did Bridgeport emerge from their series against Stamford. After a wild summer of maneuvering in the standings, the championship series, which had been scaled back to three games, promised to be entertaining.

The Bees notched the first win by jumping out to a quick 6–1 lead and holding on, 6–5, against Cabrera. At some point during that week, Bernier and Dick Kelly were caught playing for another team to earn extra cash, and the Owls suspended them for the second game of the series.

With Bernier suspended and Cabrera likely done pitching for the year, the duo bade the Owls farewell and hopped on a Sunday morning Pan American flight to Puerto Rico. Despite missing their most dangerous offensive weapon, the Owls scored four runs in the third, and Sierzega scattered four hits while O'Connell, Zwick, and LaFrance drove in two runs apiece for the victorious Owls.

Oddly, Barillari sat with Osterman in box seats behind home plate at Muzzy Field.

The winner-take-all affair was played in Bridgeport and three hundred Bristol fans traveled south to watch Wargo, who had dominated the Bees for two years, tame them with two runs on seven hits while Rutkay blasted a two-run home run in the sixth and drove home another with a sacrifice fly in the seventh.

It was fitting that in the 4–2 win, which "climaxed the greatest season in the history of Bristol baseball," Wargo, the team MVP, brought home the championship hardware. For the left-hander, it was his tenth win in ten starts against Bridgeport in the previous two seasons. He also drove in the first run of the game with a double.

*Champions Of The Colonial League*

*Bristol Owls — 1949*

Kneeling, (l. to r.) Roger LaFrance, Luis Cabrera, Guy Coleman, Ray Chew, Manager Al Barillari, Carlos Bernier, Al Prior, Rollie Zwick, Satch Escalera and John Gazzola. Standing, (l. to r.) Trainer "J. B." Buono, Ruben Gomez, Paul Wargo, John Zukowski, Dick Blow, Tony Sierzega, Joe O'Connell, Garry Rutkay, Dick Kelly, Larry Rowe, and Bat Boy Ronnie Gladowski.

In their lone full season in Bristol, the Owls of the Colonial League ran away with the pennant, set league records for attendance, and featured three future major league players—Carlos Bernier, Nino Escalera, and Ruben Gomez. Kneeling, from left to right, Roger LaFrance, Luis Cabrera, Guy Coleman, Ray Chew, manager Al Barillari, Bernier, Al Prior, Rollie Zwick, Escalera, and John Gazzola. Standing, from left to right, trainer "J.B." Buono, Gomez, Paul Wargo, John Zukowski, Dick Blow, Tony Sierzega, Joe O'Connell, Garry Rutkay, Dick Kelly, Larry "Rebel" Rowe, and bat boy Ronnie Gladowski. (Courtesy: Bristol Public Library)

Again, Barillari attended and reportedly was one of the first people to reach the dressing room celebration. Bridgeport president Carl Brunetto, once more sour over losing to Bristol, did not fire his manager this time but threatened to go one step further. "I'm going to get rid of practically every player," he was quoted as saying after the game.

Shortly after the championship, O'Connor proudly announced that Escalera, Gomez, and Bernier were signed for the following season, which certainly was great news for the fans. They had responded to higher-quality baseball, though the inclement September weather kept their attendance below three thousand total for the play-offs.

As the hot stove discussions warmed up the off-season months, there was talk that Waterbury would fold unless local investors rescued the club, and some talk that the Colonial League might merge with the New England League. Minor league baseball at the time was experiencing fierce competition from other entertainment options, and a painful reevaluation of its role in professional baseball soon occurred.

Until then, the Bristol Owls and their fans had a championship to savor.

◆    ◆    ◆

Colonial League turmoil resurfaced quickly during the off-season. Long before the ground thawed, Waterbury's general manager Henry A. Del Po was asking the city to lower its rental fees for Municipal Stadium as the team was $1,880 in arrears, owed $3,200 in taxes, and lost money in 1949.

Down in Stamford, rumors of the Pioneers leaving town started circulating in the first week of March, but the team reportedly found no desirable place that would take them.

"What has to be obtained here are fans—in quantity to keep the operation from financial disaster," wrote Maurice "Moe" Magliola of the *Stamford Advocate*.

Neither team had a manager, and at the end of March, Stamford lost their home ballpark, Mitchell Field, when the town rented it out to a group of entrepreneurs operating a drive-in theater. A few days after that news was released, Del Po resigned from the Timers to become a salesman for American Tobacco Company. In the previous three seasons, Waterbury's baseball club reportedly had lost sixty-five thousand dollars.

Eventually, Johnny Morris was hired as Waterbury's manager, but Stamford never returned to the fold. Due to the poor financial situation and lack of a playing field, the Stamford franchise transferred to Torrington.

Throughout the league, dire warnings hung heavy, except in Bristol. The Owls prepared for spring training in the small town of Federalsburg, Maryland, and McCarthy, the local columnist, predicted a season of increased attendance with good baseball and an improving local economy. Additionally, whatever disagreements that prompted manager Al Barillari to leave the team during the 1949 play-offs were resolved, as he returned to the helm.

Bernier got a jump start on spring training when he joined Springfield of the International League in mid-March. While there was speculation that the Chicago Cubs planned on purchasing him, he remained in Bristol's possession, arguably overqualified for the Colonial League. "He's definitely a Triple A player," Barillari said. "He needs only a break to make good."

The Owls sold several of his teammates early in the year: Rollie Zwick, Joe O'Connell, and Rebel Rowe went to St. Jean, Quebec, of the Provincial League while Guy Coleman went to Tampa and Gary Rutkay to Miami Beach.

Barillari was more than pleased with his current club, though, telling the local newspaper that he had "never seen a better crop of rookies at spring practice." Two of the newcomers, Warren Hurtt and Ed Meitzler, were expected to take over the left side of the infield at shortstop and third base.

As opening day approached, Scalzi, the league president, attempted to dispel rumors that his circuit was operating on borrowed time. The relocation of the Stamford franchise to Torrington, viewed as a more baseball-friendly town, reflected the strength of the Colonial League, Scalzi contended.

"Despite some of the adverse reports that have been circulated, I would definitely say our league is in much better condition financially, geographically and civically," he told the local newspaper.

Ruben Gomez started the first game of the season, but the magic of 1949 failed to carry over and the Owls were trounced, 15–4, in Waterbury. It was the start of a mediocre first month for Bristol, and the league was turned upside down in the early stages with the weakest teams of 1949 leading the pack. Two of the Owls' wins along the way came at Muzzy Field against Torrington, which featured Eddie Musial, Stan's brother, who smacked four hits, scored twice, and drove in a run in a doubleheader.

Crowds were down due to cold spring weather. When the Owls lost again to Waterbury on May 22 in front of 236 fans, it was only slightly more than had shown up a week earlier at the West End Athletic Club to hear Holy Cross All-

American Bob Cousy tell the crowd that if he did not play basketball with the Boston Celtics that winter, he would go into business, form his own team, and barnstorm throughout New England.

The first obvious fracture in Bristol's season came on May 25 when the team sold Gomez to St. Jean of the Provincial League. McCarthy, the local columnist, claimed that Gomez prompted the transaction when he threw a bat at Barillari after the manager took exception to Gomez not removing his hat during the national anthem. Gomez characterized it differently to baseball writer Sidney Fields several years later, saying that he chased O'Connor with a bat after the business manager growled at him, "Come on, get a hit, or we ship you back to Puerto Rico." Gomez said he then quit the team and offered himself to St. Jean.

Either way, Gomez's time in Bristol came to an abrupt halt, but not his baseball career. He joined the New York Giants in 1953 and became known for his wildness and brawl-inducing beanballs thrown against Carl Furillo, Joe Adcock, and Frank Robinson and his winter league skirmish with Willie Mays. He also became a highly effective pitcher for the 1954 World Champion Giants, winning seventeen games in the regular season and one in the World Series, the first Puerto Rican player to do so. In 1957, Gomez earned the win in the last victory for the New York Giants, and in 1958, he won the first game for the San Francisco Giants against the Los Angeles Dodgers in the first major league game played on the West Coast.

He notched the last of his seventy-six major league-career victories in 1962 before making an unsuccessful comeback with Philadelphia in 1967. His ten-year career ended with a 76–86 record, a 4.09 ERA, 677 strikeouts, and 574 walks.

Without Gomez, the Owls did not fare much better than they had starting the season. By early June, the team sat in last place, and their few bright spots were Escalera and Bernier, who continued to average about one stolen base per game. Frustration came to a head in Poughkeepsie when Barillari was ejected for arguing from the bench and was fined twenty-five dollars with an indefinite suspension.

Cold weather, disappointing crowds, and bad baseball finally got to Osterman that month, too. The *Bristol Press* reported on June 14 that the team might vacate Muzzy Field if the crowds did not improve beyond a paltry few hundred per game. "I am not interested in giving Bristol fans something they don't want," Osterman said after 166 fans appeared for a game against Bridgeport, a heated rivalry fewer than 12 months prior.

Similar problems league-wide, and in minor leagues nationwide for that matter, began the slow descent into oblivion for the Colonial League as television and radio shouldered the blame for decreased gate receipts.

"It wouldn't be surprising to see television banned by major league ball clubs next season," McCarthy opined on June 19. "TV is hurting the gate receipts of the big leaguers as well as the minor league outfits ... Minor league clubs can't operate on buttons and very few of the teams receive support from the majors."

An Associated Press story quoted George M. Trautman of the National Association of Professional Baseball Leagues saying 444 minor league clubs lost one million fans in the first month of the season because of major league games being televised in minor league markets.

Through the difficult month of June, Bernier and Escalera were red-hot. Bernier batted .301 with nine home runs, thirty-two RBI, forty-two stolen bases, and fifty-five runs through forty-two games. In that same time, Escalera carried a .400 average with four home runs, twenty-nine RBI, seventeen steals, and thirty-nine runs.

But the Owls were not winning and the fans were not attending, so Bristol sold Bernier and Cabrera to St. Jean at the end of the month. Bernier ended his abbreviated 1950 season in Bristol with a .287 average, 53 steals, and 67 runs, but when combined with his Provincial League performance, where he also was a dominant player, his 1950 stats were eye-opening: .316, 24 home runs, 72 RBI, 94 stolen bases, 136 runs, 136 hits, and 225 total bases in 116 games.

Despite the numbers, no major league team signed Bernier, who was twenty-three years old in 1950. He spent the 1951 season with the Tampa Smokers in the Florida International League, a Class B circuit, and led the league, by a wide margin, with 51 steals, 21 triples, and 124 runs scored as Tampa captured the pennant, according to research conducted by Steve Treder. He was then promoted to Hollywood of the Pacific Coast League, his first of several seasons on the West Coast that led to his induction into the PCL Hall of Fame in 2004. As a catalyst on another pennant-winning club, Bernier hit .301 with 65 steals, 105 runs scored, 9 home runs, and 79 RBI in 1952, earning the league's distinction as its best player.

The Pittsburgh Pirates gave Bernier his big break the next season, signing him as their starting center fielder.

"It is clear that he was voted the Coast League's most valuable player in 1952 on actual merit," states a team biography of Bernier, dubbed "Pirate Personalities," written in 1953. "Few rookies came up for major league trials this spring with more running for them."

Bernier's high-water mark in his rookie campaign came on May 2, 1953, when he hit three triples in one game against Cincinnati. But on the whole, Bernier posted numbers that failed to impress Pirates management. Appearing in 105 games, he hit .213 with 15 steals in 29 attempts, 3 home runs, and 31 RBI. The Pirates, however, were no juggernaut, finishing in last place that season with a 53–101 record.

Treder surmises that there was more to the Pirates' decision to release Bernier after spring training in 1954. "We know that Bernier did badly in his major league debut, and that the Pirates never gave him another chance," Treder wrote in 2004. "But the Pirates, under [owner Branch] Rickey's direction, were in an extreme 'youth movement' phase in the early-to-mid 1950s. There were lots of young players who performed poorly for Pittsburgh in this period, who were given second and third and even more chances ... Bernier got no such chance."

Bernier's son, Dr. N. Bernier-Collazo, believes that his father's reputation for "his aggressive style of play," and being a black Puerto Rican, the first such player for the Pirates predating Roberto Clemente by two years, was a roadblock to his major league career.

"My father's only shortfall was that he did not handle the injustices of society with the same grace and patience of a Jackie Robinson or a Roberto Clemente," Bernier-Collazo wrote in 2003.

Documented evidence shows that Bernier was a feisty player. He scuffled with Gene Mauch in PCL games and was disciplined for striking a PCL umpire and for insubordination. He also was involved in brawls in the Puerto Rican Winter League.

One published article found in Bernier's file at the Baseball Hall of Fame in Cooperstown specifically addresses one of the root causes of his demeanor, dating back to his 1948 season with the Port Chester Clippers. "Bernier was struck by a pitched ball and suffered a fractured skull in his rookie season in the minors, and suffered from chronic headaches, one of the reasons given for a quick temper that kept him in hot water much of the time," it states.

Treder continued, "To whatever degree he deserved it, Bernier became known as a combative player, and it's only accurate to say that in the 1950s and early 1960s, the chances were not good of a major league team acquiring/promoting a black Latin player who was (a) no longer very young, (b) had done poorly in a previous major league opportunity, and (c) had a reputation for aggressiveness."

Despite the slight, Bernier never slowed down. He became one of the finest minor league stars of all time, spending ten seasons in the PCL and splitting time in the American Association and International League in 1960–61 before ending his career in 1965 with Reynosa of the Mexican League. He finished his eighteen-year career in organized baseball with a .298 average, 212 home runs, 1,098 RBI, 594 stolen bases, 312 doubles, and 129 triples. He also was the Puerto Rican Winter League's preeminent base stealer before Rickey Henderson came along.

For Bernier, one of the most exciting players ever to come through Bristol, life was not kind. On April 6, 1989, at sixty-three years of age, he committed suicide by hanging himself with a rope in his home in Puerto Rico where his wife found his body, but no note. Whether caused by the pain of the chronic headaches or something else, Bernier's suicide left his native country in mourning, and its baseball games were cancelled in his honor.

"We cannot play baseball while the body of Bernier is being viewed," said Amandito Munoz, president of the country's baseball federation.

When the Bristol Owls sold Bernier and Cabrera to Quebec, the team was left with only fourteen players on their roster and was in fourth place in the Colonial League at 25–28, ten and a half games behind pacesetter Poughkeepsie. Management attempted to attract fans by bringing in baseball comedian Jackie Price for a second appearance, and the Owls pulled themselves up to 30–29, but the league clearly was fading.

During a league meeting on July 5, the owners voted to continue playing but opted for a split season. Poughkeepsie was declared first-half champions. The *Bristol Press* reported that Scalzi said "six club owners pledged to play through the season and promised to try to acquire more players in an effort to build up the circuit."

As the Owls won five of their first seven games in the second half of the season, a player mutiny developed in Waterbury on July 14. Seventeen players refused to board their beat-up bus for a game in Kingston after team president Joseph Lombard ordered them home following a Thursday night game in that city. Originally, players were told they would stay overnight in Kingston, but Lombard nixed that itinerary, probably because of money.

He fined each player one hundred dollars and suspended them indefinitely for refusing to board the bus, which players deemed unsafe in their pleadings to Scalzi. Stuart Wider, Waterbury's business manager, said Lombard's decision saved the club fifty dollars in food and lodging. An anonymous player source told newspaper reporters that six players had also been promised pay increases on June 2, but no raise had been received by mid-July.

In response to the uproar, Lombard canceled the fines, paid off the team's debt up to July 12, disbanded the club, "and bade the players God speed in their search for newer and greener pastures."

That night, the Owls defeated Torrington, 2–1, on the road, after which Torrington general manager John Gentile announced cryptically over the loudspeakers, "This is the last home game for the Torrington Braves."

The Braves threw in the towel, followed by Bridgeport, and Bristol sold off eight of their players though did not fold at that point. Only the Owls, Poughkeepsie, and Kingston remained, but the league was to collapse shortly after Scalzi said it was "in the soup."

At a meeting on July 16 at the Roger Smith Hotel in Stamford, the owners voted unanimously to shut down operations. Scalzi said there were no prospects of reviving the circuit, as it had struggled against radio, television, bad weather, and the proximity of Major League Baseball teams.

P.J. O'Hara, president of the Poughkeepsie team, told the *Sporting News* that "baseball cannot be killed because any individual quits," but the Colonial League never emerged from their difficulties. An illustration in that July 26 issue depicted major league television, in the form of a pitcher striking out a Colonial League batter at the plate while other minor league teams watched from the on-deck circle.

Bridgeport's Carl Brunetto told the *Sporting News* that he lost seventy-five thousand dollars in four years and explained to Bristol newspaperman McCarthy the reason: "Too many people now have access to television sets, and they can get all the baseball they want at home or at some grille. And even though watching a game over television isn't as good as being out in the ballpark, most fans would rather see a major league game telecast than come out and witness a Class B game."

In the wake of the fold, Osterman expressed his appreciation to the city and its fans, saying that the league's "continuation was economically impossible" after owners had poured money into a losing proposition.

"I shall never forget [the fans] and I am extremely sorry that they shall no longer have organized ball in Bristol," he told the *Bristol Press*.

Manager Barillari took a job with an independent league team in Nova Scotia while players dispersed throughout the country. O'Connor announced that all of the Owls' equipment, including uniforms, bats, balls, and catcher's gear, was up for sale to the public.

Escalera was enjoying a stellar season at that point, hitting .405 with six home runs, forty-four RBI, twenty-eight stolen bases, and fifty-nine runs scored in sixty-four games. He ended up with Amsterdam, New York, the New York Yankees' Canadian-American League entry, and several Bristol residents organized a road trip to Pittsfield, Massachusetts, in late July to watch the nineteen-year-old perform. Four years later, Escalera broke in with Cincinnati and batted .159 in seventy-three games during his only season in the major leagues.

In the ensuing weeks, the *Bristol Press* ran stories reporting that other minor leagues were suffering the same fate as the Colonial League. Television was always declared the culprit.

For Bristol baseball fans, the only competitive baseball to enjoy was coming from the city's American Legion team, which was a decent consolation prize. Post 2 was in the middle of a four-year stranglehold on the state championship title, the beginning of their current reign as the state's most successful program.

But those who appreciated the days of more noteworthy baseball events received a treat in September when local promoter Julie Larese announced the October appearance of the Mickey Harris All-Stars at Muzzy Field against the Bristol Tramps, featuring some former Colonial Leaguers. Tickets sold swiftly, especially at the Memorial Boulevard service station that Larese owned.

Following a rainout in Portland, Maine, the night before, the All-Stars arrived in Bristol on October 13 with three future Hall of Famers in their lineup: short-stop Luke Appling, first baseman Johnny Mize, and pitcher Warren Spahn.

Appling, a six-time All-Star with the Chicago White Sox, held down the shortstop position for twenty years for the South Siders, establishing a record for longevity at the position that was later broken, along with records for double plays, putouts, and assists. Though he never played in a World Series, he twice finished second in the race for American League MVP and turned in his finest individual season in 1936 when he batted .388 with 128 RBI and 111 runs in 138 games. "Old Aches and Pains" also coaxed 1,302 walks during his career, among the highest totals in baseball history. He was inducted into Cooperstown in 1964.

Mize was enshrined in 1981 following a fifteen-year career with the St. Louis Cardinals, New York Giants, and New York Yankees that included eight All-Star game nominations in nine years between 1937 and 1948 and five World Series titles with the Yankees. An impressive power hitter, Mize bashed 359 home runs in his career yet struck out only 524 times compared to 856 bases on balls. He led the league either in batting average, home runs, or RBI eight times, and he hom-ered in all fifteen major league ballparks that existed during his career.

"He was a student of hitting who relied as much on knowledge of the pitchers and an extremely graceful, well-balanced hitting style as he did on his consider-able strength," Fred Stein wrote.

The legendary Stan Musial dubbed Mize "The Big Cat" for the smooth manner in which the six-foot-two, 215-pound left-handed hitter handled himself at the plate.

Spahn is considered one of the greatest pitchers ever to play the game, and he arrived in Bristol as a twenty-nine-year-old at the beginning of his lengthy baseball career, which was interrupted by his service in World War II. A Cy Young award-winner and fourteen-time All-Star, Spahn is the winningest left-handed pitcher in baseball history with a 363–245 mark—mainly for the Boston and Milwaukee Braves—and many historians consider him the best southpaw of all time.

He started his organized baseball career with Hartford in 1942 and truly emerged in 1947, eventually becoming a twenty-game winner thirteen times, pitching two no-hitters, and leading the National League in strikeouts in four consecutive years. In twenty-one seasons, he fashioned a 3.08 ERA with 63 shutouts; he also hit 35 home runs, a record for pitchers.

He was enshrined in Cooperstown in 1973, his first year of eligibility.

Along with these luminaries, the Mickey Harris All-Stars also featured Gene Woodling, an eventual seventeen-year veteran of the major leagues and five-time world champion with the Yankees, in left field; Hoot Evers, a two-time All-Star who played for twelve years, in center field; Sam Mele, a former NYU basketball-standout-turned-baseball-journeyman, in right field; Allie Clark, who logged seven seasons in the majors with two World Series titles and finished behind Jackie Robinson in the 1947 International League batting race, at third base; an unknown player named Robertson—possibly Sherry, a teammate of Harris's in Washington at this time and nephew of team owner Clark Griffith—at second base; and Bob Swift, a fourteen-year veteran who was behind the plate when famous three-foot-seven pinch hitter Eddie Gaedel came to bat in August 1951, at catcher. George "Mercury" Myatt, who swiped seventy-two bases in seven years for the Giants and Senators, came in as a late-game replacement for Appling.

The pitchers were Joe "Burrhead" Dobson, who won 137 games in a fourteen-year major league career; Ellis Kinder, whose best season came in 1949 when he went 23–6 with six shutouts for the Red Sox, who lost the pennant to the Yankees by one game; Gus Niarhos, who was predominantly a catcher and platooned with Yogi Berra in 1948; and Spahn.

Strangely, Harris did not take the field for his namesake club, and there is no indication that he was in Bristol at the time.

Unfortunately for the fans, the eight o'clock first pitch brought with it autumnal temperatures, but fourteen hundred showed up for the exhibition.

Steve Ridzik, a rookie right-hander with the Phillies in 1950, started for the Bristol Tramps. He eventually logged twelve years in the major leagues, mostly as a relief pitcher. Former Owls players Dick Kelly, Roger LaFrance, and Al Barillari also were in the lineup, along with former Waterbury Timer Pat DeLucia.

Ridzik pitched a fine game at Muzzy, despite some wildness. In seven innings, he allowed four runs on three hits and struck out eight batters, but his nine bases on balls were a problem. The home team's downfall was their inability to hit the Harris All-Star pitchers.

The quartet of hurlers limited the Tramps to just two hits as Spahn struck out the side to end the game in his only inning of work. Offensively, the All-Stars benefited from Mele's three-run home run over the fence in right field and Clark's three hits and two RBI. Appling and Mize both collected a hit and scored three runs combined as the All-Stars rolled to a 9–1 victory.

The visitors' lineup was impressive and a fitting end to an emotional baseball season in the city.

# More Fireworks and then a Quiet Ballpark

Dissolution of the Colonial League came at the beginning of a difficult five-year span for baseball in the New England states. The New England League, which emerged most recently in the minor league boom years after World War II, folded in 1949. Two years after the Owls and the Colonial League called it quits, the Hartford Senators went bankrupt, and in 1953 the Springfield Cubs of the International League were sold and the Boston Braves moved to Milwaukee.

In 1951, though, Bristol entrepreneurs again threw their hats in the ring when the amateur Bristol Braves were formed in April. As part of the Connecticut Semipro League, the Braves did not field a team of notable names, though they did sign former New York Giants utility infielder Al Cuccinello—who played in fifty-four major league games in 1935—to the team in June.

The home opener attracted three hundred fans, and the team hoped for considerably more when the New England Hoboes were scheduled to play at Muzzy Field in mid-July. The visitors' lineup included four former major leaguers: All-Star first baseman Elbie Fletcher, who enjoyed a twelve-year career with the Braves and Pirates and accumulated a .993 career fielding percentage; former Cubs shortstop Lennie Merullo, who spent seven years in the majors in the 1940s and played in the 1945 World Series; utility infielder Al "Skippy" Roberge, who played three seasons with the Braves in 1941–42 and 1946; and Barney Olsen, who saw action in twenty-four games as an outfielder for the 1941 Cubs.

The largest crowd of the season, 698 fans, showed up to see the Hoboes break a one-all tie with four runs in the seventh inning en route to an 8–1 win. Shortstop Merullo collected two hits with a run scored; Olsen, playing third base, went 2-for-5; Roberge at second base got a hit and scored; and Fletcher, playing first base, went 1-for-4.

For the Bristol Braves, it would be the high point of the season. By the end of July, the team had disbanded after losing two thousand dollars.

Amateur baseball was the only game in town for the next two years and commanded the most attention at Muzzy Field until the Bristol Red Sox brought professional baseball back to Bristol in 1973.

The city's Legion team continued their dominance of state opponents, racking up a 52–2–2 mark from 1949 to 1952 with four straight state championships. Also during the 1950s, future major leaguers Dick McAuliffe and Moe Morhardt logged games at Muzzy Field starting in Little League for McAuliffe, of Farmington, and Legion baseball for Morhardt, a Manchester native.

Morhardt starred on the 1953 Manchester Legion team that defeated Bristol and Bridgeport for the state championship, advancing to the regionals hosted at Muzzy Field. In 1959 as a cocaptain for the University of Connecticut baseball team, the club, under the direction of head coach J.O. Christian, used Muzzy Field as training grounds before departing for Omaha, Nebraska, and the College World Series.

"I thought Muzzy Field was the best field around to play on," said Morhardt in a 2007 interview, noting the tall pine trees in the outfield and the bold green wall. "I still think it is."

Morhardt signed a free agent contract with the Cubs in 1959 and played twenty-five games with them in two seasons. His career as an amateur baseball coach in Connecticut brought him back to Muzzy Field numerous times.

McAuliffe played on a Farmington Little League team at Muzzy in 1951 and then returned several years later with the town's Legion team. It was during a tryout camp hosted by Jumpin' Joe Dugan and the Boston Red Sox in 1956 that McAuliffe remembers making quite an impression on Dugan as a sixteen-year-old when he hit a home run and a double during an intrasquad scrimmage among camp participants. Though too young to sign with a professional club that year, he inked a contract with the Detroit Tigers in 1957.

"Believe it or not, the first home run I hit that meant something was in that camp with Joe Dugan," McAuliffe said in 2007 of his first memorable moment at Muzzy Field. McAuliffe broke into the major leagues at the age of twenty in 1960 and enjoyed a sixteen-year career with the Tigers and Red Sox, including three nominations as an All-Star. For a middle infielder, he provided considerable pop at the top of the lineup with 197 career home runs and three seasons of more than 20 long balls. In 1968, he paced the American League with ninety-five runs scored for the World Champion Tigers. He was known for his unorthodox batting stance from the left side of the plate, holding his hands high and facing the pitcher until the pitch was delivered. McAuliffe then adjusted his batting position to more of a closed, conventional stance.

Near the end of his career, he joined the Red Sox and transitioned into a managerial role with the Bristol Red Sox in 1975, until Rico Petrocelli was hit in the head late in the season and Boston called on McAuliffe for their pennant run. His playing and managing career ended that year for more profitable opportunities in private business, but McAuliffe remembers Muzzy Field fondly.

"I always thought Muzzy Field was one of the great minor league ballparks that I've ever played in," McAuliffe recalled in 2007, "and I've played in a lot of minor league parks."

During the remainder of the 1950s, Bristol's ballpark hosted a few historically significant games, the most important being the June 17, 1954, appearance by legendary pitcher Leroy "Satchel" Paige and his Harlem Globetrotter baseball team against the House of David.

Paige had recently finished his career in the "white" major leagues with the St. Louis Browns and already had cemented himself among the greatest players in baseball history. While his career statistics are largely unverifiable, his impact on the game leaves no doubt, and Paige was honored with his 1971 induction into the National Baseball Hall of Fame in Cooperstown.

Unfortunately, his ballyhooed appearance in Bristol attracted a paltry number of fans, ended in disappointing fashion, and was followed by cryptic details in the local newspaper.

"Leroy (Satchel) Paige made his debut at Muzzy Field last night, and the former major league moundsman disappointed quite a number of the 453 fans who paid to see the Harlem Globetrotters edge the House of David, 3–2," the lone sentence in the lone game report stated.

When the Bristol Baseball Club, comprising former high school players, came into existence in 1955, they struggled attracting crowds in fifteen games during the summer. Then, as the devastating flood of that year demolished areas of Bristol in August, Muzzy Field was inundated by the engorged Pequabuck River beyond its outfield, and the baseball club suspended their operations. All team equipment, which had been stored in Frank's Stationery Store in nearby Forestville, was destroyed. The Bristol Baseball Club did not return the following season.

The highlight of the following summer was an appearance by the most popular softball attraction in history, "The King and His Court," with the jaw-dropping pitching talents of Eddie Feigner.

With a four-man lineup, the team barnstormed throughout the world, relying on Feigner's brilliant abilities and equally tremendous showmanship. The team was founded in 1946, and Feigner's career ended in 2000—at the age of seventy-five—after he pitched in more than 10,000 games, striking out 141,517 batters and pitching 238 perfect games and 930 no-hitters. It was said that he would pitch his 104-mile-per-hour fastball not only from the standard mound 46 feet from the plate but also would pitch on his knees, from behind his back, between his legs, from second base, from center field, and blindfolded in an amazing display of pitching prowess. An ex-marine with the requisite buzz-cut hairdo, Feigner also told newspapermen that he had thirteen hundred different deliveries.

When his career ended, he had traveled through six thousand towns and one hundred countries. On July 10, 1956, Feigner and his Court made their first stop in Bristol. At that point, the four-man club had compiled a 917–54–27 record dating back to 1946, and Feigner reportedly was netting fifty-five thousand dollars per year with the team.

The Bristol All-Stars provided little competition for the King and His Court, despite their five additional players on the field. In front of twelve hundred fans, Feigner allowed three hits and two walks and struck out sixteen batters—two while blindfolded—in the four-man team's 3–0 victory. Feigner certainly lived up to expectations.

About a month later, another attraction arrived with the Brooklyn Dodger Rookies, a team managed by former Boston Brave Tommy Holmes, who hit a home run at Muzzy Field in 1943 during the Braves' intrasquad scrimmage there. Only one of Holmes's players who appeared in front of 700 fans at Muzzy actually made it to the major leagues—catcher John Orsino, who played 7 seasons and 332 games for 3 different teams, including the 1962 World Series runner-up San Francisco Giants.

Feigner's return to Muzzy Field in 1957 was the final notable moment of the decade at Muzzy Field. Though the short game report revealed little about his performance, Feigner allowed one run, and his team rallied for three runs in the seventh inning for a 4–1 victory. The novelty of his traveling show might have worn off a bit from the year before as 708 fans paid to see him.

Fifteen years after the Bristol Owls played their final game, the city was involved in negotiations with the Springfield Giants, San Francisco's Double A affiliate in the Eastern League, about relocating and bringing minor league baseball back to Muzzy Field. In 1965, the city agreed to spend twenty-seven thousand dollars upgrading Muzzy Field's facilities, playing surface, and lighting system.

A tentative plan called for the Giants to pay a flat rental fee of three thousand dollars plus an additional fifteen hundred dollars for a maintenance man at every game. The ball club would be responsible for cleaning up the ballpark after each game, leaving the parks department responsible only for maintaining the playing surface and lighting system.

Support for the team's arrival included the Chamber of Commerce and the Legion baseball program, the full-time tenants of Muzzy Field during the summer.

Parks department superintendent Joseph J. Riley Jr. noted that "every effort should be made to get this ball club into Bristol." Double A baseball would put the city and its ballpark back on the map.

But there was a glaring problem in the plan: a city ordinance prohibited the sale and consumption of beer and other alcoholic beverages in city parks. Local clergy and other opponents protested strongly against a proposal to change the ordinance for Giants games only, concerned that a change would lead to beer sales in parks throughout the city.

The city's clergy conveyed to Springfield Giants general manager Charles "Chick" O'Malley that they were opposed to beer sales, not the Giants, but the city's former finance commissioner Thomas P. O'Brien instituted legal action to keep the Giants from violating the Muzzy Field deed. He believed that a professional ball club charging admission for their games violated the municipal nature of the ballpark.

Throughout the winter, the saga continued until four weeks before the season opener was scheduled. Tired of the fight, O'Malley abandoned the plan to relocate to Bristol in March 1966 in a "hastily-called session" with Bristol mayor Henry J. Wojtusik due to the "complications and legal entanglements," the local newspaper reported. Instead of bringing minor league baseball back to Bristol, the Giants took it to Waterbury to the great disappointment of Riley.

"The starch has been taken out and the enthusiasm is dead," a *Bristol Press* editorial stated on March 22. "All that remains is resentment ... Bristol lost face with its citizens, with the State of Connecticut and heaven knows where else."

Around the same time that the Giants ruled out Bristol as a home, the city's downtown was deep into the 1960s-era redevelopment project that forever changed the landscape with massive demolition of older buildings to make way for a large shopping mall surrounded by acres of parking lots. It was an attempt to keep pace with commercial growth in the northern part of the city along Route 6, but the development plans were mired in construction delays and political bickering and decades later, the initiative was widely considered a failed vision that robbed Bristol of its downtown identity.

Bristol was receiving the short end of others' decisions, not the least of which was the state's decision in 1967 to end Route 72 on the doorstep of Bristol's city lines. Bristol officials believed the limited access highway would link its city center to the interstate system, but ambitions of becoming more of a regional destination were dashed when Waterbury and New Britain received more attention in highway planning and thus growth in retail. Bristol became an isolated city that found it difficult to attract visitors. Forty years passed before the state announced (at the time of this writing) funding to extend Route 72 to Middle Street in Bristol.

Despite the setbacks in the 1960s, there was optimism about Muzzy Field, because as Riley had told O'Malley the day the Giants left town, the "door would always be open for baseball to land in Bristol."

The city forged ahead with the planned upgrades to Muzzy Field starting in September 1966. Along with enhanced locker rooms and restrooms, a new green wooden fence standing seven feet high was installed around the outfield, giving the ballpark a crisp, attractive look.

Another minor league team was courted in the early 1970s, and the relationship was a long-standing one that came to define Muzzy Field for the majority of those who are familiar with it. When Joe Buzas's Pawtucket Red Sox of the Eastern League were searching for a home in January 1973, Bristol made its overtures to the team after Meriden's town council voted down a financial commitment to attract the team to the Silver City.

In bidding for a minor league team, this time Bristol emerged victorious.

A total of $53,205 was spent upgrading Muzzy Field for the Red Sox arrival with $27,000 coming from an endowment established for park improvements in the city. The city picked up the rest of the tab, except for thirty-five hundred dollars that came from the team's lease agreement with the city.

Along with the normal reconditioning of facilities, the majority of the money (forty-five thousand dollars) went toward a new mercury vapor lighting system. The deal between Buzas and the city also allowed beer to be sold during Red Sox games only and called for the team's control of concessions during Red Sox games plus a cut of concessions sold during Legion and high school games.

As part of the rehabilitation, home plate was moved about fiften feet closer to the grandstand area while new bleacher seating was erected down first base line. The old West End ballpark was becoming a desired destination once again.

"We believe Muzzy Field will be one of the best parks in the Eastern League," general manager Joseph Helyar told reporters in 1973.

It was the beginning of a ten-season period when Bristol residents witnessed future Hall of Famers and future major league stars in the early stages of their careers. The first Bristol Red Sox club, managed by Rac Slider, featured Jim Rice and Fred Lynn, and the team finished fourteen and a half games out of first place.

Improvement on the field occurred immediately the next season when manager Stan Williams led the Red Sox, with catcher Ernie Whitt, to a first-place finish at 74–61, but they faltered in the first round of the play-offs when they lost to Willie Randolph and Thetford Mines. The team enjoyed a slight uptick in attendance to 47,969.

The 1975 campaign ushered in two consecutive years of declining numbers at the gate for Bristol but also their first Eastern League championship after finishing with a composite mark of 81–57, good for second place. It would be the most wins for a Bristol Red Sox club during their stay in the city as managers Dick McAuliffe and Bill Slack guided the team to a second-half championship. Facing runners-up Reading in the championship series, the Red Sox, behind Whitt and Butch Hobson, swept the Phillies in three games. McAuliffe, however, was not around to see it. He had been called up by the parent club to fill in at third base after Rico Petrocelli was suffering headaches, inner ear trouble, and vertigo, "possibly the result of a 1974 beaning," author John Cizik wrote. McAuliffe, who had played sparingly in 1974 and was on the verge of retirement, shook off the rust and logged seven games with Boston with two hits in fifteen at-bats. He stayed with the team through the end of the regular season but was left off the postseason roster. He retired from baseball that year.

After dropping to an era-low 38,637 fans during the 1976 season and missing the play-offs, despite a 74–60–1 mark under John Kennedy, Bristol increased attendance to more than 57,500 the following season. At 72–67, the Red Sox again missed the play-offs, but recovered in 1978 behind manager Tony Torchia, who with Bruce Hurst and talented young hitter Wade Boggs led the team to a first-half championship and a second Eastern League championship over Reading in two games.

Two more play-off droughts followed in 1979 and 1980 with the team winning seventy-three and seventy-nine games respectively and attendance hovering around the sixty-six thousand mark. Hurst, Boggs, and Rich Gedman were the hometown heroes while Reading's Ryne Sandberg left the cleat marks of a future Hall of Famer in the Bristol ballpark's infield.

Tony Torchia managed the team to their third and final Eastern League championship in 1981 after the club won the second-half championship, fashioned a 76–63 composite record, and then rolled past Reading and Glens Falls in the play-offs. The more than seventy-seven thousand fans who saw the team play at Muzzy Field were the high-water mark during the team's stay. They bowed out the next season at 75–65, missing the play-offs while pitcher Dennis "Oil Can" Boyd posted fourteen wins before becoming a memorable part of Boston's starting rotation.

Financial disputes between Buzas and the city regarding the lease and upgrades to Muzzy Field, not to mention the dearth of parking around the ballpark, prompted Buzas to uproot and relocate to New Britain where a brand new facility awaited with easier highway access off of Route 9. The desertion occurred a year before Boston drafted decorated University of Texas pitcher Roger Clemens in the first round; instead of a brief stint in Double A baseball at Muzzy Field, Clemens pitched at Beehive Field in New Britain.

When the team moved before the 1983 season, the city mourned the loss: "The point of all this is clear: the Bristol Red Sox will be missed, both by fans and by the city which operates the park where the team played," stated a March 1983 editorial in the local newspaper. "But the departure of the Brisox will not make a tomb of Muzzy Field. With an energetic effort to attract other types of events, and with the ambitious renovations scheduled to begin this year, athletes will continue to perform—and teams will continue to compete—at Bristol's Muzzy Field."

Indeed, it took no time before Muzzy Field and the city of Bristol aligned themselves with a newly formed conference of major East Coast universities—the Big East—and their postseason baseball tournament. A relationship that started in 1985 brought to the West End ballpark several future major leaguers.

In 1987, one of the most powerful teams in Big East history arrived with arguably the greatest three-pronged offensive attack in college baseball history. That season, Seton Hall was built on phenomenal power and speed, posting a .355 team average with ninety-two home runs and scoring more than eleven runs per game and stealing more than four bases per game on average.

The Pirates lineup devastated opposing pitchers due in large part to a trio dubbed "The Hit Men," which included freshman Maurice "Mo" Vaughn, who hit .429 with 28 home runs and 90 RBI; junior Craig Biggio, the offensive spark plug with a .407 average, 14 home runs, 30 stolen bases, and 97 runs scored; and junior Marteese Robinson, who turned in one of the finest individual seasons in college baseball history with a .529 mark, 16 home runs, 90 RBI, 58 stolen bases, and 126 hits.

The only home run ever hit out of Muzzy Field that could rival Babe Ruth's legendary blasts came off the bat of Seton Hall's Mo Vaughn in 1987. (Courtesy: Seton Hall University Archives & Special Collections Center)

Robinson collected the player of the year awards while Vaughn matched the school's career home run record in his debut season. Also on coach Mike Sheppard's team was a slick-fielding, low-profile infielder named John Valentin, who with Vaughn and Biggio, became household names and major league stars after college.

Seton Hall tore through conference play winning sixteen of eighteen games and posting a 41–8 mark in the regular season, climbing the national rankings as the most feared team in the East. The Pirates earned the top seed in the tournament pool of Connecticut, Villanova, and the well-respected defending champions, St. John's.

Their first game against Connecticut, televised regionally and played under the lights, proved to be one of the most memorable in Muzzy Field history.

Connecticut pitcher Charles Nagy, the Big East pitcher of the year as a freshman, took the mound for a talented club that was 23–15. He delighted the pro-Husky crowd of about fifteen hundred when he struck out Biggio and Vaughn in the first inning.

But when Vaughn came up again in the third, Nagy was less fortunate. On a two-strike count, Vaughn connected as solidly as he ever had and blasted a monumental, towering home run to right field that observers say was still ascending as it cleared the wall and the lordly pine trees.

"Seeing the white ball going up was something out of the movies, like *The Natural*," Nagy told author David Siroty. "He hit it really well and it kept going, going, going and going into the darkness."

Whether it was a hanging slider (said Vaughn) or curveball (said Nagy), the ball was never found, and Vaughn's blast must rival Babe Ruth's shot in 1919 as the longest ever hit at Muzzy Field. It has become legendary.

"It's still talked about in New England," Nagy told Siroty.

Vaughn's eye-popping smash propelled Seton Hall to a 6–2 victory over Connecticut, and the hits kept coming as the team scored twenty-eight runs in two wins over Villanova for the Big East championship and automatic berth into the NCAA Tournament.

Several years before he began posting Hall of Fame numbers for the Houston Astros, Craig Biggio was an offensive spark plug for the Seton Hall Pirates on the school's immensely talented 1987 team, which won the Big East tournament at Muzzy Field. (Courtesy: Seton Hall University Archives & Special Collections Center)

Unfortunately for Sheppard's club, their weakness was pitching (4.87 ERA) in 1987, and it caught up to them in the regionals in Alabama when they gave up thirty-four runs in three games. They finished the season with a sparkling 45–10 record and have not won a tournament title since.

Ensuing years brought a host of talented Big East players to Muzzy Field while St. John's, Villanova, and Connecticut consistently were capturing titles through 1995. Unfortunately, Muzzy Field's cozy relationship with the Big East ended that year when the conference announced that it was moving its tournament to the brand new Thomas J. Dodd Stadium in Norwich, home of the Navigators of the Eastern League. Attendance had been up and down for the previous five years, and the Big East was expanding to include Notre Dame, Rutgers, and West Virginia at the time, which meant an increase to a six-team tournament field. More games meant more chances for rainouts because Muzzy Field was not equipped with a tarpaulin.

Bristol and Muzzy Field again lost out to a shinier ballpark with an Eastern League presence.

Since then, Muzzy Field has existed in the spirit of its original, intended purpose—that of a city park whose activities are centered on amateur sports and local programs.

The history of the Bristol Red Sox and events and players that followed remain, for now, in the modern day conscience, but few of those details have been transferred to the generation that is approximately once removed from the debut of the Red Sox.

Even cloudier is the earliest history of the ballpark, but that is where Muzzy Field shines as one of the finest in New England, a testament to the power and appeal of Bristol and its hometown teams stretching back almost one hundred years. It was the time of Babe Ruth and Martín Dihigo, Vince Lombardi and Don Hutson, the Pittsburgh Pirates, Boston Braves, Boston Red Sox, and New York Yankees, and the phenomenal female athletes Margaret Gisolo and Jackie Mitchell.

The field itself has existed as an athletics ground since 1912; its first unofficial game was hosted in May 1913 after about a year of field preparation. In the chronology of classic ballparks, Muzzy Field stands between Boston's Fenway Park (1912) and Chicago's Wrigley Field (1914) as one of the oldest active ballparks in the country. Unlike its big-city contemporaries, Muzzy Field has never served as the full-time home to a major league team, and while it is much less celebrated in general baseball discourse, it is no less significant to the game's history or less romantic in its presentation and atmosphere. It is simply unknown by comparison, tucked away on quiet streets in a midsize old factory town whose gilded days, for now, are behind it.

These are not the thoughts of the high-school-aged youth who populate the grounds for three seasons out of the year. Their concerns are of a more immediate nature. But in the late afternoon shadows, in the whispers of towering pine trees, in the quaint grandstand with wooden bleachers, the tales are told. They are the stories of Hall of Famers who have attained immortality in the pantheon of sports heroes; the stories of the men and women whose celebrity was fleeting; and the stories of the athletes who may never have been known outside of the city limits.

All of them are vital to the Muzzy Field legacy, leaving their footprints where future generations stride on common ground, if only for a moment.

# Bibliography

Altavilla, John. "Schoolboy's Day: Hartford Native Left His Mark In The Negro Leagues." *Hartford Courant.* April 15, 1997.

Anthony, Mike. "It Was Good To Be The King: Feigner Can Still Bring It, Just Not From The Mound." *Hartford Courant.* July 6, 2006.

Associated Press. "Reds Beaten, 8 to 6, In Slugfest." *Washington Post.* April 5, 1931.

"Babe Ruth's Auto Totally Wrecked At Yalesville." *Bristol Press.* October 1, 1920.

"Babe Ruth Comes Through At Bristol." *Hartford Courant.* September 21, 1919.

"Babe Ruth Due In Town Tonight." *Hartford Courant.* September 30, 1920.

"Babe Ruth, Home Run King, Here." *Hartford Courant.* October 2, 1920.

"Babe Ruth Home Run King Is Here Saturday." *Bristol Press.* September 28, 1920.

"Babe Ruth Makes First Homer On Muzzy Field." *Bristol Press.* September 22, 1919.

"Babe Ruth Will Become .400 Hitter In 1920." *Hartford Times.* September 15, 1919.

"Babe Ruth With Poli's At Muzzy Field Saturday." *Bristol Press.* September 29, 1920.

Bachman, Lou. "800 Reserved Seats Sold, Chairman Breckbill Says." *Bristol Press*. April 2, 1943.

Bachman, Lou. "Record Crowd Expected To See Braves Here Tomorrow." *Bristol Press*. April 3, 1943.

Barnett, Bob. "When The Packers Went to War." *The Coffin Corner* reprinted from *The Packer Report*, Vol. V.

Barnhart, Tony. *Southern Fried Football*. Chicago: Triumph Books, 2000.

"Baseball Fans Will Crowd Muzzy Field Saturday Afternoon." *Bristol Press*. September 29, 1920.

"Baseball Grounds at Muzzy Field Christened by Business Men Yesterday." *Bristol Press*. July 9, 1914.

Baseball Library. http://www.baseballlibrary.com.

Baseball Reference. http://www.baseball-reference.com.

"Baseball Season Opens At Muzzy Field Tomorrow Afternoon." *Bristol Press*. April 24, 1920.

Bennett, John. "Jimmie Foxx." Society for American Baseball Research. The Baseball Biography Project. http://bioproj.sabr.org.

Bennett, John. "Max Carey." Society for American Baseball Research. The Baseball Biography Project. http://bioproj.sabr.org.

Bernier-Collazo, Dr. N. "I Remember Carlos Bernier," Baseball Library. http://www.BaseballLibrary.com.

"BHS Baseball Star To Get Workout With NY Yankees." *Bristol Press*. September 24, 1945.

Bjarkman, Mark and Peter C. Rucker. *Smoke: The Romance and Lore of Cuban Baseball*. Kingston: Total Sports, 1999.

"Boston Red Sox Had Easy Time With New Dep'ture." *Bristol Press*. July 17, 1922.

"Boston Red Sox Here Sunday." *Bristol Press*. July 12, 1922.

Brandt, William E. "Girl Pitcher Fans Ruth And Gehrig." *New York Times*. April 3, 1931.

Braunwart, Bob. "All Those A.F.L.'s: N.F.L. Competitors, 1935-41." Professional Football Researchers Association. http://www.footballresearch.com.

"Bristol Council To Decide Big Deal." *Hartford Courant*. October 2, 1916.

"Bristol High 14, Southington High 8." *Hartford Courant*. June 5, 1913.

"Bristol New Departures Trim Pittsburgh Pirates." *Hartford Courant*. June 14, 1926.

Brophy, Henry L. "Top Athletes Played At Muzzy Field." *Bristol Press*. October 12, 1971.

"Builders Of Bristol: Adrian J. Muzzy." *Bristol Press*. April 14, 1976.'

Butler, Bill. "Player Strike Speeds Colonial Loop Foldup." *The Sporting News*. July 26, 1950.

Caruso, Gary. *The Braves Encyclopedia*. Philadelphia: Temple University Press, 1995.

Cesar Lopez's Cuban Baseball. http://www.cubanball.com.

Cizik, John. "Dick McAuliffe." Society for American Baseball Research. The Baseball Biography Project. http://bioproj.sabr.org.

Clouette, Bruce and Matthew Roth. *Bristol, Connecticut: A Bicentennial History, 1785-1985*. Canaan: Phoenix Publishing, 1984.

Coates II, John and Merl Kleinknecht. "Historically Speaking: Martin Dihigo." *Black Sports*. November 1973.

College Football Hall of Fame. http://www.collegefootball.org.

"Colonials 7, Bristol 5." *Hartford Courant*. August 13, 1916.

Creamer, Robert W. *Babe: The Legend Comes to Life*. New York: Simon & Schuster, 1974.

"Cuban Stars Big Attraction For Tomorrow." *Bristol Press*. August 25, 1921.

"Cubans To Arrive Saturday Night." *Bristol Press*. June 29, 1923.

Dittmar, Joe. "Bill Bergen." Society for American Baseball Research. The Baseball Biography Project. http://bioproj.sabr.org.

Drebinger, John. "Yankees Beat Cubs For 3d In Row, 7-5, As 51,000 Look On." *The New York Times*. October 2, 1932.

"Eagles To Oppose New Departure Nine." *Bristol Press*. July 7, 1918.

Echevarria, Roberto Gonzalez. *The Pride of Havana: A History of Cuban Baseball*. New York: Oxford University Press, 1999.

Falkner, David. "Ruth, and Reilly, Live On." *The New York Times*. May 15, 1987.

"Fandom Will Be Out Tomorrow At Muzzy Field." *Bristol Press*. July 15, 1922.

"Fans Will See Big League Team." *Bristol Press*. July 14, 1922.

Figueredo, Jorge S. *Who's Who in Cuban Baseball, 1878-1961*. Jefferson: McFarland, 2007.

"Floods Block Roads During Heavy Storm; Worst Gale In Years." *Hartford Courant*. October 1, 1920.

Forr, James. "Pie Traynor." Society for American Baseball Research. The Baseball Biography Project. http://bioproj.sabr.org.

Fox, Jeff. "Bill Bergen." Legends of the Game: Dead Ball Era Player Guide. http://www.deadball.com.

Francis, C. Philip. "Surprising Facts." Chatter From The Dugout http://www.chatterfromthedugout.com/surprising_facts.htm.

Gallagher, Mark. "George Weiss." Baseball Library. http://www.BaseballLibrary.com.

Garrett, Bill. "N.D. Baseball And Basketball Teams Tops." *Bristol Press*. October 12, 1971.

"Girl Pitcher, 17, Fans Ruth, Gehrig, Walks Tony, Quits." *Washington Post*. April 3, 1931.

Greenleaf, Dave. "ND And Sports Played Prominent Role In Bristol." *Bristol Press*. September 29, 1978.

Gregorich, Barbara. *Women at Play: The Story of Women in Baseball*. San Diego: Harcourt Brace & Co., 1993.

Grosshandler, Stan. "The Brooklyn Dodgers." *The Coffin Corner*. Volume XII.

Grosshandler, Stan. "The Nadir." *The Coffin Corner*, Volume XV.

"Hartford Eastern League Baseball Club To Train In Bristol." *Bristol Press*. March 16, 1944.

"Hartford Trims New Departure In Opening Game." *Bristol Press*. April 24, 1922.

Hawkins, Joel and Terry Bertolino. *Images of America: The House of David Baseball Team*. Chicago: Arcadia Publishing, 2000.

Heise, Kenan. "John F. Moore Sr., 89; played center for Cubs." *Chicago Tribune*. April 10, 1991.

Holtzman, Jerome. "Turn back the clock ... 1943: owner William Cox, the last man banned before Pete Rose." *Baseball Digest*. August 2004.

Holway, John B. *Blackball Stars: Negro League Pioneers*. Westport: Meckler Books, 1988.

Kavanaugh, Jack. "Ruben Gomez." Baseball Library. http://www. BaseballLibrary.com.

Krosky, Bill. "Weather, Major Aircasts Halt Colonial Loop." *The Sporting News*. July 26, 1950.

Laponte, Louis, in discussion with author. March 2004.

Lardner, Ring. "When Girl Pitcher Struck Out Babe." *Chicago Tribune*. April 6, 1931.

Latino Baseball. http://latinobaseball.com

Lautier, Jack. "Bristol's baseball tradition well established at turn of century." *Bristol Press*. May 16–18, 1988.

Lautier, Jack. "Recalling the miracle at Muzzy." *Bristol Press*. June 13, 1991.

Leach, Gail and Steven Vastola. *Images of America: Bristol*. Charleston: Arcadia Publishing, 2001.

LeMonnier, Skip. "Red Sox Await Council Decision." *Bristol Press*. January 4, 1973.

Lipshez, Ken. "25 years of pro ball in New Britain." *New Britain Herald*. May 10, 2007.

"Local Fans Eager To Welcome Babe Ruth." *Bristol Press*. September 30, 1920.

Lowitt, Bruce. "Once a revered ritual, pepper becomes passé." *St. Petersburg Times.* July 26, 2003. http://www.sptimes.com.

"Maderos With Cuban Champs, At Muzzy Field." *Bristol Press.* June 30, 1923.

Major League Baseball. http://www.mlb.com.

*Manchester Herald.*

Maraniss, David. *When Pride Still Mattered: A Life of Vince Lombardi.* New York: Simon & Schuster, 1999.

McAuliffe, Dick, in discussion with the author. May 2007.

McCabe, Jack, in discussion with the author. May 2004.

(McCabe, Jack, unpublished data.)

"McCabe Threatens To Bolt Sale." *New Britain Herald.* September 10, 1909.

McNeil, William. *Cool Papas and Double Duties: The All-Time Greats of the Negro Leagues.* Jefferson: McFarland, 2005.

Monahan, Tom. "Muzzy Field Gets Face Lifting." *Bristol Press.* September 23, 1966.

Morhardt, Moe, in discussion with the author. April 2007.

Morin, Francis. *The Shadow of Bristol.* Franktown: Glacier Publishing.

"Muzzy Field After Red Sox." *Bristol Press.* March 14, 1983.

"Muzzy Field Fence To Be Erected At Cost Of $5,825." *Bristol Press.* July 25, 1935.

"Muzzy Field Grandstand, Now Complete, Said to Be One of New England's Best." *Bristol Press.* April 27, 1939.

National Baseball Hall of Fame. http://www.baseballhalloffame.org.

National Football League. http://www.nfl.com.

"N.Ds. Trim Polis With Babe Ruth In Line-up." *Bristol Press*. October 4, 1920.

Neft, David S., Richard M. Cohen, and Michael L. Neft. *The Sports Encyclopedia: Baseball, 2004*. New York: St. Martin's Press, 2004.

"Neiman Smashes Homer To Deep Right Center." *Bristol Press*. April 3, 1944.

Newman, Zipp. "Alabama's 1934 Squad Considered Greatest of All Southern Teams." *Birmingham News*. November, 30, 1934.

"New Departures Capture Two." *Bristol Press*. September 5, 1922.

"New Departure Out Hits Cubans But Lose Game." *Bristol Press*. September 27, 1921.

"New Haven And Manchester Clash In Battle For State Soccer Cup Tomorrow At Bristol." *Hartford Courant*. May 30, 1920.

Palau, Andy, in discussion with the author. October 2004.

"Park Board Talks More On Baseball." *Bristol Press*. October 19, 1965.

"Park Commission Tables Muzzy Field Grandstand Issue." *Bristol Press*. May 19, 1938.

"Park Commissioners Vote For Chain Wire Fence To Enclose Local Ball Field." *Bristol Press*. July 18, 1935.

"Paul Mooney Will Hurl For House Of David." *Bristol Press*. September 1, 1922.

Peck, Epaphroditus. *A History of Bristol, Connecticut*. Hartford: Lewis Street Bookshop, 1932.

Pepper, Al. "The Bill Bergen Shrine." Al Pepper. http://members.tripod.com/~alpepper/billbergen.html.

Phillips, H.L. "Dumm and Dummer." *Washington Post*. May 3, 1931.

"Pirates Will Show Wares To Fans At Muzzy Park, Bristol, Today." *Hartford Courant*. June 13, 1926.

"Pittsburgh World Champions Will Play New Departures At Muzzy Field Tomorrow." *Bristol Press*. June 12, 1926.

"Poli's Has Three Strenuous Games." *Hartford Courant*. October 1, 1920.

Pro Football Database. http://www.databasefootball.com.

Pro Football Hall of Fame. http://www.profootballhof.com.

Redmount, Robert Samuel. *The Red Sox Encyclopedia*. Champaign: Sports Publishing LLC, 2002.

"Red Sox's Coming Gives Joy To Local Fans." *Bristol Press*. September 18, 1919.

"Regular Players Of Pittsburgh Pirates In Bristol Sunday." *Hartford Courant*. June 11, 1926.

Retrosheet. http://www.retrosheet.org.

Riley, James A. *The Biographical Encyclopedia of the Negro Baseball Leagues*. New York: Carroll & Graf Publishers, 1994.

Rives, John. "Joe Wilhoit." Society for American Baseball Research. The Baseball Biography Project. http://bioproj.sabr.org.

Roach, James. "Women In Sports." *New York Times*. May 3, 1931.

Rose, Franklin. "A Kitchen Table Chat With Andy Palau." *Gridiron Greats*, Vol. 3:8, 18–21. 2004.

"Royal Giants Win Though Out-Hit." *Bristol Press.* September 12, 1921.

"Ruth Gets Homer In Bristol Game." *Hartford Times.* September 22, 1919.

"Ruth Plays With Poli's, Springfield." *Bristol Press.* September 29, 1920.

Simmons, Pop. "Bud Metheny Homers Twice To Spark Bombers Attack." *Bristol Press.* September 26, 1945.

Siroty, David. *The Hit Men and the Kid Who Batted Ninth.* Lanham: Diamond Communications, 2002.

Smelser, Dr. Marshall. *The Life That Ruth Built: A Biography.* New York: Quadrangle/New York Times Book Co., 1975.

"State League Winners: Bristol Baseball Club Makes a Proud Record In Its Play During the Season of 1901, Which Closed To-day." *Hartford Times.* September 7, 1901.

Stevens, Brian. "Babe Adams." Society for American Baseball Research. The Baseball Biography Project. http://bioproj.sabr.org.

(Taylor, Estelle, unpublished data.)

"The Bristol Giants Is Dead." *Bristol Press.* March 22, 1966.

"Tell How Philly President Bet On Games." *Chicago Tribune.* November 25, 1943.

Thompson, Jim. "Giants Leave Bristol." *Bristol Press.* March 22, 1966.

Treder, Steve. "Carlos Bernier." The Hardball Times. http://www.hardballtimes.com.

"To Honor League Presidents." *Hartford Courant.* June 13, 1926.

(Vincent, Fay T., Jr., unpublished data.)

Weiss, Bill and Marshall Wright. "Top 100 Teams: Team #45—1918 Toronto Maple Leafs." Minor League Baseball. http://www.minorleaguebaseball.com.

Weiss, Bill and Marshall Wright. "Top 100 Teams: Team #57—1916 New London Planters." Minor League Baseball. http://www.minorleaguebaseball.com.

Weiss, Bill and Marshall Wright. "Top 100 Teams: Team #99—1944 Hartford Laurels." Minor League Baseball. http://www.minorleaguebaseball.com.

Wells, Robert W. *Vince Lombardi: His Life and Times.* Madison: Wisconsin House, 1971.

Westcott, Rich and Frank Bilovsky. *The Phillies Encyclopedia.* Philadelphia: Temple University Press, 2004.

Westcott, Richard. *Diamond Greats: Profiles and Interviews with 65 of Baseball's History Makers.* Westport: Meckler Books, 1988.

Wheeler, Orlin. "3,036 Paying Customers Watch Braves' Yannigans Trip Regulars, 10-8." *Bristol Press.* April 5, 1943.

"Work On Thomas A. Tracy Grandstand Almost Completed." *Bristol Press.* January 18, 1939.

"World Champions Outplayed By New Departures." *Bristol Press.* June 14, 1926.

"Yanks' Homers Owe Much To West Wind." *The New York Times.* October 2, 1932.

Yantz, Tom. "Big East Baseball To Norwich." *Hartford Courant.* August 9, 1995.

# Index